The Historic Murder Trial
of George Crawford

The Historic Murder Trial of George Crawford

Charles H. Houston, the NAACP and the Case That Put All-White Southern Juries on Trial

DAVID BRADLEY

McFarland & Company, Inc., Publishers

Jefferson, North Carolina

LIBRARY OF CONGRESS CATALOGUING-IN-PUBLICATION DATA

Bradley, David, 1961–
    The historic murder trial of George Crawford : Charles H.
Houston, the NAACP and the case that put all-white southern
juries on trial / David Bradley.
        p.   cm.
    Includes bibliographical references and index.

    ISBN 978-0-7864-9468-2 (softcover : acid free paper) ∞
    ISBN 978-1-4766-1637-7 (ebook)

    1. Trials (Murder)—Virginia—History—20th century.
2. Jurors—Virginia—History—20th century.   3. Racism—
Virginia—History—20th century.   4. States' rights (American
politics)—History—20th century.   5. National Association for
the Advancement of Colored People—History—20th century.
I. Title.

HV6533.V8B73 2014
364.152'3092—dc23   2014013531

BRITISH LIBRARY CATALOGUING DATA ARE AVAILABLE

On the cover: George Crawford wanted poster, Loudoun County,
Leesburg, Virginia, January, 19, 1932

Printed in the United States of America

McFarland & Company, Inc., Publishers
    Box 611, Jefferson, North Carolina 28640
    www.mcfarlandpub.com

Acknowledgments

I am indebted to the staffs of the Manuscript Room at the Library of Congress; the file room at the Loudoun County courthouse (especially David Eddy); the Thomas Balch Library in Leesburg (especially Kiera Nolan); the George Mason University Library; the University of Wisconsin Library; the Golda Meir Library at the University of Wisconsin-Milwaukee; the Department of Special Collections at the University of North Dakota's Chester Fritz Library; the W.E.B. Du Bois Library at the University of Massachusetts Amherst; and the offices of the Loudoun County Commonwealth's Attorney, Loudoun County Sheriff's Office and Middleburg Police Department.

Thanks for repeated help to Kenneth Mack, professor of law at Harvard Law School; historian Deborah A. Lee; John Kneebone; Elaine E. Thompson; Carol Parker; Henry Baxley Jr.; Donna Bohanon; and Robert Mosko. Thanks also to Kristie Miller, Katrina McCormick and Henry Baxley, Jr., for the time they shared with me.

Thanks are always due to John Geddie and Beth Miller, the editor and publisher of the *Loudoun Easterner*, where my first attempt at telling this story was published in three installments in July and August 2002. They were great bosses, great friends and great inspirations.

And thanks to Sue, Adam, Annie and Emily for listening to me talk about this story for a very, very long time.

Contents

Preface

I first heard about the trial of George Crawford in the spring of 2002, more than 70 years after the murders of Agnes Ilsley and Mina Buckner.

I was in the file room in the basement of the Loudoun County courthouse complex in Leesburg, Virginia, researching another, more recent case for the *Loudoun Easterner*, where I was the lone news reporter, when I overheard two clerks—one new to the job, the other a veteran of many years—talking about a Depression-era trial that had brought Thurgood Marshall to the courthouse. It was a murder trial, they said; it had been national news and it had helped to end the practice of excluding African Americans from juries.

My curiosity was piqued. I had lived in the area my entire life and yet had never heard of the trial. I asked for the case file and over the course of the next several weeks spent whatever free time I had at that basement table, poring over the small collection of court documents, photographs and mysterious floor plans, piecing together the forgotten story that had once made Loudoun's county seat the center of a national debate. I filed a lengthy feature story at the *Easterner* and it ran as a three-part series while I was away on vacation that summer.

I might not have given it much more thought if there hadn't been a stack of letters from readers waiting for me when I returned. None of them had heard of the Crawford trial, either, and they all wanted to know more about the case.

So I dove deeper. There were stacks of contemporary accounts of the murders and subsequent legal battle in Loudoun's two Depression-era newspapers—the *Loudoun Times-Mirror*, which was published in Leesburg, and the *Blue Ridge Herald*, which was published in nearby Purcellville—and dozens of stories in the *Washington Post*, the *New York Times* and other papers across the country. There were detailed records in the papers of the NAACP at the Library of Congress, and insightful tidbits in the papers of W.E.B. Du Bois and General William "Billy" Mitchell. There were local legends and rumors about the trial still floating around Leesburg and Middleburg, though firsthand accounts were not to be found so many years later. All of the significant players had died decades ago. For some time it seemed that I would never reach the bottom of the mountain of research and references that I'd stumbled upon.

And it seemed that the story would have no real hero. Ilsley and Buckner exited the stage before the story had hardly begun; Crawford revealed himself to be a manipulator and a robber (at the very least); and Marshall, as it turned out, had only a minor role in the story, the vaguest prelude to what would turn out to be one of the most significant lives of the 20th century. Mitchell, an icon of what at that time was still called the Great War — and a prescient predictor of a second World War — bullied and blustered his way across the stage, while several other characters played incomplete parts, stepping in and out of the spotlight only long enough to add to the mystery of the story.

The overlooked hero was, in fact, the only man who was willing to stand by Crawford until the final scene: Marshall's teacher and mentor, Charles Hamilton Houston. And like so many real life heroes, Houston wasn't spectacular or flashy. He worked tirelessly, showed up when others would not, and did what was right and best for his client even when it was inconvenient or distasteful for himself. He accepted no pay for his service and was rewarded only with public ridicule from critics who had little understanding of the inner workings of the case.

Today, Houston's name is rarely mentioned outside legal circles, but he captained a series of legal challenges to Jim Crow, was the chief architect of the NAACP's legal battle for civil rights in the 1930s and 1940s, and his disciples — including Marshall — sang his praises even as they continued his work into the 1960s. When he died at age 54 in April 1950, there were many, including his father, who believed that Houston had literally worked himself to death.

I've tried to place the Crawford murder trial in some kind of context, side by side with relevant events of the time. The few 21st-century references to the case have been brief and concerned only with its legal implications — which are significant — but the NAACP's fear of mob violence at the trial is only understandable when one knows that lynchings had occurred in the county in the recent past, and were occurring across the region even as Crawford's extradition battle was being fought. Loudoun County redeemed itself over the course of the legal battle in Leesburg, but the fact that Virginia sent heavily armed guards to accompany Crawford to the courthouse makes it clear that even Governor John Garland Pollard thought a violent outcome a possibility.

Despite Houston's pleas to Loudoun County authorities to preserve the records of the Crawford trial — "there is no telling when they may become important," he once wrote to the clerk of the circuit court — there is surprisingly little documentation of the case in the Leesburg courthouse. The file is small, a single manila envelope about two inches thick, marked "Com. Vs George Crawford." For decades, it also contained a sliver of fragile paper, about the size of a playing card, that had been torn from a calendar — "January, 1930."

Scratched on it with an awkward hand were a few words: "Mr. Noke, Box 87, Herndon VA." At some point during research for this book, the note, on which one man's fate had hinged and a small step in the epic battle for civil rights had turned, disappeared from the file.

Introduction

By the time he came to Leesburg, Virginia, in 1933, to defend ex-convict George Crawford for the murders of Agnes Boeing Ilsley and Mina Buckner, Charles Hamilton Houston was a pillar of African American society: a World War I veteran; Dean of the Howard University Law School in Washington, DC; a member of the District's School Board; and always—always—a consummate professional. He was both a product and a symbol of Washington's Striver neighborhood, home to the District's African American elite. He attended M Street High School, an African American college-preparatory high school; graduated from Massachusetts' Amherst College Phi Beta Kappa in 1915 (he was the only African American in his class); was an honor graduate of Harvard Law School, where he was elected to the editorial staff of the *Harvard Law Review*; and studied at the University of Madrid. His grandfather had been a slave and his father one of the first African American attorneys in Washington. The Howard students to whom he taught law—including Thurgood Marshall and other towering figures of the civil rights movement—respected him, feared him, loved him, and would call him their mentor throughout their lives. But white America had taken little notice of Houston or his work.

"Separate but equal" was more than legal doctrine in the 19th and 20th centuries, it was a common practice carried out across every level of society. But while the culture was decidedly "separate," it was rarely, if ever, "equal." The Striver area was nearly self-contained, as separate from the surrounding white neighborhoods of downtown Washington as possible. The same was true of Leesburg's Black Bottom community. The benefits America had to offer its citizens—economic, educational, legal, cultural—were rarely extended to those African American enclaves.

Houston had no illusions about "separate but equal" or what it would take for black America to move closer to true equality. He had grown up in relative affluence, but court-endorsed segregation had limited his achievement. The U.S. Army remained segregated when he signed up at the beginning of World War I. His first assignment was to a blacks-only officers' training camp at Fort

Des Moines, Iowa. Stationed in France during the war, Houston and other black officers found themselves portrayed by their white counterparts as ignorant, dishonest, cowardly, and sexually degenerate. When they returned to America following the Armistice, they found Jim Crow laws as firmly in place as ever. The popularity of the Ku Klux Klan was on the rise, as was the frequency of lynchings.

Jim Crow in all its manifestations would only be repealed through the courts, and there would be no easy victories there, Houston warned his Howard students. Denied membership by the American Bar Association, African American attorneys in 1925 formed their own National Bar Association; Houston was a founding member of the affiliate Washington Bar Association.

In Leesburg, less than 40 miles from the Howard University campus, so little was known of Houston — and of African American jurisprudence in general — that the *Loudoun Times-Mirror* felt the need on the eve of Crawford's first murder trial to publish "Houston, Crawford Attorney, One of Leaders of Race in Nation," a short story meant to introduce the newspaper's white readers to the "colored attorney of Washington."

Whether Houston changed many minds about race during his time in Leesburg isn't clear. The first newspaper reports of his appearances at the courthouse focused on apparent amazement that an African American could be educated and articulate. Houston and the legal team he had gathered to defend Crawford were "described by county officials who came in contact with them as being courteous and well qualified as lawyers," the *Times-Mirror* reported in March, 1933. After Crawford's conviction and sentencing, the newspaper went so far as to say that "the accused negro was represented by exceedingly able counsel."

Real advances for civil rights and race relations were still decades away, but something *did* seem to change in Leesburg during the Crawford trial. Whether Houston's work truly convinced observers that African Americans were being shortchanged, or the trial simply coincided with some pivot point isn't clear. The *Times-Mirror*'s editor argued that Virginia's African Americans were satisfied with their treatment in general and had never expressed any interest in serving on juries in particular; Baltimore's *Afro-American* characterized the average Virginian as corrupt, bloodthirsty and irredeemable. Obviously, neither was accurate, and if the trial revealed anything about the community it was held in, it was that neither white nor black Loudoun was an easily categorized monolith. Examples of courage and cowardice, belligerence and humility, were displayed in all corners. But the NAACP's fears of mob violence in the days before the trial — which were perfectly reasonable, considering the spate of lynchings across the country, including one in neighboring Fauquier County — evaporated during the proceedings, and by the end of the trial Judge James McLemore, prosecutors led by Loudoun County Commonwealth's Attorney John Galleher, and Houston's NAACP defense team spent so much time praising each other in open court that one witness compared the exchange to a "love feast." When Crawford was returned to Leesburg in February 1934, for the murder of Mina Buckner, only a handful of citizens turned out to witness the brief hearing. Whatever the reason — emerging recognition of the injustice of lynching, segregation and the one-race jury system; the eloquence of Crawford's legal team; an enduring belief in the American legal system; or simply the passage of time — the more radical voices in the region, who had demanded the impeachment of Federal Court Judge James Arnold Lowell when he had released Crawford and questioned Virginia's ability to conduct fair trials, were nowhere to be heard as the courts finished with Crawford.

Instead, anger came from members of the NAACP and the African American press, and was directed at Houston and NAACP executive director Walter White. The NAACP defense team had considered limiting Crawford's sentence to life in prison a victory, especially after they became convinced of his guilt, but critics, most of whom had observed the case from afar, accused them of sacrificing an innocent man for the sake of expediency, or for fear of fully confronting the white power structure. For Houston, a man who had dedicated his life to the legal battle against inequality and had spent most of the previous two years in a tireless— and unpaid — struggle to defend a double-dealing and guilty man, the public denunciations must have stung bitterly.

But Houston had made believers among Loudoun County's African American community. When African Americans subsequently formed the County-Wide League (CWL) to fight for better schools for minority students, they turned to Houston. The county's Board of Supervisors approved plans for a new high school for African American students only after the CWL raised enough money to buy a few acres of land and Houston persuaded the State Literary Fund to loan the county money to cover construction costs.

Race relations may have been changing in Leesburg in 1933, but it was a painfully slow process. Thurgood Marshall, who had assisted Houston during the Crawford trial, successfully argued against school segregation in *Brown v. Board of Education* in 1954 and became the first African American justice on the U.S. Supreme Court in 1967. But it wasn't until classes began in September 1968 that Loudoun County schools were finally integrated.

Houston's immediate goal had been to save Crawford, guilty or innocent, from Virginia's electric chair. Secondarily, the case had been fought to end discrimination in jury selection. In both instances, he had been successful. Even as motions were being filed at the courthouse in Leesburg in November 1933, the names of African Americans began to appear on jury lists across the South, in places where that hadn't occurred in decades, if ever. By June 1934, Judge J.R.H. Alexander was willing to add the name of one African American to a Loudoun County jury pool. The next year, Houston successfully challenged the exclusion of African Americans from juries in *Hollins v. Oklahoma*. In the first Supreme Court victory by an all–African American counsel, the court ruled systematic exclusions from juries unconstitutional.

ONE

The Murders

January 12, 1932

It had been cold and dry since Thanksgiving, a typical winter for Northern Virginia, but it felt harsher than usual as the Great Depression, deepening in its third year, tightened its grip. After New Year's Day the weather turned warmer and, by mid–January, record high temperatures in the mid–70's were recorded. Each morning a surprisingly strong midwinter sun burned the chilly dew away. By noon, shopkeepers in the towns and villages that dotted the landscape threw open their windows to let the sunshine and crisp air pour in.

Members of the upper class— who had lost so much more in the crash than their farmer and merchant neighbors but, as evidenced by the groomsmen who cared for the thoroughbreds in their stables; by the maids and cooks, furnace men and gardeners, janitors and chauffeurs who minded their estates while they toured Europe and the Orient and the Holy Land; by the familial empires in Chicago and Milwaukee and Long Island and San Francisco that they returned to for leisurely vacations each summer —could still comfortably afford to devote their winter days to foxhunting excursions across the fields and forests of their plantations. Those few families, who had inherited most of their fortunes and didn't have to work to retain their wealth, represented a literal leisure class and continued living some semblance of the Jazz Age even into the depths of the Depression.

Middleburg, once a secluded village of well-to-do Southern planters, had during the 1920s grown in size and reputation. Now the town was home to a wealthy elite from across the country that looked to Virginia's lush, rolling hills for a rural retreat, a haven where they could indulge in weekends of foxhunting and steeplechasing away from the prying eyes of the masses. For decades Loudoun County had been a quiet getaway destination for Washingtonians escaping the tidal Potomac's mosquito-ridden marshes; Middleburg had become a tony hideaway for some of the nation's most prominent upper crust. But the idle rich who lived and played at Middleburg were the exception; most of the county was peopled by small-plot farmers, dirt-poor laborers and merchants who scratched out their livings selling goods in one-room stores.

The rolling hills of the upper Piedmont were veined by winding country lanes cut into the red Virginia clay that were shared by horse-drawn carriages and automobiles. Driving on the smaller roads in rural Loudoun County could be hazardous at any time. They were a rough, rocky ride under the best of circumstances and a slick, sloppy mess when it rained, poorly marked, with few signs to tell drivers where they were, where they were going or how long it would take to get there. Filling stations, garages, streetlights— even traffic signals—could be found only in towns, and not in all of the towns, at that. Few roads were paved and many of the rickety single-lane bridges spanning the region's creeks still required the payment of a toll before they could be crossed.

Driving herself and a friend across those rolling hills on that crisp, moonlit January night, wrapped in a modest fur coat, her hair tucked under a warm knit cap, was Agnes Boeing Ilsley. She was 39, wealthy and popular in the area's society circles. She had been widowed a year before and, except for a brother who had come to live with her following her husband's death, she had no family closer than New York.

She had been out with friends that night, first at a party near her Middleburg home and then at a meeting of the Association of Women for Prohibition Reform, a "wet" anti-prohibition group, in Upperville, a tiny hamlet tucked into the side of a hill a few miles west of Middleburg. She left Upperville at about 11:45 p.m. Agnes had recently fired her chauffeur and so she drove the black Ford Victoria coupe across the countryside herself. She dropped her friend off at an estate just outside of Middleburg and drove the rest of the way home alone.

By the time Ilsley drove into Middleburg's west end it was after midnight. The village had no police and no streetlights. Here and there a window glowed in a home where someone was up late but, by and large, the town was dark. She drove past the few houses and little stores on Washington Street, the village's well kept two-lane main road, which was lined with large maple trees. At the main intersection, with the stone walls and white columns of the Middleburg National Bank standing silently on one corner and the rustic Red Fox Inn on another, Ilsley turned left on Madison Street and then right onto Marshall Street.

She lived on Middleburg's eastern edge, between Hamilton and Liberty streets. There was a large manor house on the property, but she had not lived in it for some time. She, her brother and her 65-year-old maid, Mina Buckner, had until recently been living in a small cottage on the same property while acquaintances who were in the area for the foxhunting season, including the daughter of a former congresswoman, rented the manor house. Just days before, the hunting party had moved out and Ilsley's brother had moved into the manor house. There were large porches on both the first and second floors of the front of the manor house and wide steps leading down to the sidewalk that lined

Washington Street. There was a back entrance facing the cottage, which sat across a grassy lot. The cottage's garage and front door faced Marshall Street and weren't visible from the manor house. Ilsley was planning to move out of town in the spring to a farm she owned in the nearby countryside.

She eased the Ford up the short gravel driveway and into the garage under the cottage, walked across the lawn, up the stairs and unlocked the front door. When she was inside, she locked the door behind her, turned off the front porch light, laid her keys on the kitchen table and went into her room to get ready for bed.

A light was on at a small house across the road from the Ilsley cottage. There were no all-night stores in the town; car traffic so late was rare; there were no airplanes in the night sky. An occasional train whistle could be heard in the distance. The town slept.

If anyone had been awake and looking toward the Ilsley property, they may have seen a figure rise up out of the tall weeds that lined the driveway. But perhaps not; there were no lights on at the cottage to cast shadows or outline silhouettes. They might have heard a pane of glass shatter, a door hinge squeak, a muffled cry in the night. But perhaps not.

Moments later, they would have heard an automobile engine turn over, seen Ilsley's garage door open, and watched as the Ford pulled out with someone — not Ilsley — behind the wheel. The coupe turned onto the town's main road and sped off eastward, towards Washington, DC. The car disappeared into the sharp, black night, leaving in its wake the little country village, still quiet and asleep. There were still several hours until dawn.

In the cottage, both Ilsley and Buckner lay dead, brutally beaten, their bedrooms awash in blood. When morning finally came, neighbors awoke to a discovery that would lead to more than two years of fear and anger, controversy and disputes, during which Middleburg would become the focus of national debate and know few such calm moments.

The search for the killer and the legal wrangling that would follow included calls for a lynching, the reopening of the state's rights debate between North and South, and congressional impeachment proceedings against a federal judge. Its outcome would alter the racial makeup of juries across the South and threaten to split the struggling National Association for the Advancement of Colored People into opposing factions. Efforts to solve the murders were nearly overshadowed by what became one of the earliest civil rights victories achieved in a modern courtroom. And the legal mastermind who engineered the victory, a hero and mentor to a generation of the most successful civil rights attorneys in American history, would be rewarded for his tireless work, unflinching courage and genius, by an avalanche of criticism.

TWO

Agnes Boeing Ilsley

The story would become so complicated that by its conclusion it would be easy to forget about Agnes Boeing Ilsley. But it began with her; with her intelligence and her outgoing nature and her wealth and her kindness to those less fortunate than her. And, some would say, it began with her progressive thinking and her naiveté, with her habit of traveling and living without a man leading the way and, despite the independent streak that had taken her so far in her life, it began with a series of decisions that brought her to a horrific death far from her family.

She, her older brother John and her younger brother, Paul, were raised by Julius and Amelia Boeing in Minto, a tiny speck of a town in rural Walsh County, North Dakota. Agnes was born in 1892, just three years after the state had been admitted to the Union.

Julius Boeing was a prosperous farmer, a pharmacist, a founding member of Minto's Masonic lodge and an active member of the state's fledgling Democratic Party. He sat on the executive committee of North Dakota's Democratic State Central Committee, was elected to the state's House of Representatives in 1902, and in 1912 served as an alternate delegate to the Democratic National Convention in Baltimore, where Woodrow Wilson received his first nomination for President.

Like her father, Agnes was energetic, a worker and a joiner, but she steered clear of politics. After graduating from high school she spent a year at St. Mary's School, a private academy run by the Episcopal church in Knoxville, Illinois, 25 miles northwest of Peoria, before moving on to the University of Wisconsin. There she was a member of the Gamma Phi Beta sorority, where her friends nicknamed her "Poky." She joined the Dakota Club and the Green Umbrella; was a member of the Consumer's League, whose purpose was "to improve the sanitary conditions of workers in sweat shops by a campaign of education and a patronage limited to the products of factories"; was elected to Wyslynx, which had been founded in 1904 "to promote good fellowship"; and took speaking parts in class plays. She majored in home economics, but she had no intention

12

of staying at home all her life. Her thesis was entitled "A Comparative Study of Drafting Systems, and their Educational Value, with Reference to the Teaching of Domestic Art."

She had dark features—when she was tired she would get dark bags under her eyes—and thin lips that curled into a sprightly smile, revealing unusually small teeth. She kept her fingernails long and manicured. She dressed smartly, but not flashy, in fashionable clothes: hats worn low over her forehead, skirts below her knee, thick stockings and high-laced shoes.

She graduated from the University of Wisconsin in 1915. That fall she became an instructor in extension work in the university's home economics department. She and her fellow instructors presented lectures and short courses on food composition, preservation and sanitation; nutrition; dietetics; home management; family financial security; housing and home furnishing; clothing and textile chemistry; art in the home; and dress design and construction. Boeing was hired as a clothing specialist working for Elizabeth Kelley, the first state leader of home economics extension. Her appointment by the U.S. Department of Agriculture gave her the title of State Home Economics Specialist.

She continued her association with Gamma Phi Beta and her work in the university's Extension Division. She was chairman of the home economics exhibit committee for the school's 1915 Exposition, and was one of five University of Wisconsin faculty members to take part in the annual meeting of the American Association for the Study and Prevention of Infant Mortality in Milwaukee.

In July 1917, she gave a lecture and practical exhibition of the canning of fruit and vegetables to the women of Brodhead, Wisconsin, at the town's high school. The presentation was one in a series made by members of the university's staff to help the region adjust to the new wartime atmosphere.

Julius Boeing was a workhorse for North Dakota's Democratic party, but the state was dominated by Republicans and, beginning in 1915, the Nonpartisan League (NPL), which advocated state control of farm-related industries—including banks—in an effort to weaken the power of corporate political interests in the northern Plains.

For years the region's wheat crop had been sent to Minneapolis, the largest milling center in the country. Looking to break that stranglehold on the market, North Dakota's legislature passed and the state's voters approved a constitutional amendment authorizing a state-owned terminal elevator. But the State Board of Control argued against construction of the project and Governor L.B. Hanna, who had supported the constitutional amendment, reversed his position. So did the legislature, which killed a bill for the state-owned elevator. Farmers who were gathered in Bismarck for the annual convention of the North Dakota Union of the American Society of Equity were enraged. After that, NPL founder and former Socialist Party organizer A.C. Townley found it easy to convince the state's farmers to join the NPL. By 1919 it had gained enough power that the legislature passed a series of laws reflecting the NPL's program, including legislation that created the Home Building Association, which would build houses costing no more than $5,000 for a 20 percent down payment and installments paid for 10–20 years.

But the NPL quickly ran into trouble. Three North Dakota officials who had been elected on the NPL ticket, including the state's attorney general, publicly criticized the organization's officers for mismanagement and corruption, and in the closing days of World War I, Townley was convicted of conspiracy to discourage enlistments. State-owned banks that the NPL had campaigned for opened with insufficient capital and were accused of misusing funds; NPL-backed mills lost money and were accused of fraud.

While the Home Building Association, funded initially through state bonds, built only one home in its first year, it had plans to build 20 houses in Fargo and more across the state in 1920. But support for the organization evaporated when details of its construction plans were made public. NPL vice president William Lemke, who was campaigning to become the state's attorney general, was getting a $12,000 house in Fargo, and several other homes were either being refurbished or built for well over the $5,000 limit mandated by the legislature. Among them was a home at 724 Broadway in Fargo, which was being built at an estimated cost of $8,325 (but would eventually cost more than $14,000) for J.W. Boeing.

In 1918 Agnes, then 26, left Wisconsin to become secretary to Harry E. Bradley at the Tomahawk Land and Boom Company in Tomahawk, a small lumber town in central Michigan. Both the town and the company had been founded in the 1880s by Bradley's father, who also was the largest shareholder in the Marinette-Tomahawk Railway and, in 1886, established one of the town's two newspapers, the *Tomahawk*.

It was in Tomahawk that Agnes met Spencer Ilsley, a 51-year-old banker from an iconic Milwaukee family. Along with his partner, Samuel Marshall, Spencer's father, Charles Ilsley, had opened a private bank with just a few thousand dollars and turned it into one of the most successful institutions in Wisconsin.

In 1840, when Wisconsin was still a U.S. territory, banking had been outlawed following a series of bank failures and frauds. When the banking ban was repealed in 1853, Wisconsin awarded the first state bank charter to The State Bank of Madison, which was run by Marshall and Ilsley; they also received a state charter for another bank in Milwaukee, which eventually became M&I Bank. By the end of 1899 the state's bank examiner reported Marshall & Ilsley Bank of Milwaukee had resources of $4.2 million; by June 1902 that amount had increased to $5.4 million.[1] Samuel Marshall was the bank's president. Spencer and his brother, James K. Ilsley, worked at the bank and were major stockholders.

Spencer's home on the upper Milwaukee River in Fox Point, Wisconsin, just north of Milwaukee, was serene, a beautiful hideaway in one of the state's most exclusive enclaves. James started the first golf course in Milwaukee with John W. Tweedy Jr. and a third partner in 1894. Spencer and his friends boarded their horses at the Milwaukee Country Club, where they were prominent members; they took steamships to Europe for extended vacations.

Through Tweedy and a growing business relationship with the Bradley Bank in Tomahawk, Spencer had grown close to Alice Bradley, whose father was president of the bank. They had moved in the same social circles for years. They and their friends were members of the Cotillion Club, the first dancing club organized in Milwaukee. In January 1891 she and her sister, Edna, attended the last cotillion of the season at the Milwaukee Athenaeum. It was a costume party attended by members of the Pabst, Tweedy, Ilsley and Bradley families and a host of other members of the city's highest echelon. Edna dressed as Audrey, from Shakespeare's *As You Like It*, Alice as the judge advocate in the musical burlesque "Faust Up to Date." Spencer wasn't at the party, having taken an ocean liner to London to begin a tour of Europe.

Spencer and Alice married in Milwaukee on May 9, 1904. Tweedy married Edna.

In addition to the Fox Point mansion, Spencer and Alice had a home in Santa Barbara, California. They were members of a moneyed class whose names made the society pages of the *New York Times* merely by their arrival in the Berkshires each summer. They left icy Wisconsin for the warmth of California or Florida for months at a time every year. When Edward Bradley died in 1910, he left each of his daughters $1.2 million.

Eventually James became vice president and John Tweedy a director of the Marshall & Ilsley Bank, while Spencer and R.B. Tweedy were both directors of the Bradley Bank. In addition to his banking duties, Spencer served as vice president of the Tomahawk Light, Telephone and Improvement Co., which was formed in February 1912 with capital of $50,000 and took over the interests of the Electric, Water and Telephone Co., including a power plant located in the yards of the Tomahawk Lumber Company. R.B. Tweedy was president and treasurer. At the end of October another company headed by Spencer and Tweedy was incorporated in Wisconsin, and purchased 44 miles of standard gauge railway lines and sidings, along with three locomotives and 47 railroad cars. The lines were leased to and operated by Tomahawk & Eastern Railway Company, which had been formed five years earlier and had the same officers—in effect, the new company was formed by the old company, bought the lines from the old company and then leased them back to the old company.

Times were good; Spencer's business interests were successful; he and Alice's comings and goings were the object of pubic interest.

"Mr. And Mrs. Jack Ilsley of Milwaukee, Wis., were the hosts to Mr. and Mrs. Spencer Ilsley, Mr. and Mrs. Jas. R. Richardson, of Providence, RI; Mr. And Mrs. Wm. Chapman, of Kansas City, MO, at a dinner party at Virginia

Inn, Thursday night," *The Winter Park Post* reported on March 7, 1918. The exclusive retreat had been a wintering spot on the shores of Lake Osceola for the wealthy ever since president Chester Arthur had visited and sung its praises three decades earlier.

"Mr. and Mrs. Spencer Ilsley of Milwaukee, Wis., left today for St. Augustine, Palm Beach and Miami en route home," the *Winter Park Post* would later report. "Mr. Ilsley is connected with Ilsley and Marshall Bank of Milwaukee. They were charmed with Winter Park and have made arrangements to return early next season. They were guests of Virginia Inn."

They and their friends were young, wealthy and privileged. In Milwaukee they attended the Episcopal Church; made subscription donations to the building fund for the Girl's Friendly Holiday House; attended private dances and private country clubs and private schools. They went to work at their father's land companies, their neighbor's railroads, their fraternity brother's family banks; they traveled to Florida, to Europe, to the Far East; they vacationed in Mexico and the Caribbean and New England; drank in Parisian cafes, yachted on Long Island Sound, raced horses across the rolling hills of Kentucky and Maryland and Virginia. It was all like an episode out of *The Great Gatsby*, F. Scott Fitzgerald's 1925 grand summation of the age. Fitzgerald's editor, Maxwell Perkins, counted among his haunts Middleburg, a rural hamlet in Northern Virginia's foxhunting country. He spent time at Elizabeth Lemmon's Welbourne estate in Middleburg, and encouraged Fitzgerald to do the same during some of the author's darker days. Middleburg was, as Fitzgerald had described Gatsby's West Egg, "a world complete in itself, with its own standards and its own great figures, second to nothing because it had no consciousness of being so."

Agnes didn't stay in Michigan long, and she kept alive her ties to the Extension Division and her alma mater. In 1919 the University of Wisconsin's College of Agriculture published her pamphlet, "Making Clothes Last Longer." When the class of 1915 prepared for its five-year reunion in June 1920, she was appointed to the Class Stunts committee. By November 1922 she was back in North Dakota, taking charge of the decorations for an alumni banquet held in Fargo, and was working as assistant leader in the North Dakota University extension division, doing home demonstration work in Fargo. She was 30 years old.

She remained in touch with Spencer, who was going through the most turbulent period of his life. Alice and James had died unexpectedly within a few months of each other. Spencer, now in his mid–50s, retired from most of his banking business, sold his Fox Point home and bought a house and a few acres of land in Middleburg. More and more of his spare time would be spent in Virginia's piedmont.

The property took up most of a town block on Middleburg's east end. There were more than a dozen rooms in the largest building on the property, a white-brick manor house. The building stretched from a two-story porch facing Washington Street, the village's main avenue, back through two wings to another two-story porch that looked out over a well-kept lawn to a separate garage, which had been converted from horse stables. The manor house was crowned by a tiny third floor cupola; its green metal roof broken by several towering chimneys; its windows framed by black shutters; English Ivy cascading down its walls; large cherry and apple trees shading its grounds. It had been built in the early 1850s and had been used as a residence and a place of business over the years. Russian immigrant Edward Potz had run a watch making and repair shop in the building; Daniel K. Smith, a salesman for a Baltimore hardware company who had served as the town's mayor a decade earlier, had made his home there with his wife, Lucy. Spencer bought the manor house from William Adams, a merchant — and Lucy Smith's father — who had lived there with his son.

At the opposite corner of the property was a smaller cottage with a garage in its basement and two entrances, one facing across the property back towards Washington Street and another with steps down to the back road, Marshall Street. The cottage had originally been built as quarters for servants who worked in the manor house.

In early 1924 Agnes left her job with North Dakota University's extension division to become director of the Educational Service Department for silk manufacturers Cheney Brothers. She traveled across the country giving lectures on the development and uses of silks, and did some work as a buyer for the Connecticut-based company. She was based at Cheney Brothers' New York City office and rented an apartment nearby, at 10 West 11th St. Her elder brother, John, lived in Great Neck, on Long Island, and was a manager in the commercial division at Recordak Corporation, a subsidiary of Eastman Kodak Co., at 350 Madison Avenue. Paul, who was several years younger than Agnes, designed furniture and furniture showrooms. And Spencer Ilsley, who traveled to Long Island regularly, began to see her more and more often.

By 1927, she was living at 140 West 58th Street, a block south of Central Park in midtown Manhattan, writing articles for fashion magazines. She married Spencer on Wednesday, June 15, 1927, in a ceremony attended by a few close friends and family in the Cathedral of St. John the Divine in Manhattan. Spencer was 60; Agnes 35. She left her job immediately.

For a short time the newlyweds lived in Milwaukee, and they would continue to return there for several weeks every summer, but they quickly decided to make Middleburg their home. Spencer had made friends there in the years since his retirement, and Agnes's cousin, Charles Oliver Iselin, Jr., was in the village too. Originally from Glen Head, Long Island, Iselin was active in the local Democratic Party and was on the board of directors of Middleburg National Bank. He and his wife attended Emmanuel Episcopal Church, which was just across the street from the Ilsleys' home. His grandfather had founded the banking firm A. Iselin & Co.; his father had been a founding member of the National Beagle Club in 1887, a member of the New York Yacht Club and part owner of four America's Cup defenders— he headed a syndicate to finance *Vigilant* that included some of the nation's richest and most powerful men, most with mansions on Long Island's Gold Coast: shipping and railroad magnate Cornelius Vanderbilt, Henry Astor Carey, August Belmont Jr. (developer of New York's Belmont Park racetrack), Charles R. Flint (founder of the company that was to become IBM) and Edwin Dennison Morgan. His uncle sailed *Ace* to victory in the International Championship in 1925 and the Bacardi Cup in 1927. A year after graduating from Harvard in 1915, Charles and four other men formed the Institute Corporation, bought 508 acres in western Loudoun County and leased it back to the National Beagle Club.

THREE

The Age-Old Divide

From its earliest days, Middleburg had little in common with Leesburg, the county seat, and even less with northern Loudoun County. The farmers around Middleburg owned larger plots of land, had more money, had kept more slaves and were, for lack of a better term, more Southern than the rest of the county. They were a separate society, more culturally attached to neighboring Fauquier County, Richmond and the Carolinas than Loudoun County, Georgetown or Philadelphia. Over the years the people of Middleburg and Leesburg would find little to agree on.

The county had been settled by Southern planters who came north from the Tidewater area and Northern Germans and Quakers who came south. The northerners opposed slavery on religious grounds and, being small parcel farmers, craftsmen and merchants, had little need for African field hands. The southern plantation owners, on the other hand, owned larger tracts and plantations, and had both the need and financial means to embrace slavery.

Early on, the line of differing opinion on slavery and other issues was drawn roughly through the county's middle, from east to west, with Leesburg straddling that line, both geographically and philosophically. The county was fractured by differing religious beliefs, economic structures, national backgrounds and, eventually, by secession and racial tensions. Slave auctions were held on the steps of the Leesburg courthouse and slaves performed most of the unskilled labor in Loudoun, but there were also Loudouners, including Charles Fenton Mercer, a U.S. Congressman and co-founder with James Madison, of the American Colonization Society, who supported repatriation of Virginia's African population. Quaker Samuel M. Janney published and distributed abolitionist literature from his home near Purcellville, west of Leesburg.

By 1835 Leesburg had about 50 houses, two dozen general stores, and three churches: one Presbyterian, one Methodist, and one Episcopalian. A red brick courthouse and adjacent jail had been built on the northeast corner of the intersection of the county's two main roads, at the center of the town.

As the Civil War approached, Loudoun was becoming one of Virginia's wealthiest counties, thanks to the popularity of its grain crops. There were about 22,000 people living in the county in 1860 and nearly a quarter of them were slaves. In Middleburg and Fauquier County, nearly half the population lived in chains. The area had supported Whig candidates for some time, but in 1860 the party was in collapse. Of the 2,942 votes cast in Loudoun County in the presidential election that year, 69 percent went to John Bell, the Constitutional Union Party candidate from Tennessee. Bell owned slaves but was considered a moderate on the slavery issue. John Breckinridge, the leader of a group of Democrats who had split with the party and supported the continuation of slavery, received 778 votes. Another 120 votes went to Stephen Douglas, a mainstream Democrat who believed each state should be allowed to choose whether it would allow slavery. Abraham Lincoln, whose name did not appear on the ballot in Virginia that year, received just 11 write-in votes in Loudoun County. Bell carried the state by fewer than 200 votes. Lincoln won the national election, and the Union was split.

Loudoun threatened to split with it. The county's representatives to Virginia's 1861 Secession Convention voted against secession, even as a mass meeting in Leesburg endorsed the Ordinance of Secession. The county's 1,626–726 vote to leave the Union exposed again the age-old split; the northern Lovettsville and Waterford districts voted to stay in the Union, while Middleburg voted unanimously for secession.

Virginia seceded; just across the Potomac River, a divided Maryland chose to remain in the Union, as did several counties in western Virginia, which split from the Commonwealth to form the new state of West Virginia. Loudoun was left a Confederate peninsula jutting north into a sea of Union sentiment.

When war came, Loudouners remained split. In Waterford Samuel Means organized two companies of cavalry, which became the only organized Virginia units to fight on the Union side. Other Loudouners made their way across the Potomac to join the Potomac Home Brigade and the Battalion of Maryland Calvary, Union units operating on the river's northern shore.

But a majority of Loudouners followed Virginia into the Confederacy. More than 20 Confederate units were formed in the county, most operating in Turner Ashby's 7th Virginia Cavalry. In Middleburg in July 1861 Burr Powell Noland was appointed Quartermaster General of the Confederate Army. Noland volunteered to serve without pay, and he donated 3,000 bushels of wheat and 150 head of cattle to the Confederacy. Asa Rogers, one of the original trustees of Middleburg's Emmanuel Episcopal Church, became a Brigadier General in the Confederate States Army. The Confederacy eventually adopted a flag designed by Rogers' son, Major Arthur Lee Rogers. The "blood stained banner" improved on the second flag of the Confederacy — the "stainless banner," which had the familiar "stars and bars" battle banner in its upper left corner on a pure white field — by placing a vertical red bar on the right side of the flag, to avoid the appearance of a flag of surrender. Emmanuel Episcopal's rector, Ovid Kin-

solving, was arrested by Union forces in 1863, charged with preaching seces-
sionist sermons, and sent to Capital Prison in Washington, DC.

The county would be an easy target for the Federal Army, with the Potomac
easily fordable at many locations. Southerners burned bridges between Loudoun
and Maryland, built three small forts around Leesburg, and stationed as many
troops as they could afford in the area in the first days of the Civil War.

There was sporadic action throughout the county all during the war.
Though no major battles were fought in Loudoun, it was a crossroads for armies
of both North and South, a stepping off point across the Potomac between
Union and Confederacy and, as such, it saw dozens of minor battles and skirmishes, including the battle of Ball's Bluff, a humiliating Northern defeat fought
at the Potomac river near Leesburg. And Loudoun became the hunting ground
for one of the war's most controversial figures.

Vilified and feared by the North, mythologized across the south, Colonel
John S. Mosby and his 43rd Battalion of Virginia Cavalry — the Partisan Rangers
or, more commonly, Mosby's Rangers— raided and skirmished in an area cen-
tered at Middleburg. They fought a classic brand of guerrilla warfare, harassing
the supply lines and communications of their northern enemy while living off
the land and the accommodations of their own families, friends and neighbors.
Mosby's men cut telegraph wires, stole supply wagons, warped railroad lines
and were a constant thorn in the side of Federal efforts to calm Northern Virginia,
subdue the Shenandoah Valley, and protect the exposed underbelly of the Union
in Maryland and Pennsylvania. His legend as the "Grey Ghost" of the Confederacy, able to appear behind Union lines to create mischief and then disappear
again into the night, created a panic in border towns. During a raid into Fairfax
County, Mosby pulled a half dressed — some said half drunk — Union officer
from his bed in the middle of the night; in nearby Herndon, Mosby's men dis-
guised themselves as Union soldiers to sneak into a public house, where they
captured unsuspecting federal soldiers as they ate their dinners.

Among the northerners who hunted unsuccessfully for Mosby was Herman
Melville. In April 1864 the author of *Moby Dick* joined about 100 Union cav-
alrymen commanded by his friend and fellow poet, James Russell Lowell, and
spent three days tracking Mosby through Loudoun County. Lowell's command
captured a handful of Mosby's men, only to be ambushed by the main Ranger
force as they entered Leesburg. After the war, Melville wrote at great length of
the adventure in "The Scout Toward Aldie."

> The cavalry-camp lies on the slope
> Of what was late a vernal hill,
> But now like a pavement bare —
> An outpost in the perilous wilds
> Which ever are lone and still;
> But Mosby's men are there —
> Of Mosby best beware.

Over the course of 106 stanzas Melville described Mosby's Rangers as phantoms, ghostly apparitions slipping in out and of the Virginia forests while Union troops trailed them, always one step behind. Northern soldiers stumbled, blind and confused, through the Virginia night, so spooked by Mosby's ghostly reputation that they were startled by a rabbit, frightened that Mosby's sharp eyes would see the reflection of the moon off their uniform buttons, fearful that all of "Mosby-land" was spying and setting traps for them.

> All spake of him, but few had seen
> Except the maimed ones of the low;
> Yet rumor made him every thing—
> A farmer—woodman—refugee—
> The man who crossed the field but now;
> A spell about his life did cling—
> Who to the ground shall Mosby bring?

Eventually a trap was set. The Rangers struck and, before the Union soldiers could return fire, Lowell's command "parted like boats in a raging tide." Seven Confederate prisoners escaped, and "Mosby's men [were] off like the wind."

In the closing months of the war Mosby, by then promoted to Colonel, and George Custer, a 24-year-old Union Brigadier General two decades removed from his infamous end at the Little Big Horn, each summarily executed men captured from each other's commands. And both the southern Army of Northern Virginia and the northern Army of the Potomac had laid waste to much of the Potomac's southern shore.

After the war, Congress reimbursed some Loudouners—Union sympathizers, mainly Quakers in the northern portion of the county—for losses they had suffered. Mosby was given permission by the Circuit Court in Leesburg to practice law in Loudoun County. His men returned to their pre-war lives as farmers and merchants across the Virginia countryside and were welcomed harmoniously into the newly re-formed American Union, some with notable success. John Henry Alexander, an A Company officer, earned his law degree at the University of Virginia and practiced in Leesburg before moving to California, where he became the State's Attorney General in 1895. John Ballard became the Commissioner of Revenue in neighboring Fairfax County.

In cities and towns across the South, African Americans lived in separate neighborhoods, on the edges of—or occasionally, in defined areas within—larger and better maintained white communities. In the 1880s Thomas Glascock, a former slave owner who held vast tracts of land in both Loudoun and Fauquier counties, began selling off portions of his less valuable holdings to former slaves that he and some of his neighbors had owned. At $20 an acre, the land, located just west of Middleburg, was attainable by many former slaves. Within 20 years Glascock's property had been converted into the village of St. Louis, one of the largest African American enclaves in the region, with its own school, stores and Baptist Church. In Leesburg the African American population was centered in the Black Bottom neighborhood along the town's southern edge. And there was a large African American community in central Loudoun, on a knob officially called Negro Mountain. On some old maps, and in common usage, it was more often labeled Nigger Mountain.

One burr in the side of those Middleburg residents who had sought secession was the local office of the Freedmen's Bureau, which opened its doors on North Jay Street, one block off the town's main road. The work done by the Union officers who staffed the Bureau—and the steady stream of newly freed slaves who lined up at its doors—was a nagging reminder of the South's humiliation. And while Leesburg's primary burying ground for white residents was called Union Cemetery, its name came about to indicate that it was open to all religions, not necessarily to all political viewpoints. The cemetery's focal point was a memorial to Confederate dead that was erected among the headstones in October, 1877. The obelisk, erected on the sixteenth anniversary of the battle at nearby Ball's Bluff, was inscribed with a dedication to the Confederate soldiers who had fallen during the daylong skirmish. No mention of the Union dead was attached to the monument.

With the end of reconstruction and the withdrawal of Federal troops from the South, racial tensions in the 1880s increasingly took a violent turn. Newspapers of the day were filled with stories of crime, violence, even murder, but mobs were incited to violence only in cases of black-on-white crimes.

On January 19, 1880, a mob in Fauquier County lynched Arthur Jordan for miscegenation—race mixing—which Virginia's legislature had attempted to make illegal. Jordan's death came just a week after another man was lynched in Poolesville, Maryland, just across the Potomac River from Loudoun County. And, on February 18, Page Wallace became the first man to be lynched in Loudoun County.

The *Washington Post* had actually forecast Page's lynching two weeks earlier. He was accused of raping Mary Morman, a white schoolteacher, after escaping from the Leesburg jail, where he had been held on a lesser charge, and was believed to have crossed the Potomac into Maryland. "Wallace has not yet been caught, though the county is being scoured for him by a large party of men armed with knives, pistols and shotguns," the *Post* reported on February 20. "When last seen, he was between Point of Rocks and Sandy Hook, and, if captured, a lynching may be expected." Days later he was arrested in Washington County, Maryland, and sent back to Leesburg on a train accompanied by Loudoun County Sheriff James Caruthers and an armed deputy.

"A body of 200 men, nearly all masked, met the train as it stopped at Point of Rocks, took possession of the Sheriff and the prisoner, and acted as guard as all marched to the ferry and crossed the river," the *New York Times* reported. Morman was with the mob. "As soon as they landed on the Virginia shore, about dusk, the Regulators took the prisoner by force from the Sheriff, placed a rope around his neck, marched him to the spot where he had outraged Mary Morman. Hooting at his piteous appeals for mercy, they hanged him to the nearest tree. After the rope had been fastened, the Regulators marched off 20 paces, turned and fired three volleys of bullets into his dangling body." Morman was then handed a gun and fired her own shots into the corpse. "The crowd then dispersed, and Wallace's body was left hanging," according to the *Times*.

Though Congress had attempted through the 13th, 14th and 15th Amendments and the Civil Rights Act of 1875 to end segregation and establish voting rights for African Americans, civil rights for former slaves and their descendants were far from guaranteed. Court decisions and the acts of state, county and local governments across the country often flew in the face of the Federal Government's official positions.

In 1880 the U.S. Supreme Court upheld the convictions in Virginia of two African Americans who had been tried before an all-white jury. The *Virginia v. Rives* case made official an unwritten policy that had been in place across the South for generations: there could be no blacks on juries. The Court declared that the racial make-up of a jury did not deny a defendant their rights.

In May 1883, 17 delegates elected at the Colored Mass Meeting in Leesburg presented a petition to Circuit Court Judge James B. McCabe requesting his recognition of their right to serve as jurors and as judges of elections. "We desire in the future a fuller recognition of our rights and privileges which the laws of the land have guaranteed to us, hence we respectfully petition your Honor in the future, to recognize our rights," they said.[1] McCabe denied their right to be election judges, but allowed that blacks could serve as jurors. Still, it would be more than a half-century before any African American would be seated on a jury in Loudoun County.

On November 14, 1889, Leesburg's newspaper, *The Mirror*, printed a report about another lynching—"a terrible warning," according to the newspaper— that had occurred in the town on November 8. Nineteen-year-old Owen Anderson was accused of attempting to rape 15-year-old Mary Leith, a white girl and "daughter of a most respected gentleman of this county," as she walked home from school in Hamilton, a small village west of Leesburg. There were no witnesses and the girl could not identify her assailant but, based on the discovery of a sack found near the crime scene that was said to be Anderson's, and other circumstantial evidence, he was jailed.

There were those in town who said Anderson was guilty of nothing more than playing a Halloween joke on a young friend. Anderson had worn the sack over his head, they said, to scare the girl as both walked down the road. But, according to *The Mirror*, "The knowledge of the fiendish assault aroused the wildest indignation in the community where it occurred, especially when it became known that Anderson had confessed his crime, and was securely ensconced behind the bars of our new jail. A feeling of violent indignation asserted itself, and a band of resolute men, determined that however much their action might be deplored by those preferring that the law should take its course, they would themselves become the avengers."

Sometime after midnight as many as 40 men on horseback rode into town. They took prisoner the town's night watchman, W.R. Webb, when he approached them at the corner of Loudoun and Church streets. "I did not know or recognize any one of the entire party, either at the corner or on the hill," Webb said. "All but one had their faces concealed, some with handkerchiefs and some with rags. Would not know any of the party if I were to meet him anywhere. Did not recognize the voice of any one, nor the horse of any one."[2]

When they arrived at the town jail, three of the men bluffed their way in by posing as a pair of lawmen and their prisoner. They had no official documents commanding jailor C.F. Laycock to accept a prisoner, and he did not recognize any of them — the "lawmen" were wearing masks — but Laycock, carrying only an oil lamp and a set of keys, unlocked the jailhouse doors and led the trio to an empty cell. At that point they pointed pistols at the jailor and took his lamp and keys.

"Then they went in, found Owen Anderson, put a rope around his neck, and left with him," Laycock would later testify. "That was the last I saw of them."[3] Webb went to wake Sheriff H.H. Russell, who came to the jailhouse to investigate. But by that time the mob, it's members "masked, some with white and some with black cloths, with holes cut for eyes and mouth, and some seem to be painted," had already hung Anderson and riddled his body with bullets on the freight depot of the Richmond & Danville Railroad, a few blocks south of the jail.

Members of the lynch mob were seen riding out of town but, still, none were recognized and they were not pursued.

"I could not recognize any of these parties now, if I should meet them," Laycock said during a subsequent coroner's inquest. "I know none of them at all. I have no suspicion even of who any one of the party was, so as to put an officer on the track of him."[4]

The coroner's jury heard testimony from both white and black witnesses, none of whom could identify any of the men in the lynch mob.

"A band of men have taken upon themselves the fearful responsibility of going outside of the law and themselves meting out to the offender their own idea of justice," Judge R.H. Tebbs told a grand jury which had been convened in the courthouse to hear the charges against Anderson. "It may be said that rape is a greater crime than murder, that woman's purity is dearer than man's life; that the offender had but met his just doom and that an innocent girl has been spared a terrible ordeal.

"Yet, gentlemen, it must be remembered that the law is the safeguard and protector of our order and well-being; that if men once acquire the habit of meting out their own ideas of justice in defiance of the law, then we may bid farewell to safety and good order."[5]

The Anderson case was removed from the jury's docket. Anderson was buried in a pauper's cemetery a mile east of the courthouse and jail, on the opposite side of town from the Union Cemetery.

"The offense that thus fired men's breasts and the summary visitation of punishment were alike fearful, and the fate of the self-confessed author of the outrage should serve as a terrible admonition to the violators of law for the protection of female virtue; the holiest and most sacred of earthly jewels," *The Mirror* warned its readers. "Who the raiders were, or where they came from, are mysteries that will probably never be solved."

In 1902 delegates to Virginia's fifth constitutional convention put in place a poll tax, placed minimum age, residency and literacy requirements on all voters, and required any man wishing to vote to be able to read or understand the Constitution, have paid taxes on property valued at $333 or more, or be a U.S. or Confederate veteran or the son of a veteran. All of the changes were designed to eliminate black voters from the election process. The new state constitution also officially segregated Virginia's public schools.

At the end of that July Charles Craven, an African American with a reputation as a panhandler and a petty criminal — he'd already spent time in jail for barn burning and there were reports that he had robbed a man on the road just days before — was accused of robbing and shooting to death William H. Wilson near Loudoun's eastern border with Fairfax County. Neighbors said Craven had been begging for food at their doors that Tuesday morning and was "enraged" when they wouldn't give him any. Wilson was shot at about 1 p.m. There were no witnesses and Wilson died before he could describe his killer.

Wilson lived on a farm near Herndon with his wife and son. He had been a Confederate soldier, leaving his original regiment in the closing days of the war to join Mosby's Company H, and was planning to attend a reunion of Mosby's men in Leesburg that week.

According to *The Mirror*, posses that had formed in Herndon, Sterling and Leesburg coalesced into one large mob of nearly 300 men — among them Loudoun County Sheriff Russell and Leesburg Mayor B.V. White — when they met at Goose Creek. Bloodhounds — including a pack run by Hurricane Branch, who was something of a celebrity tracker up and down the East coast, searched for Craven across the area, but a drenching rain hampered the pursuit. Craven's brother's home in Ashburn was being watched. "At Dranesville the hounds were allowed to smell a coat and other clothing which Craven discarded. The animals caught the scent and tracked the negro in the direction of Ashburn," the *Washington Post* reported. A group of men surrounded a cornfield near Sterling after Craven was reported seen there; a Leesburg police officer said he fired three shots at Craven near Goose Creek. It was believed he would try to cross the Potomac into Maryland.

On Wednesday afternoon the weather cleared. The Leesburg chapter of the Daughters of the Confederacy was hosting a reunion of Mosby's men on the courthouse lawn in Leesburg. Mosby himself could not attend that year, but hundreds of the faithful enjoyed a huge banquet, music and speeches by "many prominent members of the Confederacy," according to *The Mirror*. The opening of the summer session of the Circuit Court, and August Court Days — an annual festival which brought most of the county's residents into town — were to begin the next day, as was Emancipation Day, an annual celebration held by the county's African Americans at the county fairgrounds.

That night a reporter from *The Mirror* noted that investigators were about to renew their search for Craven "and no doubt before this paper goes to press the fiend will be caught, and if caught, will probably be lynched." According to the *Washington Post*, Sheriff Russell was likely to "do all in his power to prevent the posse from killing Craven. Rumor has it that the negro will by lynched if caught in Fairfax County, where Wilson was killed. Wilson was a much-respected Confederate veteran, and the people of his county feel that no death can be too severe for the man who committed the crime charged to Craven."

At about 10 a.m. on Thursday Craven, barefoot and wearing only a sleeveless undershirt and a pair of yellow overalls, was found hiding in a straw stack near Ashburn. As word got out that he had been found, dozens of men gathered at the Ashburn depot, shouting threats at the prisoner as he and his guards waited for a train to take him to the jail in Leesburg. "Craven was hurried into the train and the conductor pulled away from the station before the disgruntled crowd could get possession of the negro," the *Washington Post* reported. Further east, in Alexandria, 31 members of the Army National Guard's 29th Infantry Division received orders from Governor Andrew Jackson Montague to prepare to take the train to Leesburg to protect Craven.

The news of Craven's capture had been telegraphed ahead to Leesburg, and another crowd of riotous men met the train at the station. The mob had to be held back by authorities as the terrified prisoner was marched up the street to the jailhouse. In a short time a crowd of 300–500 armed men on horseback — "from Fairfax County," according to *The Mirror*— had swarmed into the county seat. Mayor White quickly ordered every bar in town to close its doors. "Whisky shan't hang anybody here today," he said.

White and Russell called on the gathering crowd to disperse, but still they came.

"Most of the men wore working clothes and were armed with muskets and shotguns," according to a *Washington Post* report. "Rusty pistols protruded from the belts of most of the farmers. Leesburg had not seen such a demonstration since the war.

"Young men predominated among the armed horsemen. The badge of

Mosby's men, who held a reunion in Leesburg Wednesday, fluttered from the hickory shirts of some of the men and indicated that there were veterans in the party who were not strangers to warfare."

Now come a hideous confluence of disparate public displays. With the angry mob swirling around the jail, many of them having spent the previous afternoon reminiscing about their days in Mosby's Rangers— and, despite White's move to close the bars, the town having been awash in beer for two days— members of the Emancipation Day parade, celebrating the release from slavery of themselves and their families 40 years earlier, came marching into town, led by the Sugarland Colored Band, which was playing "America the Beautiful."

"Taunts and jeers greeted the colored marshals, who wore gay sashes and headed the procession. Some of the armed horsemen got into an altercation with some negroes who tried to force their way through the crowd, and police officers were called to prevent trouble," according to the *Washington Post*.

Others in the mob attacked the jailhouse's front door with sledgehammers.

"Men, remember you are wiping out every law of Loudoun County when you do this deed," said the Reverend E.S. Hinks, the rector of nearby St. James Episcopal Church. "There's not a jury in the United States that would not convict the man. Why take the law in your own hands when it is certain that the man will be punished?"[6] Laycock and his wife, who lived in the jailhouse, refused to give the mob their keys, but the armed men forced their way into the building and on toward the cells.

"A shout went up and scores of excited men forced their way through another iron door into the corridors surrounding the steel cages. Half a dozen negro prisoners who were in jail for minor offenses pleaded for mercy," the *Washington Post* reported.

"For a time the lynchers were unable to locate Craven. He concealed himself in a dark part of one of the cages and his pursuers were unable to distinguish him. Finally guns were thrust through the bars of the cages and the excited men demanded that the prisoner be turned over to them or they would shoot all the men in the cage ... hundreds of farmers, armed to the teeth, had surrounded the jail for two hours, and were urging the men on the inside to deliver Craven over to them. Escape would have been impossible." Craven pleaded his innocence as the rioters used their sledgehammers to break the locks on the cell door.

"Frightened negroes stood a safe distance from the prison and looked on with ill-concealed alarm," the *Washington Post* reported. "The Emancipation Day celebration, which was being held in the fair grounds, had lost its attractions for the colored people. They deserted the exercises and came to town to watch one of their race meet his fate. Colored men and women stood in groups and discussed the mob's action in whispers. They voiced no protest. It would have been useless.

"'This is an emancipation day hanging!' members of the mob shouted as the negro was led to his death.

"A rope was thrown about Craven's neck as soon as he was taken from the jail. Demands were made that he be strung up on one of the electric light poles which line the pike near the prison, but the citizens of Leesburg were insistent and urged that non-residents should spare the reputation of the town."

Russell and his deputies did not follow the mob as it roared out of the town square. Instead, the Sheriff sent a telegram to the National Guardsmen in Alexandria, telling them they need not come. It was too late to save Craven.

The mob dragged Craven to the potter's field burial ground just outside of the town limits, where Owen Anderson had been buried 13 years earlier. They hung him from a small tree among the crumbling headstones, some of which dated back to 1839. His body "was riddled with bullets, probably 400 shots being fired," the *Brunswick Herald* reported.

Later the same day, Coroner H.O. Clagett ordered Craven to be buried just a few feet from the spot where he had died. No African Americans were willing to take the job of digging the grave.

"The murder was unprovoked, cold blooded and dastardly, and the man guilty of robbery a few days before and many other crimes—but that is no excuse for outlawery and mob law," Leesburg resident Ida Lee Rust confided to her diary that night. "It is a blot upon Loudoun's fair record."[7]

A coroner's inquest and a grand jury were immediately called. But many of the witnesses already had trouble remembering who they had seen on the courthouse lawn just 48 hours earlier.

Eventually, Scott Bradley, George Williams and a Leesburg saloonkeeper, Charles Lowenback, were identified by witnesses as having been leaders of the mob that dragged Craven from the jail. Loudoun County Treasurer T.H. Vanderverter testified that the incident might never have occurred if the crowd hadn't been whipped into a frenzy by news that Montague had ordered out the militia. Cecil Connor, a lawyer who testified only after being threatened with contempt of court, said that Bradley, Williams and Lowenback were the only men in Leesburg who had not tried to prevent the lynching.

But Fairfax County authorities resented the implication that the mob had come from their jurisdiction.

"I was standing on the jail steps when the mob approached, did all in my power to protect the prisoner, and can state of my own knowledge that there were but few Fairfax men present, and that the men engaged in the lynching were unknown to me," said J.R. Allison, Fairfax County's deputy sheriff and deputy treasurer. He continued,

> One reason why more Fairfax men were not present was that Craven, having committed the crime in Fairfax, was pursued by a large force of Fairfax County men for two days near the scene of the crime. The fugitive fled on the evening before his capture far up into Loudoun County, and the weary citizens of Fairfax were unable to continue the chase in large numbers. Consequently, the crowd was made up largely of Loudoun County people from the vicinity of Goose Creek, where Craven was last seen before his capture.

Fairfax County never had a lynching. Mr. Wilson was a citizen of Loudoun County, as was also his murderer, who had committed many crimes in said county, and at the time of his arrest was wanted by the authorities of his county for robbing a boy near Leesburg.

The true reason why Craven was lynched was the feeling engendered by Craven's past bad record, added to which was the murder of a highly respected citizen of Loudoun County.[8]

On August 5 the Grand Jury indicted 10 men in connection with the lynching.

"Rumors have been circulated to the effect that an attempt to prosecute any of the men who are said to have been connected with the hanging of Craven will result in the delivery of the prisoners from the jail," the *Washington Post* reported. "Men who assisted in hanging Craven have boasted that they will not see any members of the mob suffer for bringing the negro to speedy justice."

And they were right. No witnesses would testify against the indicted men, and they all went free.[9]

In the midmorning of an exceptionally hot day in late May, 1908, hundreds of Loudouners and guests from around the state, including Governor Claude Swanson, a clutch of aging Confederate veterans, along with members of Daughters of the Confederacy, Sons of Confederate Veterans and Children of the Confederacy, gathered on the courthouse lawn in Leesburg. The Bluemont Band struck up "Maryland, My Maryland." Singing along with the battle hymn, which had urged Maryland to rise up against the Union during the Civil War ("Dear mother, burst the tyrant's chain/Virginia should not call in vain/She meets her sisters on the plain/'sic semper' is the proud refrain/that baffles minions back amain/arise in majesty again/Maryland, my Maryland"), the crowd marched to Union Cemetery. There they sang "Nearer, My God, To Thee" and placed flowers on the graves of Confederate dead.

At noon the crowd, by now numbering in the thousands, returned to the courthouse lawn, where the Daughters of the Confederacy and the Sons of Confederate Veterans hosted a luncheon. The Loudoun Chapter of the Daughters of the Confederacy had rooms across the street, over the Peoples National Bank, where members were available to offer some succor to lady visitors suffering from the heat.

Beginning at 1 p.m., Swanson and U.S. Senator John W. Daniel, who were introduced by Circuit Court Judge C.E. Nicols, made lengthy speeches. Harry T. Harrison of Leesburg read a poem he had written for the occasion ("Today to us who gather here/you are that someone our hearts hold dear/That father, brother, husband, lover/at peace with God beneath the sod/who heard the call, who walked the way/the soldier of right who wore the gray...").[10]

Finally, the grandson of local Confederate hero Colonel Elijah B. White and members of the Loudoun, Middleburg and Blue Ridge chapters of the Daughters of the Confederacy unveiled a bronze statue of a confederate infantry man cocking his musket, standing guard in front of the courthouse atop a large granite base. The monument, which was the creation of Richmond sculptor Frederick William Sievers, had been paid for through the efforts of the Daughters of the Confederacy and Sons of Confederate Veterans, helped in no small part by a $500 donation from the Loudoun County Board of Supervisors.

The Ku Klux Klan of the 1920s was a popular, mainstream institution that presented itself as a wholesome, family-friendly pillar of society. The Klan fielded amateur baseball teams and appeared in newspapers more often than not in stories about community picnics. But membership was limited to white, Protestant, "native" Americans and, at its core, the Klan remained a white supremacist organization dedicated to racial purity and the subjugation of immigrants, blacks, Catholics, and other minority groups.

In Loudoun County the Klan sometimes tipped the sheriff's office off to the location of stills, and at other times allied itself with bootleggers. In 1923 the Klan was involved in a gunfight near Aldie, a few miles east of Middleburg, with Methodist preacher H.C. Marsh, who was president of the county's League of Law Enforcement, which had been organized to combat the illegal liquor trade. At about the same time, local newspapers printed a letter sent by the Klan, threatening to kill a black Baptist minister who had been preaching in the Middleburg area. The minister did not return to Middleburg. When Middleburg drug store owner W.H. Bradfield hired an African American to work behind the counter at his soda fountain, members of the local Ku Klux Klan picketed the store.

The Ku Klux Klan met at Ashburn August 15, 1923, initiating 15 new members before a burning cross and approximately 2,000 onlookers, and in November another Klan rally was held in Herndon.

That fall, Loudoun County Sheriff E.S. Adrian led several of his deputies on a raid of a still set up near Daysville on the Potomac river, "the largest and most complete one that has ever been captured in the county," according to the *Loudoun Times.* The local Klan had tipped Adrian off to the location of the still. In a second raid that week J.D. Lambert Jr., a special prohibition officer — who also ran a garage in Leesburg — was shot and killed while chasing moonshiners near Ashburn.

In 1924, after decades of attempting to outlaw miscegenation, the Virginia General Assembly approved a Racial Integrity Law authorizing county clerks to deny marriage licenses to couples who could not prove that they were of the same race. The law required all Virginians born before 1912 to carry a certificate declaring their race — the choices were "white" or "colored." Only those who could show they had no more than one-sixteenth American Indian heritage, and no African heritage, were qualified to declare that they were white, and the new law made it a felony to falsify the certificates. Also adopted that year was

Virginia's Sterilization Act, which called for the compulsory sterilization of the "feebleminded ... insane, idiotic, imbecile, or epileptic."

Jim Crow laws already in place in Virginia included mandatory poll taxes, which were used to deny the right to vote by tying suffrage to income. Every man and woman over the age of 21, whether they intended to vote or not, had to pay the poll tax six months prior to election day; no vote could be cast until one had paid the poll tax for three straight years.

The Knights of the Ku Klux Klan regularly ran recruitment ads in local newspapers ("A Call to Real Americans: Are you a native born, white, Gentile, American Citizen?") and "A Klansman's Creed" was published on the front page of Fairfax's *News-Observer* in August 1925. The treatise ("published by request") presented the Klan as a free-speech, free-press, anti–Papal, anti-union, pseudo-religious organization that believed in public schools, separation of Church and State, and limits on both immigration and the rights of immigrants. The creed also claimed that the KKK did not support mob violence, though it believed "laws should be enacted to prevent the causes of mob violence."

On a chilly Saturday evening in Purcellville in November 1925, nearly 500 men and women dressed in full Klan regalia were entertained by speakers, including E.F. Randolph, a Grand Klaliff—a state leader—from North Carolina, before rising for a torch-lit parade through the town. For days Purcellville had been overwhelmed by an influx of Klansmen, including groups from Alexandria, Ballston, Winchester and Harrisonburg in the Shenandoah Valley, and others that had crossed the river from Maryland, and Washington, DC. They drove to town in cars and trucks and were delivered by special trains, gathering at the auditorium just after dark, where "the ladies of the Methodist Church South served a well arranged supper," according to an approving review of the event published that week in the *Loudoun Times-Mirror*.

"The parade was headed by six white robed horses with riders. Then followed the Ballston brass band, Purcellville and Ballston men and women, the 'little red school house' and Brunswick Kitchenette Band. Close behind came other knights of the order until the line of parade could be seen in the far distance only as a moving mass of white robed objects."

Purcellville's ties to the Klan lasted for years. In 1926 Purcellville Klan No. 113 drew another large crowd when it called for a gathering of the faithful "neath the uplifted fiery cross" to "hear Americanism spoken." In a large announcement published in the *Loudoun Times-Mirror*, the organization invited "All Klansmen, Junior Klansmen, Klanswomen, Tri-K girls and the general public" to the event. In neighboring Fairfax, Klan No. 2 was a major sponsor of the annual fair, providing a robed parade, Klan team baseball, speakers and fireworks for the three-day event in September 1927. "Let us all cooperate to make this Fair the greatest in the history of our progressive county," Fairfax County secretary R.R. Buckley said in ads published prior to the fair. At the end of the third day, "a blaze of red lights flashed across the midway and the big parade was on," according to the *News-Observer*. "This was headed by the Grand Dragon of the State, the Grand Titan and other dignitaries who marched to the judge's stand at the racetrack, where the scene was lighted by the torches of the guard." More than 3,000 people heard a speech from the Grand Dragon, which was followed by the fireworks, "and the Klan Day was over." And intimidation by the local KKK continued: the Klan burned a cross near Merrifield, in Fairfax County, in April 1931.

In the boom years of the mid- and late–1920s wealthy families from New York, New England and the Midwest began buying property in and around Middleburg, drawn by the rolling Virginia foothills and the area's growing reputation as a haven for foxhunting. But Loudoun remained, for the most part, a dusty backwater. Its population, scattered across a few hundred thousand acres of rocky hills, more than 2,000 farms and a few tiny hamlets, had remained at about 22,000 for decades.

Democrats were the conservative party of the day. Most Loudoun County farmers considered Republicans too Northern and too liberal. Blacks were not allowed to vote in Democratic primaries across much of the South (the bylaws of the Virginia Democratic Party declared that "all white persons who are qualified to vote at the next ensuing general election" were eligible to vote in the Democratic primary). Not that the African American vote could have swayed any elections: Charles Fisher, a blacksmith who ran a shop in Middleburg with John Wesley Wanzer, was the only African American registered to vote in the county.

Virginia's economy, which was dominated by agricultural interests, was hit hard by the Great Depression, and by a severe drought that halved tobacco prices in 1930. The Depression was worsening in 1931; by summer, farm incomes had dropped by more than a third. The unemployment rate would hit 19 percent by the summer of 1932.

Loudoun County was a smaller, quieter, slower place then, crisscrossed by a confusing array of unpaved roads shared by thousands of horses and a few hundred cars. Grumbling was heard from some Loudoun residents about that year's $52,671 county budget. There were 19 students—all of them white—in the graduating class at Loudoun High School in 1932, though African Americans made up about 9 percent of the county's population. The few black children lucky enough to get a formal education went to separate schools. The only school for African Americans in the county seat was the Leesburg Training School, which had opened its doors in 1884. Conditions there were so bad that the state refused to grant accreditation to the school. In 1933, with the Depression deepening and budgets being slashed, the county school board would vote to keep white schools open nine months a year, while "colored" schools would operate for only eight months.

A rail line connected points as far west as Round Hill with Washington. It took more than two hours to make the trip from Alexandria to Leesburg, with stops at Arlington Mills, Carlinsville, Falls Church, Vienna, Hunter's Mill, Thornton's, Herndon, Guilford (now Sterling), Farmwell (now Ashburn), and Leesburg. Ridership on the line fell during the 1920s as more and more automobiles began appearing on area roads, but the train still carried milk to Alexandria from Northern Virginia farms, and a growing proportion of the railroad's revenue came from carrying freight.

The courthouse in Leesburg sat at the county's major intersection, where King Street and Market Street met; Market ran East/West, connecting the farms in Loudoun and points further west with markets and ports around the nation's capital; King ran North/South and, at a bridge a few miles north of town, was the region's doorway to Maryland and the North. The town's dusty streets— some paved, some still rough red Virginia clay and stone — were lit by occasional lights, bare bulbs strung by wire at a few of the town's major intersections. There were still hitching posts in front of every building, but automobiles were replacing horses as the popular mode of transportation.

The courthouse, built in 1894, was made of red brick, with four white Corinthian columns and a large clock and bell in its belfry, the tallest building in town. The county clerk's office was housed in another large red brick building behind the courthouse. The broad lawn in front of the courthouse, which served as Leesburg's town square and was home to memorials to the area's war dead — including the confederate statue dedicated in 1908 — was also faced by the Leesburg Inn.

For a block or two in each direction around the courthouse, the streets were lined by two and three story brick buildings, most built a century or more earlier, where drug stores, dry good stores, clothes stores, shoe repair shops, lunch counters and more operated on Depression-era shoestring budgets. The intersection was dominated by the courthouse and the huge Loudoun National Bank building, three stories tall, with its lobby door opening at the corner of King and Market streets and its limestone walls stretching far down the block along both streets. Built in 1871, the building looked out of place, more of an urban cornerstone than the little country town warranted. The upper floor and limestone veneer had been added to the building during the boom days of the 1920s, and the new facade lent the bank an aura of strength that depositors found reassuring. The bank's polished stone floors and the massive door of its walk-in vault, clearly visible to customers stepping into the cool, quiet lobby, offered them stability and security.

While the Loudoun National building appeared to have been cut from a single block of cold grey American rock, the People's National Bank, which stood on the other side of the intersection, was a pastiche of warmer, more rural — some would say European — architectural styles, a hodgepodge of arched windows and doorways, stone masonry on the first floor, red brick on the second and third, topped by a sharp peak and ornate details. Loudoun National catered to wealthy landowners; People's National was the bank of the little man: farmers, laborers, and clerks. It had been formed in the 1880's by Elijah B. White, who had been commander of the Confederate 35th Battalion of Virginia Calvary during the Civil War and had served a term as Loudoun County Sheriff after the war.

Directly across Market Street from the courthouse stood the Leesburg Post Office and, next to that, on a plot that had been a stable until just a few years earlier, was an automobile showroom, one of the first in the area. The large front windows, which looked out onto the courthouse grounds, displayed Dodges, and a row of garages behind the showroom offered service to Loudoun's auto enthusiasts. Just around the corner, south of the courthouse on King Street, John Hill Carter operated a garage where he and a handful of employees put the finishing touches on new Fords for sale.

There were three electrified traffic signals in town. The Leesburg Town Council had voted in 1927 to install signals on King Street at Loudoun Street, Market Street and Cornwall Streets to deal with an alarming increase in automobile traffic and minor accidents.

The town's two newspapers, *The Mirror* and the *Loudoun Times*, had merged in 1924 to become the *Loudoun Times-Mirror*. Written and printed in a small brick building at 21 North King Street, just across the street from the Leesburg Inn, the paper boasted the "largest circulation in Northern Virginia; therefore the best advertising medium." There were other, smaller newspapers in the county — the *Blue Ridge Herald* was published weekly in Purcellville, for example — but with more than 3,000 paid subscribers and many more copies sold on the town's streets each week, the *Times-Mirror* was the paper of record in the county seat. It was fiercely partisan, reflecting the dominance of local Democratic politics, but it was generally filled with small town news, stories of petty crimes, livestock and crop prices, and wedding and funeral announcements. By 1931, former Governor Westmoreland Davis, who lived on the 2,000-acre Morven Park estate on the edge of town, had bought the *Times-Mirror* and supervised a small staff, as few as eight people. They were a rough and tumble bunch. Editor Robert T. "Speedy" Corbell, a former *Richmond Times-Dispatch* reporter, once got in a fistfight with a political opponent in the street outside the *Times-Mirror* offices.

One block south of the courthouse, at the intersection of King and Loudoun streets, was a huge red brick building that housed on its ground floor the offices of the Leesburg town government, a few retail stores and the town's fire department. The second floor of the building was a theater, which had a balcony and room for more than 400 folding chairs. It was called the Opera House, but never staged a single opera. It showed movies during the silent era, and was the only venue in the area where large crowds could gather for seasonal dances or to see touring speakers. In April 1923 "a large and well pleased audience" was regaled by two nights of performances by a minstrel show put on by the Leesburg Band. The minstrel troupe held "the undivided attention of the audience, which gave them hearty applause and frequent encores."[11]

Leesburg's tiny downtown area was almost exclusively white. The businesses were owned and operated by whites, some of whom lived on the second floors above their shops, and they catered to white customers. Those few shopkeepers who would accept the business of the town's African Americans forced them to come to back doors or side windows, which were not visible from the street. When the Tally Ho movie theater opened two blocks west of the courthouse in September 1931, all of the downstairs seats in the Art Deco building were reserved for whites. Black moviegoers had to buy their tickets at a separate window and sit in the hotter balcony at the back of the theater.

Most of the county seat's black population lived in its southern end, across the banks of the tiny Town Branch creek from white Leesburg. They attended their own schools; owned and shopped at their own stores; ate at their own restaurants; had their hair cut at their own barbershops. Their world was tucked into a rough end of town that was also home to the Washington & Old Dominion freight and passenger rail station, a lumberyard, a power plant, a factory that manufactured blinds, and several mills. One of the predominantly black neighborhoods was Murderer's Bay, which gained its colorful name from the days when it had been home to the town's gallows. Local officials demanded that police crack down on trouble in another African American neighborhood — "Black Bottom," on lower Wirt Street — and debated plans to develop a "White Way" to attract visitors to another part of town.

On the border between the African American community along Royal Street and the white center of Leesburg, near the corner of Loudoun Street and Wirt Street, stood the Do Drop Inn, the most popular African American restaurant in town. Florence Simms operated a beauty parlor catering to Leesburg's African American women on the second floor, and for a short time Dr. Henry Ladray, one of only a few African American doctors in the area, practiced medicine there.

But even the most successful, most prosperous of the area's African American families were something less than second class citizens; shunned by white society, limited in their ability to participate in the school system, in the judicial system, in elections or government or any other facet of traditional American life. Outside of their own small circle, black Loudouners were eyed with suspicion, shunted to back benches, balconies, shadows and side streets; unemployable except as laborers and servants; not even allowed to be buried in the same cemeteries as whites. For each of the county's black business people, there were a dozen more who struggled to hold onto jobs cleaning out horse pens or pumping gasoline or mowing lawns, growing what food they could on small plots of land they rented and earning what they could doing occasional odd jobs.

A mile or so east of the courthouse a desolate pauper's graveyard was still the final resting place for the area's homeless and outcast, for lonely strangers who met their end on its roads, and for the bodies of unclaimed criminals.

FOUR

"My dear little darling"

In 1924 a group of Middleburg's prominent citizens, led by Daniel Cox Sands, formed the Middleburg National Bank. They paid a construction company owned by William Hall, the area's most successful African American businessman, to build an impressive home for the bank on the corner of the tiny town's main intersection, using locally cut stone. The bank's offices became the town's de facto government, and over time a string of businesses were established along the southern side of the street east of the bank building: the Middleburg Real Estate company, a pair of grocery stores — Sanitary Grocery and the Great Atlantic & Pacific Tea Company, side by side — Luck's filling station, a restaurant, a plumbing and heating business.

From the front steps of their manor house on Washington Street the Ilsleys could see the Middleburg National Bank a block and a half to the right; directly across the street was Emmanuel Episcopal church. It was the most well attended church in town, but even after undergoing renovations in 1927, it was only big enough to seat about 70 parishioners. The Gothic Revival building, complete with buttresses and rose-tinted arch windows, hosted Middleburg's annual memorial service for Confederate dead. The Reverend David Campbell Mayers and his wife, Josephine, who lived in a house next door to the church, welcomed the Ilsleys to Emmanuel Episcopal. Thin lipped and bespectacled, Mayers had been born in the British West Indies in 1885. In addition to his duties at Emmanuel Episcopal, he was president of the local Parent Teacher Association and a key member of the village's de facto government.

Isabel Tibbs lived in a tiny house in the woods across Marshall Street from the Ilsley's cottage; Harry Leonard and his wife to the east at the corner of Washington Street. On the northwest corner of the block stood a large house, stable and icehouse owned by Mrs. Arthur White; on the southeast corner — at the intersection of Liberty and Washington streets — were the Iron Jockey Tea Room and the Middleburg Cleaners and Dyers.

Less than two blocks to the east of the Ilsley's was Confederate Hall, home to the Middleburg chapter of the United Daughters of the Confederacy, which hosted a library, motion pictures, plays, graduations ceremonies and even wrestling matches in the building. The old Freedman's Bureau office, where former slaves in the Middleburg area had gone for help in the days following the Civil War, still stood two streets east of the Ilsley's cottage, though it had been converted to a private home.

The list of friends the Ilsleys made in Middleburg was long and included many of the town's most prominent citizens, including retired airman William "Billy" Mitchell, one of the most colorful and controversial figures of the era, who lived on the 120-acre Boxwood estate just south of town.

Mitchell was intelligent, ambitious, volatile, and abrasive. Those who followed him called him a visionary, single-minded and ahead of his time. Opponents, including many stung by the public criticism Mitchell habitually dished out, said he was high-handed, disrespectful, tactless, a military Barnum with no concern for the damage and embarrassment his words brought to the military establishment.

His grandfather, Alexander Mitchell, emigrated from Scotland in 1837 and went on to become a millionaire banker and railroad tycoon in Wisconsin. Alexander Mitchell was a Democrat, powerful in both state and national politics, who had fought for the Union during the Civil War. The wealth he accumulated through his Wisconsin Marine & Fire Insurance Company Bank allowed his son, John Lendrum Mitchell, to attend universities in Europe and go on to become a United States Senator. The power John Mitchell held, and the wealth passed down generation to generation created a world of privilege and opportunity for Billy Mitchell.

Born in France in 1879 and raised in Milwaukee, Mitchell learned to ride at an early age — his father raised horses on the family's 480-acre Meadowmere estate — became fluent in Spanish, French, German, and the Philippino language Tagalog. Over the course of his life, he made friends and enemies in the highest levels of society, the military and government in Washington, Europe, and at home in Wisconsin. He was sent to an Episcopalian boarding school at age ten and moved on to the prep school at Columbian University (now George Washington University) in Washington, DC, five years later. At the outbreak of the Spanish-American War in 1898 he left college to join the Army.

His father's intervention gained him a quick commission as a 2nd Lieutenant in the U.S. Army Signal Corps. He was the youngest Captain in the Army at age 24 and, after serving in the Philippines and Alaska Territory, became the youngest member ever assigned to the General Staff, at age 32.

He had a high-pitched voice and was of average height, but from the beginning he had the air of a commander about him in all situations, whether they be military, business or social. Like his childhood friend Douglas MacArthur, Mitchell wore uniforms that he designed himself, combinations of military efficiency and fox hunter's flash, with high boots and scarlet ribbons.

In 1916 the Army declared Mitchell, then 36, too old for flight training.

Convinced that airplanes were the key to future military power, he paid for his own flying lessons. At about the same time he became friends with Orville Wright. By the time the United States entered World War I, Mitchell held the top U.S. aviation position, Chief of Air Service of the Group of Armies, commanding American combat units in France. He believed even before the war began that victory would become ever more dependent on air superiority, a theory refuted by most military leaders. By the end of the war Mitchell had earned the Distinguished Service Cross and the Distinguished Service Medal, had been promoted to Brigadier General and was America's most famous pilot. When the war ended and the size of the military was reduced from its wartime high, Mitchell and thousands of other American officers saw their rank reduced to pre-war status; Mitchell was reduced in rank to Colonel. He considered it a humiliating insult and a personal affront.

He was outspoken, publicly criticizing the then-popular belief that World War I had been the war to end all wars and its logical extension, the demilitarizing of the former allies and massive cuts to American military spending. He gave speeches, made radio addresses, wrote articles and books, and carried on a one-man publicity campaign to have aviation recognized as a vital cog in the United States' military machine. Military and political leaders chaffed at the harshness of his attacks.

Following tours of Hawaii and Asia — tours arranged by superior officers to keep Mitchell from speaking to American newspaper reporters — he returned to the United States in 1924 with a 324-page manuscript in which he predicted war between the United States and Japan. Included in the report were claims of American Naval vulnerability in the Pacific and an uncanny prediction of a Japanese air attack on Pearl Harbor.

In 1925 he was transferred to Fort Sam Houston at San Antonio. The transfer didn't silence Mitchell. When five pilots were lost near Hawaii and 14 crewmen died in the crash of the Navy dirigible *Shenandoah* in Ohio, Mitchell issued a lengthy statement in which he claimed that the incidents were "the direct result of the incompetency, criminal negligence and almost treasonable administration of the national defense by the Navy and War Departments."[1] Commanding officers in Washington, and President Calvin Coolidge, on vacation in Swampscott, Massachusetts, were livid. A court martial was scheduled in Washington in the fall of 1925. Mitchell and his wife drove from San Antonio to his estate in Middleburg in September, shipping ahead more than 800 pounds of documents he planned to produce as evidence at his court martial.

The seven-week military trial was followed closely by millions of Americans who tuned in to daily updates on the radio and read stormy newspaper reports filed by a swarm of reporters who filled the makeshift courtroom in a Navy-owned warehouse in Washington. In the end, he was found guilty of insubordination and was sentenced to a five-year suspension from duty without pay. He resigned from the Army February 1, 1926.

He had married Caroline Stoddard in 1903; they had three children before divorcing in 1922. In October 1923 he remarried, this time to Elizabeth Trumbull, a Michigan socialite. He and Betty, as he called her, had two children, Lucy and William Jr. After resigning from the Army, Mitchell moved to Boxwood, which Elizabeth's father had bought for the couple as a wedding gift. There, on the border between Loudoun and Fauquier counties, surrounded by thoroughbred horses and hunting dogs, Mitchell continued to campaign for increased funding for American military aviation. He occasionally flew his personal plane to and from a landing strip near Boxwood. On one of those flights he took the first aerial photograph of Middleburg.

At home and around town, he dressed as a rather dandy gentleman farmer, wearing breeches and tailcoats, his hats cocked to the left, and carried a swagger stick, riding crop or walking cane wherever he went. He did not smoke or eat red meat; slept only five or six hours a night and drank heavily — he believed Prohibition was a "dismal failure"[2] — kicking off most evenings with a cocktail hour and pouring himself drinks late into the night. He drove fast, scaring passengers when he would reach 60 miles per hour on the country roads near Boxwood. He owed money to everyone, including tailors in London and Paris. His views on race were harsh, if not unusual for the time: he thought black American soldiers had performed in a cowardly fashion during World War I, and predicted that "the white and yellow races will be brought into armed conflict to determine which shall prevail" in Asia. "The policy of the United States and, in fact, of all the white countries having their shores washed by the waters of the Pacific Ocean, is to keep their soil, their institutions, and their manner of living free from the ownership, the domination and the customs of the Orientals," he wrote after a tour of Asia. "We are faced with a problem much greater than it appears on the surface: that of maintaining not only the political supremacy but also the very existence of the white race."[3]

The century-old fieldstone house at the center of his Boxwood estate sat on a terraced hill on Plains Road, less than two miles from the Ilsley's manor house. Mitchell had several servants, including a nanny for the two children, and his personal secretary, Maydell "Blackie" Blackmon. Mitchell participated in foxhunts, joined the village tennis club and entered his horses in the Hunt Cup races. He was elected vice-commodore of the Capital Yacht Club in Washington, and sailed a 56-foot cabin cruiser that he christened the *Canvas Back*. He fought endlessly with Isaac Waddell, a sharecropper who rented a few acres at Boxwood.

There were those in Wisconsin who wanted Mitchell to come home and run for Senate, and there were attempts to launch a "Mitchell for President Club," Democratic "Billy Mitchell Volunteers" organizations, even an "Aviation Party" with Mitchell as its head. But Mitchell preferred to throw his support behind other candidates. In 1928 he campaigned for New York Governor Alfred E. Smith, campaigning mostly in Wisconsin. Smith lost to Herbert Hoover. As

Franklin Roosevelt's fortunes rose in New York, Mitchell became an outspoken supporter.

Like the Ilsleys and so many members of Middleburg society, the Mitchells attended services at Emmanuel Episcopal. In 1928 they and the Ilsleys joined other Middleburg elites— Mrs. Thomas Atkinson, Mrs. William Holbert, Mrs. Oliver Iselin — to found the Hill School, a private, all-white elementary and high school.

They were a small, closed group; an elite and rich clique, almost none of them native to the area, most of them away from the village for months of every year; few of them having any contact with the sea of working class people that lived all around them, other than those moments when they, as employers, crossed paths with their servants.

Electricity had come to Middleburg in the 1920s, but central water and sewage wouldn't be connected until the mid–1930s. The town's first automobile service station was built next to the W.W. Welch five-and-dime store in 1924. A generation earlier, when it had been a sleepy farm town, there had been plenty of African Americans in Middleburg. The horse farms and plantations around the town had been owned by whites who hired the blacks for manual labor. But as its reputation as a foxhunting attraction for America's elite grew, fewer African Americans remained in the village. More and more, their homes would be found in nearby St. Louis or along the lonely roads between towns, where a cabin could be bought or rented for less money.

"Once a dusty, drowsing Piedmont village, the foxhunters have now taken it over lock, stock and barrel (lots of barrels)," *Fortune* said of Middleburg in November, 1930. "Almost every available property has been snapped up and painstakingly outfitted with the hooked rugs and Alken prints which Northern taste believes indispensable in a Southern hunting community." Nothing in the area was open all night; by the time the sun went down, most businesses had shut their doors.

But the Depression was taking its toll even in tony Middleburg. By April 1931 Middleburg Saddlery, the Hill and Poole drug store, the Iron Jockey and the Red Fox tavern and theatre had all closed their doors. The Iron Jockey reopened in June 1932 and the theater the following month as the Middleburg-Hollywood Theatre. Manager Elizabeth Altemus Whitney bragged to friends that she operated the first air-conditioned building in the county; African Americans were relegated to the balcony. The Red Fox, located a block west of the manor house, was converted into rental apartments, catering to the out of town foxhunting clique.

Spencer and Agnes were wealthy but, by Middleburg standards, not unusually so. People who stayed at the Ilsley's home said it was a little shabby; a country place that was more of a hunting lodge than a home. Dogs begged at the dinner table and cats slept in the eaves. They had room in their garages for several vehicles, but owned a single automobile: a trendy green V-8 LaSalle. Even as the world economy sunk into the Great Depression in 1930, the Ilsley's Middleburg manor was valued at $60,000 and, despite the fact that neither of them worked, they remained wealthy enough to pay three live-in servants. Their maid, Dorothy Paine, was 16; cook Matilda A. King was 55. They even had room for chauffeur Charles A. Riemes, his wife and their 11-year-old son, who had followed Spencer east from Wisconsin. At the end of 1930 the Ilsley's extended their Middleburg holdings, paying $25,139 for the 211-acre Francis Mills Farm Estate in nearby Mountsville. Agnes would build new stables there and, eventually, would plan to make the farm her primary residence.

Agnes was popular in Middleburg, described as "a woman of great charm,"[4] who dressed smartly — but never flashy — in clothes that others admired: hats pulled down low over her forehead, snug skirts that covered her knees. She was a member of the Middleburg Hunt Club, a group of wealthy foxhunters who rode and ran hounds on the rolling foothills surrounding the village. She was still a joiner: she gave her time and money to Emmanuel Episcopal, the Hill School, the 4-H Club, the Red Cross, and a variety of charities in the area. She and seven other women, including her neighbor, Edith Kennedy Sands, formed the County Conservation Committee to rid the county's roadways of advertising signs. She had several entries in the Washington Horse Show, kept a half dozen hunter horses and employed several grooms and stablemen at the Francis Mill Farm.

Spencer and Agnes rode their horses and often went to parties with friends. In November 1929 they were in Fairfax County for the first hunt — "a decided success," according to the *Washington Post* — of the newly organized Fox Hunt Club of Sunset Hills. In May, 1930, they traveled to Media, Pennsylvania, for the Rose Tree Hunt Club's steeplechase Spring feature. The rainy day was brightened somewhat when the Ilsley's horse, a four-year-old named Bellfont, came in second in the third race, a 2.5-mile course over brush. William du Pont Jr. awarded the Corinthian Plate to the first place horse, Autumn Bells, owned by George Brooke III.

Just after Christmas, 1930, Spencer's health failed him. He died of pneumonia at Emergency Hospital in Washington on New Year's Day, 1931. He was 63.

Agnes accompanied Spencer's body on the train trip back to Milwaukee. His funeral was held at Forest Home cemetery on January 3.

Thirty-eight years old and widowed after only three years of marriage, Agnes returned to Middleburg, hundreds of miles away from her family and all the life she had known before marrying Spencer. She was independent, enterprising, headstrong, and very much alone; a single woman in a world dominated by men.

Her brother, Paul Boeing, who had lived in Minneapolis and New York after leaving North Dakota, moved into the manor house with Agnes following Spencer's death. He made few friends in Middleburg, where he was described as "dapper" and "high strung." Roy Seaton, who lived with his mother on Madison Street, about a block from Agnes, would say Boeing was "the queerest man I ever knew. He is effeminate and dresses immaculately. He takes more trouble over his appearance than a girl. He is very dark, with dark eyes, dark skin and coal black hair."[5] He was a small, slender man with a rather large, sharp nose, his voice "soft, cultured, well modulated."[6] He had little to do with most of Agnes's friends and neighbors, but grew especially close to Katherine Elkins Hitt, who ran the Red Fox Inn.

Katherine and William F.R. Hitt, who had married in 1913, divorced in 1921 and then remarried in 1923, lived between Middleburg and St. Louis. Their Homeland estate, which had a half-mile racecourse for their horses, became a frequent haunt of Boeing's. William was the son of Illinois congressman R.R. Hitt; Katherine was the daughter of Stephen B. Elkins, who had been President Benjamin Harrison's Secretary of War and a United States Senator, and the granddaughter of another Senator, Henry Gassaway Davis, who was the Democratic nominee for Vice President in 1904. In 1908 there were rumors that she had secretly married the Duke of Abruzzi, the cousin of King Victor Emmanuel of Italy. Katherine did little to stop the rumors or their publication in newspapers worldwide. The rumors, it turned out after some time, were untrue.

Like so many of Middleburg's young elites, Katherine was an avid horsewoman. One of her horses, Irish Laddie, had won the first Virginia Gold Cup steeplechase in 1922, and her horses dominated the prestigious race throughout the 1920s.

Katherine counted among her closest friends Alice Roosevelt Longworth, the only child of Teddy Roosevelt, who had won the presidential election in 1904.

Though Agnes was due to inherit an estimated $325,000 from Spencer's estate when it closed in January 1932 — and she still held all of the Middleburg properties, a stable full of horses and had several employees working for her — the mansion house and everything needed to keep it running were more than she wanted to deal with. She released all of the servants who had lived with her and Spencer, rented out the larger building during the fox hunting season, and moved herself into the cottage with Mina Buckner, her new maid and the only live-in servant on her payroll. Buckner was white, 65 years old, and, during the summer, lived on a farm in Rockville, Maryland, with her husband, Florian. The job provided her with room and board and some extra money, but even a wealthy woman like Ilsley did not pay domestic help a large salary during the Depression. Buckner made a single bank deposit between August 1931 and January 1932.

Agnes had a few other servants around the estate. There was Birdie DeNeal, a tiny 41-year-old African American who lived on Pot House Road, not far from the Ilsley estate, with her husband, eight children and one grandchild, who came in to cook and do some cleaning up. She had been working for Richard Holt, a Middleburg doctor, before Agnes hired her.

In March Agnes and Holt hired George Crawford, a former convict, to run errands, mow the lawn and drive and service their cars. Ilsley provided him with two dark grey chauffeur's uniforms, with matching overcoat and chauffeur's hat, to wear when he drove her on errands. She had first met Crawford when he was working on a chain gang at a work camp in Loudoun County. She had been doing volunteer welfare work for the prison system; Holt, a general practitioner, was frequently called in to do medical work for prisoners and guards.

Crawford's background, at least until he entered Virginia's prison system, is obscure. He was born on February 2, 1897, but where is unclear. Various reports identify his place of birth as Richmond, or Jacksonville, Florida; or Augusta, Georgia. His parents may have been Cuban immigrants. He left school after the third grade and had only rudimentary reading and writing skills. He was a short man, only about five foot two, but unusually strong, with broad shoulders, exceptionally long arms, uneven eyes and a walk variously described as bow-legged or pigeon toed.

In 1918 he was living in Richmond with his sister, his only sibling, working at a hospital and as a chauffeur. Two years later he was married; it is unclear what became of his wife. In March 1921 things turned sour when he was arrested for receiving and concealing stolen goods and sentenced to three years in the state prison in Henrico County. He escaped on May 28, 1922, but was arrested a few months later and was convicted of stealing jewelry from an employer. He was sentenced to five years in prison, plus two years for being a repeat offender and an additional two years for escaping. In 1925 he once again managed to escape, but he was caught after only a few hours. His afternoon of freedom earned him another year added to his sentence.

In 1928 Crawford was working on a road crew in Loudoun County when another prisoner attacked a guard, slashing his neck with a knife. Crawford stepped into the frenzy to defend the guard. While fighting off the convict, Crawford was cut on the back of one hand, an injury that would leave a scar stretching from his knuckles to his wrist. He carried the guard to a car and took him to Holt, who treated both the injured guard and Crawford.

In January 1929, in recognition of Crawford's actions to save the guard, Governor Harry Byrd commuted a year from his sentence. He was discharged from prison on November 23, 1930. There weren't many job opportunities for an uneducated African American ex-con in the South during the dark early days of the Depression. Crawford went to Middleburg, where he talked Ilsley and Holt — who was living in the cottage — into paying him $6 a week to be their driver and handyman. He rented a room in a building on Washington Street, next to the drugstore. In the evenings he sat on the steps in front of the drugstore and gossiped with white men. People in town would later say of

Crawford that he was "a nice boy," and "if he had been white, we might have been chums."[7]

But from the beginning, Crawford's record and his race made him a suspicious character in Middleburg. When a store in town was broken into that spring, Crawford was questioned.

In May 1931 Billy Mitchell was one of the special guests invited to the 102nd floor of the Empire State Building to view a simulated air attack on New York by 672 Army Air Force planes. But times were tough for the aging war hero.

Mitchell met with New York Governor Franklin Delano Roosevelt in July, promising to organize Virginia Democrats to support Roosevelt at the 1932 convention. Mitchell had encouraged Harry Byrd to run for president. Despite a unanimous endorsement from Virginia's General Assembly and a tumultuous demonstration in the aisles at the Democratic Convention in Chicago—a demonstration by the delegations of eleven states, led by the former governor's brother, polar explorer Admiral Richard E. Byrd, Governor John Garland Pollard and Mitchell, along with the Richmond Blues National Guard regimental band blaring "Carry Me Back to Old Virginia" and "Dixie"—Byrd could not garner enough national support. The nomination went to Roosevelt. A brief push for an FDR-Byrd ticket also failed to gain support. After Roosevelt's November 1932 victory there were some who wanted Roosevelt to appoint Mitchell Assistant Secretary of War for Air. The appointment did not come. Mitchell instead was relegated to working on Roosevelt's inaugural arrangements.

In August 1931 Agnes traveled to Milwaukee, where she visited a cousin, Blanche Van Brunt Reilly, wife of Arthur C. Uihlein, a member of one wing of the Schlitz brewing empire. She also visited her nephew, Charles F. Ilsley, who was vice president of the Marshall & Ilsley bank, and her sister-in-law, Mrs. James K. Ilsley, and spent time with old friends at the Milwaukee Country Club.

When she returned to Middleburg, things soured with Crawford. Now he was working only for Ilsley. Holt had moved out of the cottage. There was talk around town that Crawford was having an affair with DeNeal, a scandal that separated him from the African American community—an individual outcast from an outcast society. And Ilsley told friends that Crawford had been stealing from her. He had taken a bottle of whiskey from her liquor cabinet, she said—a bold admission, with prohibition still the law of the land. Crawford denied stealing anything. He said he and Agnes had argued about the car. In any case, Ilsley fired Crawford in early September 1931. He left town. DeNeal went with him.

To take over some of the work that Crawford had been doing, Agnes hired Alex Grayson, a 34-year-old African American man who lived across the street from the cottage. Grayson, who also worked at a garage in town, was to do janitorial work around the place and tend the furnaces three times every day as the weather turned colder. Like Crawford, Grayson was an ex-con, having spent four years in jail for assaulting a man with a razor.

But Ilsley would no longer be chauffeured. On October 3, 1931, she bought a second car, a new four-passenger, 24 horsepower 1931 Ford Victoria Coupe, from the Purcellville Motor Company. It was a sharp black and blue machine, with cream interior and yellow wire wheels. From now on, she would drive herself.

As she made plans to move to the Francis Mills Farm, Ilsley occasionally rented the bigger house to hunting parties in town for the season, and she spent more and more time living in the cottage.

By the standards of white Middleburg, the cottage was a small place, but to the African Americans who worked on the property, and to most of the whites who lived outside of the village, it would have been a comfortable home. On the street side there were two large doors leading into a garage. There were two bedrooms on the basement level designed to be used by servants, along with a furnace room and a room-size coal bin. There were stairs from the ground level to the main floor on both the Marshall Street and yard sides of the cottage. The door from the road side opened into the kitchen, which in turn had two doors, one opening onto a large living room and the other into a central hallway. There were three bedrooms and a bathroom off of the hallway and, on the right, a door into a front hall, which led out onto a covered porch that ran the length of the yard side of the cottage. From the front door, the manor house, the town's main street and the Episcopal church were all clearly visible.

In late November 1931 Agnes leased the manor house to a group of women who had come to Middleburg for the foxhunting season. Among them were 27-year-old Katrina McCormick, the daughter of two members of congress, along with Margaretta Rowland, Rowland's aunt, Isabelle Rowland — a friend of Ilsley's — who acted as their chaperone, and their servants.

Katrina McCormick came from a long line of Republican politicians and newspaper people. Her uncle, Robert R. McCormick, was president of the *Chicago Tribune*, which had been founded by her great-grandfather, Joseph Medill; cousin Joseph Medill Patterson published the *New York Daily News*; and another cousin, Eleanor Patterson, was editor of the *Washington Herald*. Katrina herself wrote a column for her mother's *Rockford Morning Star*.

Her paternal grandfather was Marcus A. Hanna, a Republican who had been political manager for President William McKinley and was a twice-elected U.S. Senator from Ohio; her maternal grandfather was Robert S. McCormick, who had been appointed ambassador to Austria-Hungary by McKinley and ambassador to Russia and France by Theodore Roosevelt. Her father, Joseph Medill McCormick, had been publisher and owner of the *Chicago Daily Tribune* and the *Cleveland News*, and was a war correspondent in the Philippines in 1901. He became vice chairman of the national campaign committee of the Progressive Republican movement; was elected to the Illinois House of Representatives in 1912 and again in 1914; and served a single term in Congress before being elected to a term in the Senate. He sought a second term, but failed to receive the Republican nomination. In 1925, with only days left in his Senate term, he committed suicide in a Washington hotel room.

Katrina's mother was Ruth Hanna McCormick, also an Illinois Republican. She owned and operated a dairy and breeding farm in Illinois and was publisher and president of the Rockford Consolidated Newspapers; she was chairman of the first woman's executive committee of the Republican National Committee and an associated member of the RNC from Illinois from 1919 to 1924; she was an active worker for the suffrage amendment; a delegate to the Republican National Convention in 1928, and U.S. Representative from Illinois at-large, 1929–1931. She did not run for a second term because she had received the Republican nomination for the U.S. Senate, but she lost in the general election and returned to the newspaper business. Ruth's best friend was Alice Roosevelt Longworth. She knew Agnes's Iselin relatives through Longworth, who in her younger days had considered Arthur Iselin a potential husband.

The McCormick party rode with Middleburg's foxhunting crowd through the holidays and planned to stay in the manor house until January. In the village's close-knit confines, Katrina came to know everyone. She knew Roy Seaton and spent time with Billy Mitchell and his wife. "I didn't like him," she would say of Mitchell years later. "He was a dreadful man. He was awful to his wife," who had short legs, which made it hard for her to stay on horses. Once, when she fell off a horse, "he dressed her down in front of her friends," McCormick recalled.[8]

On Christmas Eve, 1931, while the McCormick group was away, Boeing and Ilsley were staying at the Mountsville farm, and Buckner was home in Maryland for the holiday, someone came through a window of the manor house, broke open a strongbox and stole $500 worth of clothes and jewelry, including a watch that had belonged to Spencer. There had been several robberies reported in Middleburg in the past few months.

On December 28 Ilsley went to Roy Seaton, who was a magistrate, and swore out a warrant charging Crawford with the robbery. Paul Boeing and Alex Grayson were named as witnesses. But Crawford could not be found, and wasn't taken into custody.

After New Years Day, 1932, the weather turned warm. By mid–January, several record high temperatures were set.

DeNeal was back at home with her children and husband, but there were secrets she was keeping from him. On January 8 she sent a letter to Charlie Smith ("my dear little darling"), who was staying with an old friend at 1212 North

17th Street in Richmond, saying she was "not at all well in health or mind. I have been just all to pieces.... I guess you had begun to think that I had forgotten you, but I will never be able to do that." She offered her condolences for the recent death of Smith's sister and apologized for not being able to send him any money — her husband ("this old thing") had refused to give her a penny.

The McCormick party's lease at the manor house had expired on Friday, January 8, but they had stayed over at the place through the weekend. McCormick moved out on Monday. Paul Boeing moved into the manor house the same day. Agnes and Buckner stayed in the cottage.

That afternoon, in the upstairs board room at the Middleburg National Bank, Seaton swore in Middleburg's first town council: Homer A. Spitler, the Ilsley's family physician and vice president of the bank, was named president of the council. William Jordan Luck, son of Samuel Luck and manager of his father's filling station, was mayor of the town. Mayers acted as recorder for the council. In their first meeting, the council granted a special permit for a dance to be held at Confederate Hall, tabled a proposal to install a streetlight at Pickering and Marshall Streets, and voted to hire E.W. Bosher to be "town sergeant," in response to the recent rash of break-ins. Bosher, a five-year veteran of the Washington police force, had been recommended by Mitchell.

On Tuesday morning Ilsley drove into Washington and hired the William J. Burns Detective Agency to investigate the robbery at the manor house. She had grown increasingly frustrated by Seaton and Loudoun County Sheriff Eugene Adrian's inability to find Crawford.

That night Agnes and Paul Boeing ate dinner together in the cottage. He was still there when Agnes left at about 7:30 p.m. to drive the Ford sedan to a party at the Hitt estate. Despite his close friendship with Hitt, Boeing decided to read at the cottage for a while and then return to the manor house for the night.

Mitchell was at the party. Agnes told him about her meeting with the Washington detective agency. She told him she was scared of Crawford, Mitchell would say later. She met her friend Winifred Maddux at the party and the two women drove to Upperville for a meeting of the Association of Women for Prohibition Reform, a "wet" anti-prohibition group.

Agnes dropped Maddux off at her parents' Belmont home about midnight. They had plans to go fox hunting the next day, she reminded her friend. And then she turned the car towards Middleburg and home.

FIVE

"The atrocious crime"

Just after 9 a.m., Boeing put a coat on over his pajamas and walked across the lawn to the cottage to meet Agnes for breakfast, and to retrieve some of his clothes. He found the front door locked. He rang the bell, but no one answered. He walked back down the stairs and around the house to try the back door. Finding it also locked, he reached through a broken pane of glass to open the door and entered the silent cottage.

He called to Agnes, but there was no answer. He walked down the narrow hallway that connected the kitchen to the bedrooms where Agnes and Mina Buckner slept. He came to his sister's room first.

Agnes lay in a pool of blood, her skull crushed. She was dressed in her nightclothes. She lay with her head near the bed, her feet in the doorway. Her bedside lamp lay across her body; a chair had been turned over; a blood-soaked book had fallen on the floor next to the bed. There was blood splattered on her pillowcase; on the walls; on the ceiling.

Boeing turned to the bedroom across the hall. Buckner, dressed in her nightclothes, was dead on her bed with a gaping wound in her forehead. She was in a half-sitting position on her bed, her feet on the floor. Blood was spattered on the walls and ceiling of her room.

Boeing ran for help. His first instinct was to find Duke Tyler, who lived a half block away. But there was no answer at Tyler's home.

He didn't stop to seek the help of any of his neighbors—not Alex Grayson or Isabel Tibbs, whose houses were just across Marshall Street from the cottage; not Harry Leonard or Mrs. White, who each lived just moments away on the same block, and not Mayers or W.W. Welsh or any of the other people who lived within sight of the cottage. Nor did he telephone for help.

Instead, he ran from the cottage and hurried past the manor house, past the Iron Jockey Tea Room, crossing the intersection at Liberty Street, and walked past an entire block of stores, restaurants and other businesses until he arrived at Middleburg National Bank on Madison Street.

There, Boeing found a bank cashier and Roy Seaton, who telephoned the news to Sheriff Adrian in Leesburg. Seaton also alerted Dr. Spitler and together the four men—Boeing, Seaton, Spitler and the cashier—returned to the cottage. Within moments they were joined by Grayson and Billy Mitchell.

Grayson went to the garage, located beneath the bedrooms. The wooden doors were ajar. Ilsley's car was gone.

Fear and outrage were palpable as word spread through the village. Cars raced through the streets; the telephone exchange was quickly overwhelmed; a restless crowd of men gathered on the Ilsley's lawn, including Middleburg bank directors D.C. Sands and James "Middleburg Slim" Skinner. Mitchell tried to take charge of the place, repeatedly chasing away reporters and other outsiders drawn by the news of the murders. The *Times-Mirror*'s "Speedy" Corbell was the only newspaperman allowed to view the murder scene.

Ilsley had been hit repeatedly in the head and upper body with a sharp object. There had obviously been a violent struggle in her room: the lamp and chair had been knocked over and blood had been splashed about the room. There was blood on the edge of the bed and on the wooden rail. Investigators found a hairpin clutched in Ilsley's hand, with which she may have tried to defend herself. There were bruises on her arms, probably defensive wounds received in her final moments. Adrian said the first blow probably hit Ilsley as she lay in her bed, and then she had fought her way out of bed before succumbing to further blows.

From the position of Buckner's body, investigators believed she had started up out of her bed and then been struck once by her assailant, and then again after she fell back across the bed. Adrian found bloodstains in Buckner's wash basin. The killer had apparently cleaned his hands before he left the cottage.

While blood was spattered on the walls and ceiling of both bedrooms, on the beds and floors, on Ilsley's book and in Buckner's wash basin and on the door frame in Ilsley's bedroom, detectives found no bloody footprints in the home. Still, the overwhelming amount of blood on the scene, and the fact that it had obviously flown through the air when each woman had been struck, led police to believe that the killer's clothes must have been bloodstained as well.

The most important clue found in the house was a bloody palm print on the doorframe of Ilsley's room, which investigators believed was left there by her killer. A portion of the frame was sawed out for further examination.

Fingerprints were a new tool for law enforcement in 1932, and there was no man on Adrian's force or in the office of Loudoun County Commonwealth's Attorney John Galleher who could do that type of investigative work. Galleher appealed to Washington's Metropolitan Police Department for aid. Washington sent Lieutenant John Fowler, Homicide Detective Sergeant Dennis Murphy and Detective Sergeant Fred Sandberg, a fingerprint expert, to assist in the investigation.

Even by the time Dr. John Gibson, the county coroner, first examined the bodies, shortly after 10 a.m., rigor mortis had not set in. The time of the murders was unclear — Gibson, Spitler and Dr. Oscar B. Hunter, a pathologist from Washington, said the attacks occurred sometime between midnight and 4 a.m. Gibson believed the murderer entered the cottage shortly after Agnes went to bed, but before she was asleep. Buckner had probably been asleep, was awakened by the sound of the attack on Agnes across the hall, and had been struck down as she rose out of bed to investigate.

While Galleher, Murphy and Fowler told reporters that a second man may have participated in the murders, Adrian was convinced from the beginning that Ilsley and Buckner had been bludgeoned to death by a single intruder, and he had no doubt that Crawford was the killer. Crawford was strong enough to have carried out the murders by himself, and was familiar enough with the cottage to enter and exit the building in the dark, Adrian said.

But other investigators doubted that one man could have broken into the house, killed both women and escaped without help and without anyone hearing or seeing him. An accomplice would have been needed to take down one of the women and help make a clean getaway, they said.

Investigators considered every item in the cottage a potential clue that could break open the case. They hinted to reporters that a large kitchen spoon found near a garage window might be proof that the killer had been in the house days before the murders. The spoon, they theorized, could have been used to break the garage window and the back door window to confuse investigators.

Adrian posed for newspaper photographers holding a bloodstained bootjack — a cast iron tool used to remove riding boots — that had been found in Agnes's room. He believed Ilsley and Buckner had been beaten to death with the bootjack, but there was no consensus on a murder weapon. Some investigators thought a harrow tooth — a heavy piece of farm equipment — found in the kitchen might have been used; others speculated that the killer had used a hatchet and taken it away when they left.

Consensus on a possible motive was elusive as well. Buckner's son, Walter, thought robbery was a likely motive. After checking his mother's possessions, he reported that a gold watch, a white sapphire and amethyst ring, a string of 52 gold beads and as much as $80 in cash were missing. But police quickly discounted robbery; a silk pocketbook may have been missing, but nothing else appeared to have been taken from the cottage. Valuable jewelry — rings and a wristwatch — remained on Ilsley's body; there was cash laying on her dressing table; her fur coat was draped over a chair at the foot of her bed. The cottage had not been ransacked. Some investigators posited that revenge might have been the killers' motive. Adrian postulated that Crawford had taken advantage of an opportunity to get back at Agnes for firing him and for fingering him for the Christmas Eve burglary.

Agnes had told Billy Mitchell that she feared Crawford, he told the *Mil-*

waukee Sentinel, and "there seemed no doubt but that revenge was the motive for the atrocious crime."

But despite disagreements about motive and the number of killers who had entered Ilsley's cottage, Adrian and the Washington detectives were able to agree on one thing. They named Crawford as their sole suspect in the case.

A few hours later, Ilsley's car was found in a coal yard in Alexandria, on the Virginia side of the Highway Bridge, which spanned the Potomac River into Washington. Her driver's license and a few other scraps were found in the car. A night watchman for the Colliflower Coal Company told police that two black men had left the car there before dawn. One of the men matched Crawford's description. Galleher believed Crawford had escaped by boarding a northbound freight train in nearby Potomac Yards. He wired police departments along the rail lines, asking them to be on the lookout for Crawford.

Benjamin Gunner, manager of the William J. Burns Detective Agency, revealed to investigators and reporters his meeting with Agnes the day before the murders.

"She explained no action had been taken on the warrant she had sworn out for Crawford's arrest on a robbery charge, and inquired as to our rates for handling the case for her," Gunner told the *Evening Star*. "She said she would communicate with me within the next few days."

Seaton told the *Times-Mirror* that when Ilsley had left his office after swearing out a warrant on December 28, he had followed his usual procedure, dropping the warrant on Deputy Sheriff Paul Alexander's desk. Not so, according to Alexander.

"The warrant never came into my hands," he told the newspaper. "The first I heard of it was when somebody told me that the colored man I was looking for was near The Plains," a small village in Fauquier County, about six miles south of Middleburg." A few days later, Magistrate Seaton told me he thought Crawford was again in the neighborhood and had tried to break into the Ilsley house. He told me if I ran across him to pick him up."

Adrian, too, said he had never seen the warrant. "I did not know one had been issued until I read of it in the papers," he said.[1]

"Shuddering from the horribleness of the crime, quiet little Middleburg, in the center of Virginia's fox-hunting territory, was aghast yesterday," according to the *Washington Post*.

John Boeing arrived in Middleburg late on Wednesday and took charge of his sister's funeral arrangements. Her parents were on their way to Middleburg from Delray Beach, Florida, where they had been spending the winter.

On Thursday, Hunter told Gibson that his examination of the bodies showed conclusively that they had not been the victims of sexual assault. Hunter had discovered "the presence of bits of negro hair and flesh" under Ilsley's nails during a microscopic examination of her fingers.

In the first area newspaper stories about the murders, reported in the Thursday, January 14 edition of the *Times-Mirror* in Leesburg and the *Blue Ridge Herald* in Purcellville, Crawford was the only man named as a suspect.

"Police Spread Net for George Crawford," the *Times-Mirror* reported, under a photograph of a smiling Agnes holding her pet cat, while the more subdued *Herald* reported that "Suspicion points toward one George Crawford, colored, formerly in the employ of Mrs. Ilsley as the man who committed the brutal murder."

At the top of the *Times-Mirror's* glaring front-page story, Corbell added a bulletin in bold type just before the paper went to print. Such additions were common in the days of manual typesetting, when tearing down an entire page and replacing it with new information was too time consuming. But because the practice also gave editors less time to verify eleventh hour details, bulletins were more likely to include incorrect or misleading information.

Such was the case with the January 14 *Times-Mirror* bulletin. Based on information the newspaper had obtained from a source within the Commonwealth's Attorney's office — in all likelihood, Galleher himself — the bulletin claimed that two black men, one identifying himself by the name of Crawford, had been taken into custody in Washington. In the main *Times-Mirror* story that day, police up and down the East Coast were said to be in a "feverish, determined hunt for George Crawford, negro, sought as a suspect in the double murder of Mrs. Spencer Ilsley, widely known Middleburg woman, and her companion, Mrs. Annie [sic] Buckner, in the former's home at Middleburg Tuesday night."

But even as Adrian was spreading the word that Crawford was his sole suspect, he was revising his theory of the crime, and rethinking his initial contention that Crawford had acted alone. Within days of the murders, the sheriff told reporters that he believed the women had been killed simultaneously, which would indicate that there were two killers. Adrian hypothesized that the men had broken the glass on the rear door, near the kitchen at the rear of the house, and thrown the night latch to let themselves in. Crossing the kitchen and passing down the narrow hallway in the dark, they entered Ilsley and Buckner's rooms, killing the women simultaneously. Afterward they broke into the garage, but when they found the car there was locked, they returned to the cottage, broke the basement window to lift a latch, opened the door and stole the other car.

"Fear in the case of the suspect's capture that the people would not wait for his trial was expressed by Mayor W.J. Luck," the *Washington Post* reported. "There was no talk of lynching, but a grim and thin-lipped expression on the faces of her friends, men and women, who clustered about the cottage all day long, talking quietly in small groups, indicated the depth of feeling."

Years later NAACP executive director Walter White would write of the rabid search for Crawford: "Posses had combed the countryside, and had the murderer been apprehended at the time, a prominent citizen of Loudoun County told me afterward, he would have been burned at the stake."[2] One of the posses searching for Crawford had been led by Mitchell, according to White.

"If they had caught Crawford at the time, there would have been a burning," Mitchell told one reporter.[3]

Local newspaper editors were offended by the actions of their out-of-town colleagues and any implication that Loudoun County would be anything less than fair to African American suspects.

"There is not and has not been the slightest indication of friction between the races there," the *Blue Ridge Herald* reported. "The colored population is to be highly commended upon their sensible and well-mannered behavior during this trying time. They have rendered all possible help to the authorities and have openly expressed the desire to do all in their power to bring the murderer to justice. The white people in the town are indignant that such reports as were established in certain Washington papers about 'intense feeling between the races,' 'terrified white women trembling behind barricaded doors,' and a lot of unmitigated falsehoods should have reached the public. The community could not be expected to understand the craving for morbid and alarming details that was expressed by a number of reporters to these sheets, because such things are unknown in a town of this kind."

On Thursday, the *Washington Post* reported that a fingerprint had been discovered on the rearview mirror of Ilsley's car at the Colliflower Coal Yard. Murphy told the newspaper that other evidence found in the car—he would not divulge what that evidence was—would lead to Crawford's arrest. Other investigators weren't so discreet. They told reporters that a few words penciled on a tiny slip of notebook paper were enough to prove that Crawford's motive for the break-in at the Ilsley home was robbery. According to police, Crawford had "visited a woman friend near Tyson's crossroad" on the Sunday prior to the murders "and promised to send her some money, and then wrote her address on the paper," the *Post* reported. Crawford broke into the Ilsley house to get money to repay that debt, investigators said. He had killed Ilsley when she discovered him in the house and, in turn, had killed Buckner when she was woken by the sounds of the struggle in the next room. The note, scrawled by someone with almost childlike handwriting, spelling and grammar, had prompted Galleher and Murphy to meet at "a colored settlement" about three miles from Herndon.

On Friday, the *Post* reported that five African Americans were being held in Virginia in connection with the murders. Their identities and where they were being questioned were being withheld due to a "fear of mob violence, because of the high feeling engendered in the social colony about Middleburg," according to the newspaper.

"Instructions from a 'high government official,' it was learned, have directed the Middleburg authorities in case of the arrest of the suspected principals, to take them to some large jail, preferably in Richmond, to forestall any possible reprisals against them," the *Post* reported.

SIX

The Hunt for George Crawford

Within hours of Boeing's discovery of the bodies, Middleburg residents had pooled $500 to offer as a reward; that amount would eventually grow to $2,000. Paul and John Boeing put up $1,000 of their own money for the capture of their sister's murderer. The Black Aberdeen Fellows and R.P. Dawson Elks—a 50-member, all black division of the Elks Club in Middleburg—offered $25. Two officers of the Black Elks lodge—William Hall, whose company had built the Middleburg National Bank building and a wing of Loudoun Hospital in Leesburg, and Carr Cook, who owned a roofing contracting business—made the pledge in a letter to the Middleburg Town Council one week after the murders.

"We stand ready to assist in any way," they said.[1]

The Reverend Mayers wrote a response to the Black Elks on behalf of the Town Council.

"Your communication of January 19 relative to your sympathetic interest in the cruel murder of our highly esteemed fellow citizens, Mrs. Spencer Ilsley, and her maid has been the source of great gratification to us as a representative body of this town. Your action is very commendable and we appreciate it. This is a time for all good citizens to rally to the support of law and order and to show a determination to better conditions in our community."[2]

In bold letters set aside in a box on the front page in the midst of two articles about the Ilsley murders, the *Loudoun Times-Mirror* announced on January 28 that is was offering its own reward of $100 for the apprehension and conviction of the killers.

There were calls for the Loudoun County Board of Supervisors to meet in extra session and offer at least a $1,000 reward in the case (it turned out the Board was legally limited to a $100 contribution) and requests that Governor Pollard match that amount in state funds.

The Middleburg Town Council authorized Mayor Luck to deputize a dozen men to help in the search for Crawford. Bosher asked for a motorcycle. Thousands of flyers with Crawford's photograph, fingerprints and description were circulated up and down the east coast.

Police were watching for Crawford at railway stations and bus terminals as far north as Boston, where Crawford was reported to have connections in the Roxbury neighborhood, and far into the Deep South. Reported sightings came in from Culpeper, Virginia, and Leonardtown, Maryland, where Sheriff R.L. Cooksey said two men, one of them matching the description of Crawford, were spotted in a touring car with Virginia license plates, taking the ferry to Colonial Beach, Virginia.

Reports of possible sightings came in from across the region, but no arrests were made. A few men appointed themselves guards and gatekeepers at the Ilsley property. Seaton was on guard duty at the cottage at 3 a.m. the day after the murders when a car sped into Middleburg with its horn blowing. A man leapt from the vehicle saying that he'd chased someone driving what he thought was Ilsley's missing car for miles from near Leesburg before losing him on a country road.

"The volunteer sleuth appeared greatly disappointed when Magistrate Seaton informed him, the car used by the slayer had been found some time before," Washington's *Evening Star* reported. "Nerves of the townspeople apparently were on edge last night, many of the women insisting that their husbands search their homes with shotguns ready for action before they would retire."

"The people are all worked up over the murders of Mrs. Ilsley and Mrs. Buckner, and fear further attacks," Adrian told reporters.[3]

Following up on one tip, Murphy searched the hills west of Middleburg and Leesburg, while Fowler was dispatched to Richmond to question anyone who knew Crawford about the accomplice thought to be on the run with him. Galleher went to Richmond as well, to gather information about Crawford's time in the state prison.

In Washington, "Police of all precincts have been instructed to go through the colored districts with a fine-tooth comb in an effort to uncover the murderer, who they have definitely established came to Washington after committing the crime," the *Evening Star* reported.

The day after the murders there were reports that Crawford had been seen in the District. Police said two black men, one matching Crawford's description, had been spotted driving through town. Officers gave chase, but the men got away.

The *New York Times* reported the arrest of 28-year-old Melvin Crawford in Washington. He answered the general description of George Crawford, "the Negro suspected of slaying Mrs. Ilsley and her maid," according to the *Times*.

"The man was picked up at a mission home by detectives acting on orders to search every possible hiding place. A cut on one hand was freshly bandaged. He was subjected immediately to a thorough examination." No connection to George Crawford or the Middleburg murders was found.

Traffic officer J.P. Comisky took into custody an African American, William Clifton Thomas, 31, who lived in the 300 block of D Street SW, after he was alleged to have said he was related to Crawford. Thomas was questioned by the head of the city's homicide squad, who decided that Thomas, who had once lived in Middleburg, had been drinking when he made the remarks and was not actually related to Crawford.

There were raids in Hughes Court, in northwest Washington, where nothing was found. Just outside the District, in Prince Georges County, Maryland, police questioned Howard Turner of Covington, Kentucky, after he told conflicting stories about his whereabouts at the time of the murders. Two hunters in Maryland "reported flushing a negro in the woods."[4] The man ran from the hunters, leaving behind a coat similar to one Crawford was suspected of stealing from Paul Boeing. The coat was reported to Washington police detective headquarters — Montgomery County police, who had jurisdiction over the area where the coat was found, complained that they were not made part of the investigation — but nothing ever came of it.

South of Leesburg, under the Lee Highway bridge near Manassas, state road workers found a four-foot long, $1\frac{1}{4}$-inch diameter iron pipe that they believed was stained with blood. It too was sent to investigators in Washington.

There were reports that Crawford was carrying a .45 caliber revolver and "is regarded as a cunning and dangerous negro," according to the *Times-Mirror*.

The hunt for Crawford was national news. In New York, the *Dansville Breeze* reported that authorities were searching for a "bulky Negro."

In Camden, New Jersey authorities questioned two African American men who they considered suspects — even though they didn't match the descriptions of Crawford and his accomplice — before releasing them. In Queens, a gasoline station owner and one of his customers told police a man resembling a newspaper photograph of Crawford had stopped for a cup of coffee and directions. In an amazing coincidence, the customer told police that he saw the same man, who wore a gray overcoat and fedora hat and had a scar on the left side of his face, again the next day in Cedarhurst. Police from Queens and Nassau counties, Far Rockaway and Jamaica swarmed Cedarhurst to search for Crawford.

Separately, New York state police held Wilson Pat Green in Bayshore and sent his fingerprints to be checked against Crawford's. Green matched Crawford's description, but said he'd been traveling in the Midwest for several weeks. Green was hitchhiking across Long Island to the home of the Reverend Major T. Divine in Sayville when police picked him up. "The Rev. Mr. Divine, who is known as the 'Negro Messiah,' is the leader of a large cult there whose activities have aroused villagers of Sayville and set them to devising means of ridding the community of the cult," according the *New York Times*. Green was charged with vagrancy and sentenced to 30 days in the county jail — but he wasn't George Crawford. Neither was Ernest Walcott, who was arrested at South and Jefferson Streets the same day and was also charged with vagrancy. Nor was a man charged in Brooklyn later that afternoon.

And always the specter of a lynch mob hung over Loudoun County. Investigators reported that other vehicles, driven by men not involved with the investigation, frequently trailed their cars.

After two weeks of frantic searching in vain, Adrian and his men were no closer to finding their sole suspect than they had been on the morning the bodies were found. They had interrogated a laundry list of Crawford's Middleburg acquaintances and questioned virtually every African American in and around the village — but had learned little.

At least six African Americans, including Grayson and DeNeal, had been taken into custody and held in the Loudoun County jail, where Adrian, Galleher and others questioned them. "Middleburg authorities announced the Negroes were held on the understanding that they had been in contact with George Crawford, murder suspect, both before and after commission of the crime here Tuesday night," the *New York Times* reported. DeNeal told authorities that she had not seen Crawford in Middleburg since Christmas day 1931, the day after the Ilsley home had been robbed, and nearly three weeks prior to the murders.

Grayson had come into the lower level of the cottage to fix the fire in the furnace, apparently without realizing that Ilsley and Buckner lay murdered in their rooms above him. He told Galleher that he had gone to the Ilsley cottage at 7 a.m. the morning of the murders to fire the furnace, as he did every day, before going to his job at a garage in Middleburg. He noticed a broken window in the furnace room but said nothing about it at the time. He had thought at the time that the house might have been robbed, but he didn't want to disturb Ilsley so early in the morning, so he didn't alert anyone, he told Galleher. Later he changed his story, saying he had assumed that Ilsley herself must have broken the window after losing her keys. He also told different versions of how he'd spent the night before the murders, at one point saying he had gone to bed by 9 p.m., and later saying it may have been as late as midnight. After a long second session of questioning, during which Grayson cleared the discrepancies in his story, he was cleared and Galleher order him released.

Also cleared was Ilsley's milkman, William Wynkoop, who had made his delivery to the cottage kitchen at about 8 a.m., letting himself in through an unlocked door and leaving the bottles on the table, never realizing that Ilsley and Buckner lay dead just a few feet away. That conflicted with Paul Boeing's recounting of the morning's events. Boeing had said the door was locked and the milk was sitting on the rear porch.

Aldrich Sutphin, who worked on the Ilsley farm, had also visited the Middleburg property sometime between the murders and the discovery of the bodies. He had removed garbage from the vicinity of the garage, but had not entered the cottage.

On January 25 Adrian arrested Claude Furr, a 54-year-old quarry worker from Mountville. He was charged with aiding in the murders, based on a statement from a neighbor who said Furr had given her a blood stained shirt to clean the day after the bodies were found. The shirt and Furr's coat, which also had what appeared to be bloodstains, were sent to Washington for analysis. A search of Furr's home turned up more bloody clothes. Furr told investigators he was "dead drunk" on the night of the murders, had slept at a friend's house, and had no idea where all of the blood had come from. Investigators eventually determined that the blood was Furr's, and the charges were dropped.

But, from the beginning, the investigation remained clearly focused on George Crawford. All the rest of it was little more than window dressing. Investigators were pressuring blacks for information about Crawford; whites were not interrogated.

Though they had lived on the Ilsley property at the time of the Christmas Eve robbery and right up until the day before the murders, the members of the McCormick party apparently were not contacted by investigators. By February 26 Katrina McCormick was in New Haven, Connecticut, where she was a guest at Yale's class of '33 junior promenade; Ruth Hanna McCormick was preparing for her second marriage, to Albert Gallatin Simms, another member of the Seventy-First Congress. Mitchell, Seaton and others in Middleburg had become de facto members of the investigation; the Hitts were secluded at their Belmont estate.

Buckner was buried in Rockville Union Cemetery in Rockville, Maryland. The rites were conducted by the Reverend J. Woodman Babbitt, assistant pastor of the Presbyterian Church of the Covenant in Washington. About a dozen people attended. Flower arrangements around the casket had been sent by the Mitchells and members of the Iselin family in Middleburg and Long Island.

Middleburg businesses were closed for Ilsley's funeral on Friday morning. The Reverend Mayers conducted the service at Emmanuel Episcopal Church, across the road from the manor house and within sight of the cottage where Agnes had been killed. Among the wash of flowers flooding the tiny church were floral tributes sent by the Mitchells, Iselins, Sands and former Connecticut Senator Walter Goodwin.

At the conclusion of the service, Mayers said a few quiet words to Julius and Amelia Boeing before leading the funeral procession out of the church to a hearse waiting on the street. The casket was escorted by pallbearers Sands, Mitchell, William Hitt, James Skinner, Henry Frost, Col. William Clifford, Thomas Atkinson, William C. Hurbert, George Gaither and Dr. Carey Langhorne. Agnes's body was to be taken to Washington, where with her parents and brothers it would be put on a train to Milwaukee. Spencer's relatives had not made the trip from Wisconsin for Agnes's Middleburg funeral. Instead they planned a second service, to be held at Forest Home Cemetery Chapel in Milwaukee. Agnes would be buried next to Spencer.

Photographers from the local newspapers, and from Washington, Richmond, Baltimore and New York, who gathered on the sidewalks and in the street between the church and the manor house would later claim that the Boeing brothers had told them that they could take pictures there. But when Ilsley's casket was carried from the church and flashbulbs popped, Thomas Stafford, a state motorcycle officer from the Warrenton district assigned to keep the peace at the services, waded into the crowd of newspaper men, announcing that Mayers had ordered that no pictures were to be taken.

James Williams, who had been sworn in as a deputy sheriff, and Turner Wiltshire, a Middleburg horse trader who had attended the funeral, told Stafford that he should destroy the photographic plates. Stafford ordered the photographers to hand over their plates to him.

"But we received permission from Mrs. Ilsley's family to take these pictures."

"That's alright, but Dr. Mayers said no pictures were to be made, and none will be made," the policeman replied.[5]

When *Evening Star* photographer Gus Chinn refused to hand over his plates, Stafford first threatened to smash his camera and then grabbed it and pulled out the plate himself.

Stafford grabbed the arms of two photographers—Joseph Roberts of the *Washington Herald* and Fred Cole of the E.W. Scripps-owned *Washington Daily News*—and attempted to hustle them up the street to Seaton's office to be charged. Roberts yanked his arm away from Stafford, who punched the photographer, knocking him to the ground. Other reporters claimed that Roberts' glasses fell on the ground and that Stafford ground them beneath his heel.

Eventually Stafford hauled into the magistrate's office Roberts, Cole, *Washington Times* photographer J. Abner Bealles and Robert Clark, from William Randolph Hearst's *International Newsreel*. Only after the newsmen turned over their exposed photographic plates to Williams—who promptly destroyed them—did Seaton release the men, saying he couldn't think of any charges that applied to the situation.

Before he left Seaton's office, Roberts obtained a warrant for Stafford's arrest. Adrian was called to serve the warrant on his fellow officer.

Middleburg's town council gathered in the director's office at the bank shortly after the funeral to approve a motion of support for Stafford and condemnation of the actions of the newspaper photographers.

They met again at Mitchell's Boxwood home to decide what they could do to keep anything like the Ilsley murders from occurring in their town again. Among their ideas: hire a town police officer—the town had hired Bosher to patrol its streets, but it had no regular police force—and annex the Ridge View and Windy Hill villages to increase property tax revenues enough to pay for the added security. In the meantime, Luck was authorized to deputize a dozen men, without pay. On Sunday morning the council met with state Delegate Wilbur Hall at his office in Leesburg, laying out the plans they had discussed at Boxwood.

On Wednesday, a panel of three magistrates—Seaton, Fred Stabler and John F. Kincaid, from Leesburg—met in a converted automobile dealership in Middleburg to hear the charges and counter charges stemming from the scuffle at Ilsley's funeral. Former State Senator Frank L. Ball, an Arlington attorney representing Roberts, called as witnesses several other journalists who had been at the church, including Clark, Beales and Dunbar Hare of the *Washington Times*, William W. Chance of the *Washington Star* and E.E. Lawlor of the *Washington News*. Roberts claimed Stafford had hit him without justification, and that he had not resisted arrest.

Stafford was represented by attorneys Stilson H. Hall of Leesburg, and William Horgan and W.H. Gaines of Warrenton. Luck, Middleburg Town Councilman William D. Piggot, E.C. Downs, Wiltshire and Mayers all testified on Roberts' behalf. Mayers remained unforgiving, testifying that the photographers had disturbed him during the discharge of his priestly duties.

After three hours of testimony, Stafford and Roberts were each found not guilty. Stabler said the panel believed Roberts had created a disturbance at the church, but his infraction had not reached a level warranting conviction, and the panel cautioned Stafford to use greater care in making arrests.

Virginia Motor Vehicle Director T. McCall Frazier would find that Stafford had been justified in arresting the photographers, but should not have roughed them up. While the photographers had said that one of Ilsley's brothers had given them permission to take pictures outside of the church, evidence obtained proved otherwise, Frazier said in a report to Governor Pollard.

"No permission was given to any photographers or reporters to photograph or use cameras at any incident during the recent tragedy in Virginia, and absolutely no permission was given to photograph the funeral," John and Paul Boeing said in a telegram they sent to Frazier.

Stafford would be appropriately punished, Frazier said.

In Loudoun County, Paul Boeing was widely believed to be a drug addict; there were sniggering asides and crude jokes about his supposed homosexuality. Seaton believed that Boeing was wanted in connection with a murder in Paris, but didn't pursue it.

Boeing did not stay on the Ilsley property in the days after the murders. Within a few hours of finding the bodies of his sister and her maid, he had been taken from the scene in a car by one of the Hitts, and spent the night at their home. The shock of the murders had been so great that a physician was called in to attend to him, according to the Hitts, who refused to let reporters speak to Boeing. He went to Milwaukee for his sister's funeral, but did not make himself available to investigators for nearly two weeks after the murders. It was January 23 before Boeing returned to Middleburg, and he did not make a complete statement to Galleher until January 25.

When they finally met, Boeing told Galleher he had stayed at the cottage when Agnes left for the anti-prohibition meeting in Upperville. Buckner went to her room about 9:30 p.m., and he had walked to the manor house about two hours later, taking the dog with him. He returned to the cottage moments later to get something to eat. He was in bed in the manor house by midnight. He read for a short time before falling asleep. Some time during the night, he said, a noise woke him up. The clocks in the manor house had stopped, so he was not able to tell Galleher what time this had happened. He turned on a light and got up to investigate. The noise stopped. Boeing went back to bed.

According to Boeing, there were lights on at the cottage and the front door was unlocked when he left that night. When he went back to the cottage the next morning, all the lights were off and the front door was locked. He told Galleher he had gone to the back door and found that it was locked as well. He had opened the door by reaching his hand through a broken pane of glass.

After giving Galleher his statement, Boeing wasn't seen in Loudoun County again for nearly three years.

On January 23, Galleher called a Grand Jury; five days later E.O. Russell, Clerk of the Circuit Court — a former member of the McPherson & Russell law firm, with close ties to the *Times Mirror*— subpoenaed a dozen Loudoun County citizens to sit on the panel. Receiving summons to appear on the Grand Jury for the Circuit Court's February term were C.H. Arnold, M.E. Ball, Frank Saunders, George Ankers, Alfred Dulin, George W. Laycock, T.M. Derflinger, R. Carroll Chinn, James M. Cole, Walter Leith, Fred S. Warren and H.M. Ball. Laycock was named jury foreman.

All of them were familiar with the case; some had tangential connections to it. Derflinger was a member of the board of directors of Middleburg National Bank. Leith had played on the Middleburg baseball team with Roy Seaton in the 1920s.

Others had political aspirations. Ball and Cole were both active Democrats who were delegates to the 1932 State Democratic Convention in Richmond. Most were farmers who had lived all their lives in Loudoun County and had paid taxes there, including the poll tax, in 1931. And they were all white men, as had been every member of every jury in Loudoun County history.

SEVEN

A Year on the Run

As January rolled into February and no arrests had been made, Galleher confided to *Loudoun Times-Mirror* editor "Speedy" Corbell that he was ready to indict Crawford, the only man he considered a suspect in the double murders. The prosecutor could place Crawford in the car that had been abandoned in Alexandria, and was confident that proof Crawford had committed the murders would soon be found.

"Capture Crawford and we will have solved the murders," Galleher said.[1]

In a statement that would haunt him later, Galleher told the *Times-Mirror* that indicting Crawford before he was captured would speed extradition if he were found in another state.

But, while "Loudoun has been combed in the hope of uncovering the trail of the perpetrator or perpetrators of the foulest deed in Loudoun's history," no suspects had been arrested, the *Times-Mirror* reported January 28. "George Crawford, negro, former convict, widely hunted as a suspect, remains at large."

On February 8 Galleher went before the grand jury and asked that two first-degree murder indictments be handed down for Crawford. He presented testimony from nine witnesses, including Gibson, DeNeal, Seaton and Murphy.

Galleher told the grand jury that Crawford had entered the cottage by breaking a glass windowpane to reach in and lift the back door latch. He killed the women, took Ilsley's car keys, and left the cottage through the back door. He forced open a window on the basement garage, opened the garage door, and drove Ilsley's Ford to Alexandria, he said.

Galleher and Seaton described the scene they found at the cottage the morning of the murders, and Seaton told the Grand Jury about Ilsley's burglary allegations against Crawford. Gibson described the condition of Ilsley and Buckner's bodies, and said the bootjack was probably the murder weapon. Murphy testified that Crawford was almost certainly responsible for the murders, though he still believed Crawford had operated with an accomplice.

Mack Bushrod, an African American stable hand who lived on Washington Street, said he knew Crawford, and had seen him in town the night before the murders. A second African American stable hand, G.J. "General" Jackson, said he had seen Crawford in the woods outside Middleburg at about 2 p.m. the day of the murders.

Also called to testify were Joseph Hill, Rastus Nokes and Hammond Nokes, African American men who lived in Herndon. Hammond made the most lasting impression on the jury. His testimony — that Crawford had stayed at his Herndon home January 11—was interesting enough; but it was Nokes attire that drew the attention of onlookers at the courthouse. He wore a dress, stockings and a woman's hat to the hearing. A World War I veteran, he had dressed as a woman and used the name "Annie" since before the war. His nephew, Rastus, and Hill, who was a boarder at Nokes' Herndon home, confirmed Hammond's testimony.

Perhaps the most damning testimony of the day came from DeNeal. She told the Grand Jury that she had received a note asking for food at her home some time between noon and 1 p.m. on January 12. The note was in Crawford's handwriting, but was delivered by a tall black man who she said she did not know. DeNeal also identified the writing on the note found in Ilsley's car as Crawford's.

On the final day of its term, the grand jury indicted Crawford on two first-degree murder charges. According to the indictments, Crawford "did strike, hit and beat" both Ilsley and Buckner "with a certain blunt instrument," giving each "several mortal strokes, wounds and bruises in and upon the head, the arms, the hands and other parts of the body," from which each "instantly died." Russell signed the indictments that afternoon, and 26th Judicial Virginia Circuit Court judge John R.H. Alexander issued a warrant for Crawford's arrest.

Alexander was 49 years old, thin and pale but vibrant and energetic. He was familiar with Agnes Ilsley, having traveled in the same circles as she and Spencer. Years earlier, as an attorney, he had done legal work—for the seller — when Charles Iselin and the Institute Corporation had bought land. He was a member of the Loudoun Hunt, and would eventually become its Master of the Hounds. His father had served briefly in Mosby's Rangers and been wounded in battle at age 17; had been an attorney in Middleburg and, in 1895, served an even briefer tenure as Loudoun County's Commonwealth's Attorney.

Among Alexander's duties as Circuit Court judge was the compilation of lists of potential jurors for upcoming trials. On February 19 he swore in W.H. Frazier, a former Loudoun County Supervisor from Lovettsville, as Jury Commissioner. Frazier signed an oath in which he promised to select as jurors for trials in the Circuit Court "none but persons whom I believe to be of good repute for intelligence and honesty ... in all my selections I will endeavor to promote only the impartial administration of Justice."

At the end of February, the amount of the reward for Crawford's capture, which had peaked at $3,250, was reduced to $1,250. "It was explained that large sums already had been expended in an effort to solve the crime and apprehend the guilty party or parties," according to the *Washington Post.*

In March the nation was enthralled by the kidnapping of Charles and Anne Lindbergh's 20-month-old-son from their home in East Amwell, New Jersey. People everywhere joined in a frantic search for the missing baby and his kidnapper. Police in Loudoun County, like police all across the country, joined in the search, stopping couples with babies in cars on the Leesburg Turnpike. In the county seat, a church ceremony was halted when worshippers heard what they imagined was a baby crying in the basement. A hurried search of the building failed to turn up the Lindbergh baby or any other child.

By the spring of 1932, with Lee's surrender 67 years in the past, only a handful of aging Confederate veterans remained to attend reunions. There were six known former Confederate soldiers living in Loudoun County, and only four of those — Magnus Thompson, Columbus Wenner, J.E. Copeland, and one of Mosby's Rangers, William Fletcher — made it to the Leesburg High School auditorium in April for a banquet sponsored by the Leesburg Chapter of the United Daughters of the Confederacy.

Since the murders, investigators had been scanning DeNeal's mail for any sign that she was communicating with Crawford. In March a package addressed to her, mailed from Philadelphia, arrived at the Middleburg post office. Alerted by the postmaster, Adrian brought DeNeal to the post office. Inside the package they found a coat, and pinned inside it a letter, dated March 20 and signed by "Chairl Smith," which Adrian believed had actually been written by Crawford:

"My dear Berter just a line from the one that love you so," he had written in a childlike cursive. "I am Worry to deth a bout you truly hope this leeter Will find you Well and also the children. I have a nice coat for you I will send it in a few days.

"I would like to know When is you coming Back to me. I have every thing Ready for you. rite and send me all the news. when you rite send your mail to 1066 tremont St in Boston. But I am not work in Boston at all I am work in Linny Mass."

"Plese don't say anything a bout me or mencher any thing a bout me at all, just rite Chairl Smith and I will get it and if anybody want to know who Chairl Smith, just tell them any thing. if you want to come Why let me know at once. I will send you the money...."

A mutual friend in Boston had recently died and another, Ruth Reed, wanted DeNeal to return to Massachusetts, he wrote. "Give my best love and Regard to the children honny I miss you ever so much. Rite at once and let me know his you coming to me ... well, that all the news from you Belove one."

And on the reverse side of the sheet of lined paper was written a hasty postscript to let DeNeal know a sister of Mrs. Mary Fraction of "Sferinge St" had recently died. DeNeal had told investigators that she and Crawford had stayed at Fraction's home at 205 Springfield Street in the Roxbury neighborhood of Boston — just a half block north of Tremont Street — while they were there together in late 1931.

Telegrams were flashed to Boston to hunt down Crawford, telling authorities there that he was living at 1066 Tremont Street, just across the street from St. Cyprian's Episcopal Church, under the alias Charles Smith. But when police raided the house, Crawford was not there.

And with that, the trail went cold. There was a flurry of excitement in May when police in Orangeburg, South Carolina, announced that they had arrested a man matching Crawford's description. Hopes that the case had been closed were quickly dashed when the man's fingerprints were compared to Crawford's. The lone suspect in the Middleburg murders seemed to have vanished.

Months passed. There was no word, no sign of Crawford.

At a rally for FDR's 1932 campaign held at the Leesburg Court House, Galleher, who was president of the Young Democrats of Virginia, met Louise Falligrant, who spoke on behalf of the Florida chapter of the Young Democrats Club. Falligrant was from Tampa; educated at the Georgia State College for Women, the University of Miami and George Washington University Law School; and was a member of the District of Columbia bar. She had come to Washington in 1929 as a secretary to Congresswoman Ruth Bryan Owen.

As part of the liquidation of Ilsley's estate, the Francis Mill farm was sold in September to Washington, DC, surgeon Dr. Thomas E. Neill. The selling price was reportedly less than $11,000 — more than a 50 percent discount from the price Spencer had paid for it less than two years before.

On Saturday, October 1, James J. Williams, a special deputy officer from Leesburg, was robbed in a house near First and F streets in Northwest Washington, DC. Four icepick-toting robbers took his gun and two warrants, one of them for the arrest of George Crawford. What Williams was doing in the house so far outside of his jurisdiction wasn't clear.

Thomas J. O'Conner, a young student policeman in Boston who was studying to become a fingerprint expert, dreamed of being the man who would catch Crawford. Months after the murders, he still held on to one of the wanted posters that had been distributed by authorities in Virginia, and he spent spare time at his desk comparing Crawford's fingerprints to those of every African American man arrested in Massachusetts.

On Friday, January 13, 1933 — exactly one year to the day after the Middleburg murders — police in Boston arrested an African American man for stealing $8 from a store in Roxbury Crossing. He was stocky, dressed in rags, and told them that his name was Charles Taylor. On Tuesday he and several other men who had been arrested over the weekend were taken to Suffolk Superior Court to be arraigned.

The District Attorney was about to ask that Taylor be held on bail of just a few dollars when Inspector Stanley Gas ran into the courtroom. O'Conner had spent Monday afternoon analyzing fingerprints. His hunch had finally paid off. Charles Taylor was, in fact, George Crawford, Gas said.

The court immediately granted the District Attorney's request to raise the prisoner's bail to $25,000.

"News that the long hunted Crawford had been apprehended spread rapidly through Loudoun, causing excitement and discussion," the *Times-Mirror* declared in a front-page story in its next issue. It continued,

> Later in the evening an announcement over the radio told of the arrest of the negro, and the force of the *Times-Mirror* was kept busy answering telephone calls from various parts of the county making inquiries as to the correctness of the reports. Everywhere satisfaction was expressed that the long arm of the law finally had laid firm grasp on Crawford, and that the atrocious crime, one of the most hideous in the annals of Virginia, was in a fair way to be cleared up. The double murder of the defenseless women, alone in the Ilsley cottage, by a midnight intruder, stirred Loudoun to a high pitch of excitement. In cold-bloodedness, fiendishness and diabolical intent, the crime is without a parallel in the history of Loudoun.

"Although evidence against the negro is entirely circumstantial, little doubt is felt that the state will be able to present a convincing case against Crawford," the *Times-Mirror* opined. Evidence likely to be used to prosecute Crawford included the bloody print of the killer's palm found on the doorframe of Ilsley's bedroom, the hair and flesh found under her fingernails and the note that was found in Ilsley's abandoned car.

Alerted by a telephone call from police in Suffolk, Galleher quickly forwarded a petition to Governor Pollard asking him to request that Massachusetts Governor Joseph Buell Ely hand Crawford over to Adrian and Deputy Sheriff David H. Cooley for extradition to Virginia.

Galleher also ordered Adrian to once again take DeNeal into custody. When shown photographs of the man arrested in Boston, DeNeal positively identified him as Crawford. As she left the jail in Leesburg, she told a *Times-Mirror* reporter that she had seen Crawford in Middleburg on Christmas day, 1931— the day after the Ilsley house was robbed, but more than two weeks before the murders.

In anticipation of a speedy extradition, Galleher and Adrian prepared to travel to Boston. The Commonwealth's Attorney told a *Times-Mirror* reporter that Crawford had told Boston police he was willing to waive extradition and return to Leesburg.

Adrian and Galleher were confident that Boston would set aside the robbery charge against Crawford and he would be back in Virginia by Saturday. His trial on the Middleburg murder charges would begin during the next Circuit Court term, scheduled to begin February 13, Galleher told reporters. He had hoped for an earlier trial date, but Alexander was already scheduled to hear another murder trial in neighboring Fauquier County.

Galleher came face to face with Crawford for the first time on January 19 in an interrogation room at the Suffolk County Jail in Boston. Also in the room were Suffolk Deputy Sheriff James J. Morris, who was in charge of the jail, and police stenographer Harold Kraus.

Police were not required to inform prisoners of their rights in 1933. There was no attorney to represent Crawford.

"At first," Galleher told the *Washington Post*, "Crawford denied any knowledge of the crime. Finally he admitted that we had the goods on him and that we could convict him, so he said he wanted to be 'right with his God.' He broke down, and wept and then told us his version."

Galleher immediately attacked Crawford's insistence that he had been in Boston at the time of the Middleburg murders.

"Berda DeNeal says you came to Washington, to start off with," he told Crawford.[2]

"She is lying," Crawford said. Camden Street undertaker Basil Hutchinson, for whom Crawford said he had worked until February, could vouch for him, he said. After that he had gone to work for Rogers Brothers plumbers at 1082 Tremont Street, just down the street from the home where "Chairl Smith" had told DeNeal to send his mail.

When Galleher showed Crawford the note found in Ilsley's car, he said the handwriting was not his.

"Whose handwriting is that?"

"I don't know," Crawford said.

"That note was found in Miss Ilsley's car you stole that night," Galleher said. "The night the murder was committed and you stole that car, that piece of paper was there. When you left you said you were going to send Mr. Nokes some money for spending the night there, and when this car was found abandoned down near Washington, this note was found in the car two nights afterwards. Can you account for that?"

"No, sir."

"Supposing Mr. Hutchinson says that you were not working for him? Supposing he says you were not working there until February? If he says you were not working there, are you willing to tell me the truth?"

Crawford insisted that he had been working for Hutchinson when DeNeal left Boston.

Galleher put a photograph of the Ilsley cottage on the table. Had Crawford ever seen it before?

"Yes, sir, I worked there," Crawford said. "I didn't know anything about the killing proposition until the other day. If I did, I would have come down there."

"Why don't you tell the truth about being down in Virginia?"

"I haven't been down there."

"You don't remember being out in the woods the afternoon of January 13, the little piece of woods in back of where Berda DeNeal lives?"

"No, sir, I don't remember that."

"When three different, distinct men saw you and spoke to you?"

"I would like to know who it was," Crawford said. "I don't remember it."

"You don't have to tell me one single solitary word. I've got enough evidence on you to convict you," Galleher said.

"I know it — with people telling lies about me."

And back and forth they went, Galleher insisting he had proof that Crawford had been in Middleburg on the night of the murders; Crawford insisting that he hadn't been anywhere near the town in more than a year.

Galleher turned the interrogation to the accomplice some investigators believed had broken into the Ilsley cottage with Crawford.

"What became of this man that was with you?"

"There was nobody with me," Crawford said.

"What are you going to protect him for? Do you intend to take the whole blood of this affair?"

"I've got to take it for all the lies they have pinned onto me."

Pat Harrison, who had been a neighbor of Crawford's when he lived in Richmond, had told investigators that Crawford had showed up at his house the morning of December 29, 1931. Crawford had been looking for money, and he was expecting an insurance check from DeNeal, Harrison told police.

"Said he had come from Middleburg, second time he had been to my house," Harrison said. "He had been working in the summer for Doctor Holt. He stayed at my house for seven days," leaving on January 7 — the Thursday before the murders.

"Now, why should Pat Harrison tell a lie?" Galleher asked Crawford.

"Well, he *has* told a lie," Crawford said. "I was only there once, and that was before I first come to Boston."

Eventually, Galleher called for a break in the interrogation. How long the prosecutor, the jail keeper and their prisoner were off the record isn't clear, and none of them ever said what transpired during that time. But when the interview resumed, the tone of the conversation had inexplicably changed, and Crawford was telling an entirely different story. Instead of saying he had not been in Middleburg at the time of the murders and had no knowledge of the crimes, he now declared that he was guilty and was ready to go south to be tried in Leesburg.

"This thing has been worrying me to death since I have been here," Crawford told Galleher.

"This is the square thing for you to do," Galleher said.

"The reason I am doing it, I know I am guilty," Crawford said. "I can hide it from the public, but I can't hide it from God. I am ready to go back, because it's been worrying me ever since I have been here."

After DeNeal had left Boston, Crawford had "hoboed to Washington" and then made his way to Herndon, where he stayed with "the man that dressed in women's clothes," he told Galleher.

"I was going to send him something for eating there ... that is my handwriting," Crawford said. He and another man who was traveling with him walked along the road to Leesburg and spent the night in the woods west of town, he said.

"What was his name?"

"His name was Charlie Johnson," Crawford said.

"Did you ever see him before?"

"I met him in Washington. He belonged in Washington." Johnson's mother and two sisters lived at 1616 Third Street, according to Crawford. But they wouldn't recognize Crawford's name, because he had been using the alias Charlie Smith.

Johnson had spent time at the infamous Maryland House of Correction in Jessup Cut, near Baltimore, after being charged with robbery in the city, Crawford said. He'd also been locked up for vagrancy in Raleigh, North Carolina.

The next morning they had walked south toward Round Hill, and approached Middleburg from the west. They walked through town, past the Ilsley manor house, crossing a field owned by Charles Iselin near Pothouse Road and on into the woods near DeNeal's house. It was afternoon by the time they set up a camp and started a fire. They weren't hiding—several people saw them, including General Jackson. A woman they met along the way gave Crawford a quarter.

"I saw several of the fellows I knew. I know the face, but I couldn't tell the name," he said. By the time the sun was setting, they were hungry. Crawford sent Johnson to DeNeal's house with a note asking her for food.

"He brought back a loaf of bread and some other stuff," Crawford said.

Later that night they went to Ilsley's house, cutting across the field instead of following the road back into town. He had wanted to walk back to Leesburg, Crawford said; it was Johnson's idea to follow Ilsley into the house.

"He suggested going in and robbing the place?"

"Yes, sir."

They watched Ilsley drive her car into the garage under the cottage.

"We was in the road, and fell down in the grass," Crawford said. "She didn't see us because of the tall weeds."

Ilsley closed the garage doors, went around the cottage and walked up the steps.

Crawford and Johnson went walking through the darkened town, debating what to do next. Crawford said they should walk further south, to The Plains, where they could catch a train back to Washington. But Johnson insisted that they go into the Ilsley place.

"Man, I used to work there," Crawford said he had told Johnson. "But if you want to go in, we'll go in." They walked back to Ilsley's house.

As they approached the cottage, Johnson, who was walking a step ahead of Crawford, picked up a large stone lying near the gate. Johnson followed in Ilsley's footsteps, up the stairs and onto the darkened porch. He used the stone to break a window.

A light came on at the Grayson house. Crawford dropped to the ground in the tall grass; Johnson dropped to his knees by the banister in the shadows on the porch. There was no sound from the Grayson place, but the light stayed on.

"We can't wait here all night," Johnson whispered to him. "I am going in."

"I'll wait here and watch," Crawford said.

After 15 or 20 minutes, with no sign of Grayson or anyone else approaching and screams coming from the cottage, Crawford went up the stairs, across the porch and into the kitchen. The house was dark. He walked into the hall, where Johnson, the stone still in his hand, ran into him.

"Man, they grabbed me," Johnson said.

"I said, 'Man, you've gone and hit her. You went and killed these people.' I said 'they are going to get me, because I used to work here.'" Crawford said he didn't realize Buckner had also been attacked.

"When I got in there, Miss Ilsley was laying on the floor by the bed. I said 'Man, God damn it, you didn't have to do that.' I didn't know anything about this other woman." He asked Johnson what valuables he'd been able to steal.

"I didn't get nothing much," Johnson said. He had taken five dollars from a pocketbook, he told Crawford. Crawford grabbed a small watch.

They went back into the kitchen, where they took Ilsley's keys from the table. The keys to the garage hung on the wall. At some point, Johnson threw down the stone he had used to kill Ilsley.

As they walked to the garage, Johnson hurriedly sorted items he had lifted from the cottage.

"He kept on throwing something over the fence, and when I went back to see what it was, I saw a lot of rings in somebody's yard." Investigators had never found any jewelry outside the Ilsley cottage.

Crawford got behind the wheel of Ilsley's Ford.

They abandoned the car at the Colliflower Coal yard and jumped on a freight train in Washington that was headed for Pittsburgh. They stayed at a shelter for the unemployed there, where their pictures were taken. "They generally do that when you don't live in the city," Crawford said.

From Pittsburgh, they took a B&O train to Philadelphia, where they stayed one night in a flophouse before moving on further North. In New York they paid for a night's stay in a room on 135th Street in Harlem. They spent some time living along the New York waterfront with no place to stay before heading back to Philadelphia. It was from Philadelphia that he had mailed the fur coat to DeNeal, Crawford said, and it was there also that he and Johnson had finally parted ways.

Crawford assumed that Johnson had headed back to Washington. Crawford made his way back to Boston. He sold the watch he had taken from the cottage for $3 at a pawn shop on Washington Street.

Galleher, mindful that there were some people back in Loudoun — and some editors in the African American newspapers — who were trying to tie Paul Boeing to the murders, asked Crawford about his connection to Ilsley's brother.

"He is innocent and didn't have anything to do with it," Crawford said. "Johnson and I did it. Her brother is an innocent man. He don't know nothing about it."

Galleher had close ties to the *Loudoun Times-Mirror*. Born in 1898, he'd been raised on a Loudoun County farm, attended Leesburg High School, taught in Loudoun County schools for two years, hung his shingle and practiced law in the county seat in 1925, following his graduation from the University of Virginia Law School. The *Times-Mirror* was more than the newspaper of record in Leesburg; it was quite literally the only game in town, and Galleher had haunted its offices for years. He was president of the Young Democrats of Virginia, had been a founding member of the Young Democratic Clubs of America and a member of Virginia's Democratic State Central Committee, and, like him, the paper was clearly in FDR's camp. It seemed natural to him to funnel information to the friends he'd made at his hometown newspaper. Before leaving for Boston, he promised Corbell that he would keep him informed about the proceedings. With the confession nailed down, he called Corbell with the news. In the *Times-Mirror*'s basement, printing presses that had been running the newspaper's regular edition were halted. Copies of an extra edition with a newly laid out front page, breathlessly repeating Galleher's report from Boston, were soon rolling off the presses.

"In six minutes the *Times-Mirror* extra was being cried on the streets of Leesburg by school boys, hastily summoned to the *Times-Mirror* office," the newspaper reported. "Large bundles of the extras were speeded by motor to Middleburg. Others were sent to Purcellville. The 'scoop' was complete, the *Times-Mirror* carrying the news to its readers hours before Washington dailies carrying the story reached Loudoun and before the radio announced the confession."

On Friday afternoon Adrian and deputies Cooley and S.P. Alexander left Leesburg to retrieve Crawford from Boston.

But when presented with the typed, notarized confession in his jail cell on Saturday morning, Crawford was in a surly and vicious mood, Galleher told the

Times-Mirror. He refused to sign the confession, denied he had admitted to the murders and said he would not cooperate with extradition.

The change in attitude seemed clearly connected to a visit from attorneys from the National Equal Rights League (NERL), who had been to the Suffolk jail since Galleher's last visit. NERL had advised Crawford to have attorneys fight every effort to have him returned to Virginia, a "state where colored men have for years been victims of lynching, especially when accused of crimes against white women," according to NERL secretary William Moore Taylor.

"The National Equal Rights League, on behalf of colored American citizens, calls upon you to exercise of your prerogative of granting extradition to at least first require from the State of Virginia full assurance of a fair trial," Taylor said in a public statement directed at Massachusetts Governor Joseph Ely.[3]

Virginia bristled. "The statement is an unwarranted reflection upon Virginia and Virginia justice," Lieutenant Governor James H. Price said. "It is prompted either by ignorance or prejudice, perhaps both. The sympathetic attitude of Virginia toward her colored people is too well known to require any special comment from me."[4]

The *Loudoun Times-Mirror* showed less restraint.

"It was the unanimous sentiment of the community that no difficulty would be encountered in insuring a fair trial for the accused negro. Suggestion by the Equal Rights League that Crawford might be lynched if returned to Loudoun also was decried by leading residents of Leesburg, as was the intention that bad feeling existed between white and colored people here...."[5]

Of the 1,886 lynchings in the United States between 1900 and 1931, only 26 had been reported in Virginia, according to L.R. Reynolds, director of the Virginia Commission on Interracial Cooperation. "No reasonable citizen, of course, could or would defend even this record; but it is hardly fair to single Virginia out as a place where justice is a stranger as to require a bond, that even her worst criminals will be given a fair trial," Reynolds said.[6]

Virginia had made lynching a crime in 1927, and Leonard Woods, who was killed by a mob in southwestern Virginia that November, is generally considered to have been the last lynching victim in the Commonwealth. But it is clear that there were other, unreported mob murders in the state.

In September 1932 the *Times-Mirror* reported that the body of Shadrick Thompson, a black man accused of attacking a Fauquier County couple earlier that summer, had been found hanging from a tree near Linden, less than 20 miles from Middleburg. His body "was found by Tode Kenney, a white man, in a dense undergrowth," according to the *Times-Mirror* story.

"The body was badly decomposed, and before officers summoned from Warrenton could reach the spot a large crowd had gathered and set fire to the body. Officers who went to the scene, however, were successful in saving the negro's head and a part of his clothing and from these the officers said they made a positive identification. A hole was found in the skull of the negro, according to press dispatches, giving rise to the theory that Thompson may have committed suicide, as at first thought by investigating officers." The *Times-Mirror* offered no explanation of how Thompson could have shot himself in the head and also hung himself from a tree, nor why Kenney and the others felt compelled to burn Thompson's body.

"Persons who find a dead body hanging from a tree in the woods are not apt to set fire to it before notifying the sheriff," the *Richmond News Leader* said in an editorial. The *Washington Evening Star* reported that some members of the crowd that had gathered around Thompson's body had taken home his teeth as souvenirs. But a subsequent investigation by the *News Leader* concluded that Thompson's death was a suicide, and a grand jury impaneled by Judge Alexander ruled that Thompson had killed himself.

NAACP officials were certainly not convinced by the official determination.

"I am equally convinced with you that this was a lynching and nothing else," Walter White wrote in a letter to James H. Dillard in Charlottesville. The Tuskegee Institute, in its annual compilation of lynching statistics, listed Thompson as one of eleven lynchings in 1932. Virginia was outraged. Under pressure from former Governor Harry Byrd and the *News Leader*, White backed off of the lynching determination, and the NAACP declared the cause of Thompson's death "doubtful."[7]

NERL was the first group to step forward to defend Crawford, but there were others. The International Labor Defense (ILD), an offshoot of the Communist Party of the United States, made overtures. The ILD had defended Sacco and Vanzetti and was participating in the defense of the Scottsboro Boys in Alabama. On Sunday, attorney Butler Wilson, president of the Boston branch of the NAACP — which W.E.B. Du Bois and others had founded after a disagreement over white membership in NERL — came to the Suffolk jail. Crawford emphatically denied committing the murders, confessing to them, or having waived rendition proceedings.

By Monday morning, White was putting together a legal team to fight Virginia's effort to extradite Crawford. Things were moving so quickly that White, who was relaying information between Boston and his home base in New York, hadn't yet learned the defendant's correct name.

"Have just been informed over long distance by Mr. Wilson of your agreement oppose rendition proceedings [against] Joseph Crawford with Mr. Wilson before attorney general," White wrote in a telegram to former Massachusetts Attorney General J. Weston Allen. "National office NAACP profoundly gratified your invaluable aid.... Call on us for any help we can render." The NAACP quickly obtained Crawford's signature giving irrevocable power of attorney to Allen.

According to White's sources in Northern Virginia, there was some feeling there that Crawford was being scapegoated.

"Considerable doubt among both white and colored [about] Crawford's guilt," White said in a telegram he sent to Wilson Tuesday morning. "Strong feeling he is being made a victim. General rumor that fingerprint experts declared hands of murderer not those of laboring man."

The ILD was making headlines for its work on the Scottsboro case, but the NAACP — less PR-savvy and far less radical than the ILD — was the most important anti-lynching organization in the country. The NAACP was handicapped by constant financial problems and struggled to gain a wide base of support within the African American community, in large part because much of its leadership was not African American. Its extensive efforts to have Congress adopt federal anti-lynching legislation had so far been unsuccessful.

White, who had become executive secretary of the NAACP in 1931, had begun his tenure at the organization as an assistant to then-executive secretary James Weldon Johnson in 1918. Relying on his "white looks" — he had blue eyes and light skin, and said his parents "were both so light-skinned that either could have passed for white" — White was able to gain entry into circles usually closed to African Americans, an invaluable tool in his investigation of lynchings.[8] On more than one occasion he fooled unsuspecting whites into describing lynchings in detail, including identifying participants. In 1926 he won a Guggenheim Fellowship for two anti-lynching novels, *The Fire in The Flint* (1924) and *Flight* (1926). He used the money to finance his work on an investigatory piece on lynching, *Rope and Faggot: A Biography of Judge Lynch.*

A devout Christian, a heavy smoker, diminutive, and described alternately as charming, imperious, affable and demanding, White was born in Atlanta in 1893. Both his parents had been born into slavery; his mother traced her ancestory, and her son's unusually pale skin, to Virginia, where future President William Henry Harrison was said to have fathered six children with one of his slaves.

The NAACP legal team in Boston could handle Crawford's case there, but White needed someone he could depend on to lay the groundwork for a defense should Crawford be extradited to Virginia. He turned to Charles Hamilton Houston, the 37-year-old vice dean of the law school at Howard University in Washington, DC.

Houston was a dominant force at Howard; a respected, mythologized and feared figure who dazzled students with the brilliance and eloquence of his lectures. He was intellectually gifted, meticulously educated and driven to excel, working endlessly at his office at the university and in the study of his row house at 1744 S. Street, three doors down from Langston Hughes, in the Striver section of Washington, an aristocratic African American enclave near the Howard campus.

In classrooms and courtrooms he was an imposing figure, more than six feet tall, with intelligent gray eyes, a broad forehead rising to a deeply receding hairline, and always dressed in tailored dark suits and mild, conservative ties.

His grandfather had been a slave in Kentucky and then Missouri. He escaped to Illinois and later returned to Missouri to rescue his family from slavery. He went on to become Ulysses Grant's unofficial personal bodyguard, saw action during the Civil War, and went on to work as a cabinet maker and Baptist preacher in Washington when the war was over. His eldest son, William Houston, graduated from Howard Law School, became a member of the school's adjunct faculty and was one of the first black attorneys in the District to head his own law firm. He and his wife, Mary Hamilton, were part of a small community of relatively affluent African Americans in Washington who held relatively well-paying jobs and believed in higher education for themselves and their children.

Charles Hamilton Houston was their only child. He attended M Street High School, an African American school for Washington's black upper class. He graduated from Amherst College Phi Beta Kappa in 1915 — he was the only African American in his class — and returned to Washington to teach at Howard. When World War I began he enlisted in the Army and was commissioned as a first lieutenant in the infantry, serving as judge-advocate at Fort Meade, Maryland, before resigning his commission to go to artillery school. He was recommissioned as a second lieutenant and saw service with the 351st Field Artillery in France and Germany. He returned to the States during the Red Summer of 1919, when the country was overrun by racial violence and lynchings. He entered Harvard Law School in the fall of 1919; became the first African American elected to the Harvard Law Review; was awarded a traveling scholarship upon his graduation; studied at the University of Madrid; and completed his education in 1924.

He joined his father's law firm and began teaching evening law classes at Howard in the mid–1920s. The school's president, Mordecai Johnson, appointed Houston dean of the Howard University Law School in 1929. He revamped the school — its classes, its facilities, its staff and its recruiting, bringing in young intellectuals including Thurgood Marshall and Oliver W. Hill, who would go on to become towering figures in the civil rights movement. And he brought a new attitude to the school, which was unaccredited and always short on cash. On the first day of classes, he warned Marshall and other freshmen that two-thirds of them wouldn't make it to their sophomore year.

"We nicknamed him Iron Pants and Cement Shoes ... he insisted on perfection," Marshall would say of his mentor.[9]

"I never worked hard until I got to Howard Law School and met Charlie Houston ... I saw this man's dedication, his vision, his willingness to sacrifice, and I told myself, 'You either shape up or ship out.' When you are being challenged by a great human being, you know that you can't ship out."[10]

Their legal educations would be tools to secure their race's constitutional rights, Houston would tell his students. "A lawyer's either a social engineer, or he's a parasite," he told them.[11] And African American attorneys could not look for any sympathy from the judges or juries. Any successes they achieved would come through hard work and preparation before entering the courtroom, he said. "You are in competition with a well-trained white lawyer, and you better be at least as good as he is, and if you expect to win, you better be better. If I give you five cases to read overnight, you better read eight, and when I say eight, you read ten. You go that step further, and you might make it."[12]

But the long hours of dedicated work were going to pay significant dividends for the race, Houston told one prospective law student. "There is an unlimited field in the law for young Negroes who are willing to make the fight. The lawyer is going to be the leader in the next step in racial achievement."[13]

In his office on the third floor of the school, Houston would spend his days and nights reading and writing, a green visor pulled tight on his forehead, typing most of his own work and correspondence with a rapid-fire two finger method students described as "Gatling gun." He kept a full schedule at the school and, at the same time, was working on court cases, and was a member of the District's School Board.

As far as anyone could remember, no African American (and no woman) had ever served on a jury in Loudoun County, or anywhere else in the area. Across the state — and, in fact, across most of the South — African Americans were barred from jury duty, if not by statute, then by practice. African Americans had occasionally been seated on grand juries in Lynchburg Corporation Court, Richmond's Hustings Court and both grand and petit juries in Henrico County. But even those appointments had occurred far less frequently since Virginia adopted the jury commission system in 1918. According to the amended Virginia Code, "The judge of the circuit court of each county and city, and the judge of every city court where juries are empaneled, shall, prior to the fifteenth day of February in each year, or as soon thereafter as practicable, appoint for the next ensuing year ... two persons as jury commissioners, who shall be competent to serve as jurors under the provisions of this chapter, and shall be men of intelligence, morality, and integrity ... every jury commissioner shall have a fee of five dollars a day for the time actually engaged in making out the list of jurors men...."

In a murder case arising out of Ohio County, West Virginia, the United States Supreme Court in October, 1880, had found that a statute forbidding blacks from serving on juries was unconstitutional. But Virginia saw little reason to change its ways.

On Wednesday morning, January 25, Crawford swore out a statement, witnessed by Butler Wilson, in which he said Galleher had strong-armed him to obtain his confession and had not told him that the statement could used against him in court. Crawford said he had told Galleher that he had not killed Ilsley and Buckner. According to Crawford, he had been in Boston, sleeping in Basil Hutchinson's boiler room at the time of the murders.

That afternoon, Massachusetts Attorney General Stephen D. Bacigalpuo presided over an extradition hearing at the Statehouse in Boston. Police would seek to prove Crawford's identity and that he was in Loudoun County at the time of the murders; Allen and Wilson would argue that he had been in Massachusetts. Authorities wanted Crawford to stand in a police lineup before the hearing, but the NAACP attorneys were able to block that move.

Witnesses Galleher had brought from Virginia testified that they recognized Crawford from photographs that police showed them. Repeating the testimony they'd given to the grand jury in Virginia, Jackson and Bushrod said they had seen Crawford near Middleburg the night before the murders—though Jackson seemed confused about the specific date of the killings—and Murrell Partlow, a former prison guard who lived in Ashburn, said he had seen Crawford two days prior to the murders. Adrian testified that he had seen Crawford somewhere between Middleburg and Leesburg the day before the murders. And, despite the defense team's objections, Galleher was able to enter into evidence the still unsigned confession.

Crawford insisted that he had come to Boston in September 1931 and stayed there until his arrest. He said he had changed his name because he had left Middleburg with a married woman—DeNeal—who did not want her identity known. In Massachusetts they had become Charlie and Bertie Smith.

When Allen and Wilson admitted that some of their witnesses were sick and so could not testify, the hearing was adjourned until February 7.

The delay frustrated Wilbur Hall. "There are some phases of this matter that I want to discuss with you sometime, and if you happen to be in Leesburg please drop in to see me," he wrote in a note to Billy Mitchell. "Confidentially to my mind the thing is being bungled."[14]

But to Galleher, extradition seemed assured. He sent a telegram to the *Loudoun Times-Mirror* to say he expected a decision by Gov. Ely by the end of the day. But when no decision was handed down by nightfall, Adrian and his deputies left for Leesburg. They had now traveled to Boston twice to retrieve Crawford, returning home empty handed each time. They would not return until Crawford's extradition order was in hand, according to Adrian, who told reporters that there was no reason Crawford couldn't receive a fair trial in Leesburg.

It was clear to White that, despite his claims of innocence, Crawford was likely to be returned to Leesburg, and a fair trial there was hardly guaranteed. That afternoon, White discussed the Boston hearings with Crawford's defense team via long distance telephone. Wilson and Galleher's witnesses had not seemed credible, and none of them had testified that they had seen Crawford from closer than 50 feet. Still, White worried that the NAACP would be walking into Loudoun County blind, with only Crawford's testimony to guide them in their preparations for a trial. The morning after the hearing, White called Helen Boardman, a white investigator who, along with Martha Gruening, had done plenty of footwork for the NAACP over the years — including compiling much of the information used in the association's 1919 study, "Thirty Years of Lynching in the United States, 1889–1918" — to ask that she investigate Loudoun County's attitude toward the case. He wrote letters of introduction for her to hand to Ludwell Denny at Scripps-Howard Papers and a few other people in Washington, asking them to help her with her investigation.

Denny sent Martha Strayer to Loudoun County with Boardman. They spent Saturday and Sunday talking to anyone who would speak to them, telling them that they were reporters from the Scripps-Howard news service. In an eight-page deposition taken in New York days later, Boardman said Strayer made it clear she thought Crawford was guilty.

In Leesburg they spoke with Adrian, Galleher and Russell, who all said they expected no mob violence if Crawford was brought south. Crawford would be held at the Alexandria jail, they said, because "the Leesburg jail was a flimsy structure and he might escape from it," according to Boardman.[15] While Boardman and Strayer were talking with the County Attorney, Billy Mitchell telephoned Galleher's office, "apparently expressing great interest in having Crawford brought to Middleburg and offering assistance." Gibson told Boardman that he didn't have time to speak to her.

In Middleburg that evening, J.W. Mitchell, who had an auto accessory store in the village, told the women "that the day after the crime, all the people on the streets were armed and that in fact there were so many guns it was hardly safe to be out," Boardman said. "He felt that if Crawford had been found that day he would have been lynched. Now, he said, it is not likely, as feeling has calmed down and people are anxious for legal procedure." More than a dozen other people told them similar stories, she said.

A man in a plumber's told them he was not convinced of Crawford's guilt and said that Crawford did not stand a chance of acquittal. Something in the case was being covered up — but he did not care to discuss it with reporters.

On Sunday, they spoke with Roy Seaton.

"He said that at the time of the murder there was great excitement and mob violence would have been certain if Crawford had been found," Boardman said. "Probably nothing of the sort will happen now, he said, as people in general are opposed to it. He said there were many facts in connection with the crime that had apparently been suppressed. Mrs. Ilsley's brother, Paul Boeing, he said, was said to be a drug addict and a pervert and had had some very serious trouble in Paris quite recently (before the crime). He brought a queer sort of man back to America with him, who lived with him for a short time and then disappeared. Mrs. Ilsley had sent her brother abroad for medical treatment and had tried very hard to break him of his habit. He was financially dependent on her and they were known to have quarreled frequently about money. After the crime, he was terribly unstrung and would not talk about it. When questioned by officials he became hysterical. Local gossip connected him with the crime and he hired an attorney from New York and threatened to bring action against several people. Mr. Seaton said that in his opinion there was no doubt that this brother knew much about the crime which he had never told." Boeing did have an attorney from New York on retainer, but most of Seaton's other allegations were not corroborated by others.

Boardman and Strayer also spoke with Billy Mitchell, Hitt, Luck and Sands, who all said there may have been trouble if Crawford had been caught immediately after the crime—"If we had found him then, there would have been a burning," Boardman reported Mitchell saying. Luck said that there had "been talk of that sort, especially since the lynching last October in the next county [the Shadrick Thompson lynching in Fauquier County in September 1932]. He said the influential people in Middleburg did not want trouble and will try to prevent it."

According to Boardman, there was some talk that Crawford had been given shelter on Swann Street in Washington's Striver section, near the Howard University campus, an area "where some of the finest colored people in the city resided."

The danger of mob violence still simmered in Middleburg, according to some of the people Boardman and Strayer spoke with. "The longer they keep him in Boston, the more excited people get," one man told them. "I hear a lot of talk, and they're hot under the collar, the way Boston's holding him back."

On Tuesday, Boardman returned to Middleburg and spoke again with Seaton, who "said he thought it was time the true story was published somewhere. He said that in his opinion there is more evidence against Paul Boeing than against Crawford. He said he was the only person in the village who had the nerve to say this. 'The rich people have been riding me pretty hard for saying it. Paul Boeing is their own kind. If they thought he was likely to be implicated, they would let Crawford go and hush it up.'" Boardman then repeated Seaton's growing list of allegations against Boeing. According to Boardman, Seaton had said that

> "Paul Boeing is the queerest man I ever knew. He is effeminate and dresses immaculately. He takes more trouble over his appearance than a girl. He is very dark, with dark eyes, dark skin and coal black hair."
>
> Mr. Seaton explained the interest of the wealthy estate holders in Paul Boeing on the ground that he was a particularly intimate friend of Mrs. Hitt, who was the daughter of Senator Elkins and a close associate of Alice Roosevelt Longworth.... Mr. Seaton said that they had threatened him repeatedly because he was so outspoken in regard to his suspicion of Boeing.... "I [Seaton] do not feel sure that there will be no mob violence if Crawford is brought here, even though he will be taken to Leesburg and not to Middleburg. I do feel certain that if tried he will be railroaded to the chair as sure as fate. They are doing it to protect Paul Boeing. I

think his friends would rather drop the case than have him implicated and might go so far as to engineer a lynching to prevent this.... I believe Paul Boeing is connected with this and either committed the crime or planned and hired it done. I have heard and I believe that Paul is wanted in Paris for murder. He was sent there by his sister for treatment for venereal disease. He was always queer. Mr. Ilsley did not like him and objected strongly to his being allowed on the place but after Mr. Ilsley's death, he went there to live permanently." He was believed to be a kleptomaniac, Seaton said.

During his interview with Boardman, Seaton said Boeing told him he had spent the evening of the murder in the cottage to guard it as it was empty; undressed and put on pajamas there, and at 11 p.m. went to the big house, where he slept on the third floor in a room facing Washington Street, on the opposite side of the house from the cottage. The morning after the murders, Boeing had arrived at the bank in pajamas and overcoat, but when he, Seaton and a man from the bank went to the cottage, there was no sign of worn clothes or other evidence that Boeing had undressed there the night before, according to Seaton. With the bodies of his sister and their maid lying in their blood-soaked bedrooms, Boeing had grabbed fresh clothes from his room, and was driven away from the crime scene by Mrs. Hitt.

Seaton said he believed "a very fine pair of men's shoes" that had been found in the getaway car were Boeing's. Boeing had confessed to the crime in front of others and told Leslie Ferguson, one of the men who had been guarding the cottage in the days after the murders, that the murder weapon was a piece of iron pipe hidden in the basement of the big house. John Boeing, the Hitts and others had interfered, and reporters and others away from Boeing. Seaton said he had gone with Ilsley to the Burns detective agency the day prior to the murder.

"Why, that nigger doesn't stand a chance," Seaton told the women. "The rich people are against him, and they'll send him to the chair. That's all right if he's guilty — but if he isn't guilty? Well, he doesn't stand a chance." That opinion had earned Seaton the disdain of his neighbors, and some threats, he told Boardman.

Ferguson thought Crawford was guilty, but said "there was certainly something extremely strange about Paul Boeing, and that he had several times collapsed in his presence following the crime. Whenever he was near the cottage, he was hysterical and had difficulty in talking or in controlling himself." Ferguson's wife had said that many people thought Boeing was implicated and said "he was strange and has something like insanity," according to Boardman. "He was thought to be a drug addict ... she said that money was circulated in unusual quarters after the crime and people known to be poor previously bought cars in 1932, etc. She stated that the witnesses who testified in Boston were not reliable."

And there were a few people, almost all of them African Americans — and none of them willing to speak on the record — who saw something more sinister in the case. The only reason the Middleburg elite would protect Crawford from lynching, they said, was because they needed him to be convicted and executed by the state in order to protect one of their own from arrest.

"Ain't it true that if they convict him, no one else can be accused? That's what I hear," one Middleburg resident told Boardman and Strayer. "Well, in that case, they don't want a lynching." A clerk at the drugstore told Boardman that he too believed Boeing was connected to the crime.

Boardman said Corbell had told her "if we get Crawford back next week, there will be some trial here. They seem to love a nigger in Boston, but we'll get him and put him in the chair, I hope."

On February 3, the NAACP Press Service issued a statement summarizing much of Boardman's work. But, flustered by possible legal repercussions of the charges laid out against Boeing in the piece, NAACP Assistant Secretary and Director of Publicity Roy Wilkins sent telegrams to the *Pittsburgh Courier, Afro-American, Norfolk Journal and Guide, Philadelphia Tribune, Washington Tribune* and *Kansas City Call,* asking them to "chop Paul Boeing references from Ilsley story in later editions."

On March 8, *The Nation* published Boardman's account of her investigation in Loudoun County, and it included some electrifying anecdotes. After Boeing reported the murders he was taken to the Hitt estate "in a chattering state of hysteria," she wrote. One Middleburg resident told her that Boeing was found in the attic of the manor house days after the murders, wrapped in a bloody blanket from his sister's death bed, "gibbering to himself." On the day of the murders, Billy Mitchell "dominated the scene, directing, suggesting, questioning," Boardman said. "Onlookers crowded about, buzzing with suspicion and surmise ... who could have done it? It must have been a nigger. Then the cry arose, 'George Crawford! Get George Crawford!'" Middleburg's white population formed posses and "searched with minute thoroughness" Windy Hill, the African American section of the village. Crawford was the only suspect ever pursued, Boardman said. "During the weeks of the hunt, which stretched to months, no other theory appears to have been seriously considered."[16]

Not all *Nation* readers were swayed by Boardman's rhetoric.

"I have been in many parts of the country, but I have yet to find a more law-abiding and well-ordered country section than Loudoun County and its county seat, Leesburg, a small and quaint town whose history extends back to pre–Revolutionary days," Charles Tittmann, an assistant solicitor for the State Department who was a part-time Leesburg resident, wrote in a letter to *The Nation*'s editor, continuing:

> If Crawford is returned for trial, undoubtedly the prosecuting attorney will exert all his powers to secure a conviction. But that does not mean an unfair trial. It must not be overlooked that the present judge is a well-educated gentleman, an experienced lawyer, and a man whose character and family traditions would not

allow him to conduct a trial unfairly in his court, especially when the accused is one of a race which in that part of Virginia still looks to the gentry for leadership and protection. Further, undoubtedly the jury would be a fair cross-section of the local white population, namely, farmers and business men. The jury will certainly not be of that type of park-bench semi-morons which, as a lawyer, I have often dealt with in juries in some of our large cities.

As for real danger of lynching, that is all past now. It is planned to protect Crawford by at least fifteen extra police and troops if necessary. I have no doubt that if Crawford is extradited, Virginia will see that no just criticism can be made of his trial or treatment.[17]

And Ludwell Denny was not happy with the exposure Scripps-Howard was receiving for Strayer's part in the investigation. He complained to White that the NAACP and Boardman had misused his reporter.

On Saturday, February 4, Galleher and Louise Falligant married in St. Thomas' Episcopal Church in Washington. The reception was held in the home of Congresswoman Ruth Bryan Owen of Florida. The two attorneys had scheduled their wedding and honeymoon to fall on a date when the Circuit Court was in recess, but the Crawford trial had tampered with their plans. Galleher had traveled from Boston to Washington for the ceremony and the couple would cut short their honeymoon to return to Massachusetts.

On February 7, Crawford's extradition hearing was continued, this time at the Suffolk County Jail. Allen and Wilson called a series of witnesses whose testimony indicated that Crawford had been in Boston since September, 1931. Crawford was so desperately poor that he couldn't have afforded to travel to Middleburg, they said. Eighteen-year-old Irving Washington told the court that he and Crawford had both slept in the boiler room of Basil Hutchinson's Camden Street undertaking establishment for three weeks in January, 1932, including the night of the Middleburg murders.

Boardman's testimony lasted nearly three hours. She recounted her story of traveling through Loudoun County, painting a picture of a community that was unapologetic about having sought to lynch Crawford in the days following the murders, and still seeking to railroad him into the electric chair to cover the guilt of one of their own. Interestingly, Boardman testified that Boeing was the man people said was being protected, but the *Loudoun Times-Mirror* reported only that she had named a person "and said he was a known drug addict who was well known to the victims of the slaying," without using Boeing's name in the story.

When word of Boardman's testimony reached Middleburg, Sands said the investigator had misrepresented him. Luck said he had never even met Boardman. Seaton told the *Times-Mirror* that he had been "misquoted, insomuch as I do not know any Helen Boardman, and ... I am not a justice of the peace or any kind of peace officer for the county or the state [Seaton had, in fact, resigned as Justice of the Peace for the Mercer Magisterial District on Oct. 3, 1932]. Also, there have been no threats against me, so far as I know, regarding this case. Furthermore, I see no reason why he, George Crawford, should not get a fair trial just like anyone under the same circumstances and conditions."

Mitchell said that Boardman had distorted his comments and, frustrated by what he and others in his neighborhood felt was Governor Pollard's reluctance to protect Virginia's honor, fired off a telegram to Pollard.

"This community much concerned over the turn the Crawford matter has taken in Boston," Mitchell wrote to the governor. "We hope every effort will be made by the state to obtain extradition."

Crawford took the stand when the hearing was continued Wednesday morning. He said he had been in Boston at the time of the murders, and his account of his whereabouts over the past 18 months matched some of the details of the preceding day's testimony. Some of the conversation between he and Galleher in the unsigned confession was accurate, he said, but he denied that he had confessed to the murders, denied that he had been placed under oath by Galleher, denied that he had been in Virginia in January 1932, and denied that he had committed the murders. Galleher had bullied him to get him to sign the confession without being allowed to read it first, Crawford said. He had come to Boston with DeNeal in the fall of 1931 and hadn't been south since then, he said.

And with that, the extradition hearing closed. Bacigalpuo sent his report to Governor Ely the next morning.

On Thursday, February 16, Wilson and Allen met with Ely, who expressed his sympathy with African Americans seeking justice in the courts of southern states. "I feel that, personally, he will act on his conscience and the law," Wilson wrote to White.

But Ely announced the next day that he would grant Crawford's extradition to Virginia. He was convinced that Crawford was the man wanted for the Middleburg murders and would receive a fair trial in Virginia.

The *Loudoun Times-Mirror* was once again offended. "The governor's comment as to Crawford's trial was regarded as entirely uncalled for, the contention being that it was not for the governor of another state to question the manner in which Virginia trials are conducted. The opinion freely expressed here is that the sole question to be determined by Governor Ely was whether Crawford is the man under indictment."[18]

The warrant for extradition was issued on Saturday. In Middleburg, Mitchell and others were already searching for prominent southern lawyers to assist Galleher in the coming murder trial.

White wanted the NAACP legal team to keep its cards close to the vest. On February 21, he wrote to a Richmond attorney that the legal team's opposition to Virginia's practice of barring blacks from jury service should be kept confidential, "as our Boston attorneys fear that in order to forestall successful action on application for a writ of habeas corpus, authorities might put one or two Negroes on a jury between now and the time when the hearing is held."

Wilson sought advice from sympathetic lawyers in Virginia about the practice of seating African Americans on juries there. Richmond attorney Alfred E. Cohen told him that juries for criminal cases in the state were selected from lists of qualified voters.

"Owing to the failure of negro citizens to pay their poll tax and qualify themselves for the election franchise, generally the names of negroes are seldom drawn from the jury box in the cities of this state," Cohen said.[19]

Another Virginia attorney, Leon A. Reid, told Wilson that black voter lists appeared to be "entirely ignored upon the selection of the venire men from which the juries are selected."[20]

In an effort to block the extradition, Wilson applied for a writ of habeas corpus. In the petition, the NAACP claimed that the indictment was invalid because it was brought by a grand jury that blacks had been excluded from, according to long standing Virginia custom. "This exclusion of Negroes, as a class, we claim is the denial to them of a right given by the Fourteenth Amendment of the Constitution of the United States," Wilson said.[21]

On Thursday, March 2, Wilson wrote to White, recommending that a lawyer examine the list of grand jurors who had indicted Crawford, to see if they had been seated according to Virginia code, and to see if the jurors were qualified to sit on a grand jury.

"If in calling the venire, etc., the Virginia authorities erred as many times as they did in the copy of the indictment"—Wilson had noted several misspellings and other minor errors in the indictment—"we may get some very material help," he wrote.

The next hearing—at which Bacigalpuo's office would have to prove that Crawford was actually the man wanted in Virginia—was scheduled for March 13. The attorney general of Massachusetts later put it off until Friday, March 24.

The NAACP continued to run short on funds for Crawford's defense. Butler had to request that White send him $25 to pay the filing fee for the habeas corpus. Morgan Bradford, a private investigator who lived and worked out of the Hotel Chatham in midtown Manhattan and claimed 33 years of Secret Service experience, approached the NAACP to offer his services, but had to be turned away because of a shortage of funds. Bradford said he had met William Hitt on the streets of Washington a few days after the murders, and Hitt had told him that he believed Boeing was the killer. Bradford wanted $350 to conduct a 10-day investigation. The NAACP balked at the price. "Arthur Spingarn [head of the NAACP's legal committee] and I doubted whether he could get anything we could not get ourselves," White told Houston.[22]

White was scrambling to find legal precedents of any kind to block Crawford's extradition. In an effort to buttress the NAACP position, he sent a telegram to New Jersey Governor A. Harry Moore, who in 1932 had refused to return to Georgia a fugitive from a chain gang.

Robert Burns had been sentenced in Georgia to six-to-ten years for stealing $5.81 from a grocery store with two other men. He escaped and made his way to Illinois, where in 1922 he became editor and publisher of *Greater Chicago Magazine*. Seven years later he was arrested and returned to Georgia. Again he escaped, this time making his way to New Jersey. When he was arrested in Newark in 1932, Moore refused to extradite him.

"My decision was in the following words," Moore said in his response to White. "I have listened carefully to the arguments of the counsel. I cannot agree with counsel for Georgia that the Constitution controls my decision; in fact, quite the reverse is true under the opinion of Chief Justice Taney of the United States Supreme Court in the case of Kentucky vs. Dennison [an 1861 case in which Taney ruled that the court did not have the power to force states to comply with extradition requests from other states] ... I am constrained, therefore, to deny the request for extradition."[23]

White would suggest that Houston find a way to demonstrate that Virginia was not prosecuting crimes against blacks as enthusiastically as it was pursuing Crawford. But he waited until Monday to write to Houston, asking him to be the attorney to examine the venire in Leesburg. "We are up against a most difficult situation at a critical stage," White wrote.[24]

"All the evidence tends to indicate that Mrs. Ilsley was killed by her brother, Paul Boeing, a dope addict, and that Boeing is being protected by the wealthy society and fox-hunting landed gentry around Middleburg. It is equally evident that they are attempting to make Crawford the goat ... legally our case is a weak one, in that the alibi witnesses for Crawford who swear that he was in Boston at the time of the murders are humble people."

White suggested that Houston ask Claude Swanson, Roosevelt's Secretary of Navy, for a note of introduction to take to Leesburg. Swanson was a relatively progressive Virginia Democrat, who had served seven terms in Congress, one as the state's governor and four in the Senate, before heading the Navy.

White also apologized to Houston for the NAACP's inability to pay him a fee.

"Unfortunately, we are absolutely strapped and have already spent more money on this case than we could afford. We cannot pay a fee but we will, of course, pay expenses."

Houston responded on Wednesday. He would take the assignment.

"I did not bother Mr. Swanson because he is now Secretary of the Navy, and hard to reach ... I think I will have to go without any letter of introduction. But I am carrying my certificate of membership in the bar, and that may be sufficient with a little diplomacy.

"I will try to locate in Leesburg or in the county some reputable attorney who can testify as to the practice in empaneling grand juries. This is likely to be a hard job because the reputable attorneys will probably be identified with that class of people apparently anxious for Crawford's conviction."[25]

Houston also asked White to have Crawford sign a power of attorney over to he and Edward Lovett, a Washington attorney he had recruited to help him with his investigation. Crawford's case, Houston had come to believe, offered the NAACP a chance to use extradition to force the South to open juries to African Americans. If Virginia wanted George Crawford returned from Massachusetts, it would first have to end its all-white jury system.

The national coverage the Crawford case was receiving attracted a flood of advice and tips, much of it from anonymous sources. Most of it was worthless. But a few were interesting enough to pursue.

"Will former Virginia woman who wrote *Amsterdam News* early in 1932 regarding Ilsley case communicate immediately with National Association for Advancement of Colored People, 69 Fifth Avenue, telephone Algonquin 4-6548," the NAACP said in a personal ad White ran in the *New York Times* on three occasions in the spring of 1933. "Will treat matter strictest confidence. Vitally important as life of innocent man at stake."

On March 7, John Boeing met with White in New York after seeing the *New York Times* ad. White told Boeing the NAACP was not interested in protecting a guilty man from justice, and asked Boeing what evidence he knew of that proved Crawford was in Middleburg at the time of the murders. Boeing told White that "persons retained by himself and the family" had a note written in Crawford's hand that had been found in Ilsley's car the morning after the murders. "The writing gave the address of a house in a town near Middleburg at which, according to information transmitted to Mr. Boeing, Crawford and another colored man stayed approximately two nights before the tragedy," White wrote to the NAACP legal team in Boston.[26]

In a March 8 letter to Arthur Spingarn, White described his meeting with Boeing:

> He was affable enough, and seemed most interested in trying to find out if we had evidence against any person other than Crawford. I played dumb — not a difficult process at all — and told him that if he had any evidence that Crawford was guilty, we would not continue to oppose rendition; but that we would have to have specific evidence. He fell nicely into the trap and is having the Burns detective agency supply me with a statement of the evidence they have gathered against Crawford. From his recital of it, it does not seem terribly impressive.

"Mr. Boeing's approach to you is rather extraordinary, and such conferences are dangerous," Wilson wrote back to White. "In all such procedure, my reaction is to 'trust no gift-bearing Greeks.'

"We are not disturbed about the slip of paper mentioned by Mr. Boeing. The Va. Dist Att'y did not make a very impressive effect in the attempt to get it before the Asst. Att'y General."

In Leesburg and Middleburg on March 9, Houston and Lovett spoke with Alexander, Adrian, Russell and others, who confirmed to them that no African American had ever served on a Loudoun County jury. "Cordial reception there, but folks quite sore about Mrs. Boardman," Houston wrote to Wilson that night.

At Russell's office they inspected the indictments against Crawford, the minute entries of the proceedings of the grand jury on February 2, 1932, and the lists of qualified taxpayers of the county for the years 1928, 1929, 1930 and 1931.

According to Virginia state law, prospective grand jurors were to be selected "from the male citizens of each county ... twenty-one years of age and upwards, of honesty, intelligence, and good demeanor, and suitable in all respects to serve as grand jurors ... each grand juror shall be a citizen of this state, twenty-one years of age, and shall have been a resident of this state two years, and of the county or corporation in which the court is to be held one year, and in other respects a qualified juror...."

All eleven members of the grand jury had been white men. Russell also said "that no question had ever been raised about a Negro serving on a jury in Loudoun County, that the Negroes evidently were satisfied with the justice they received at the hands of white juries, and that it was just the custom not to put Negroes on the jury," Houston and Lovett said in an affidavit.[27]

Alexander told them that "he knew there were Negroes in Loudoun County who met the common law and statutory requirements of grand jurors, and had no doubt there were Negroes in the County who further measured up to the standard which he himself in his discretion had established for grand jurors of the County, but he had never investigated the qualifications of any Negro with the purpose of determining his fitness for jury duty; that no question had ever been raised about Negroes serving on any jury in Loudoun County; that the Negroes of Loudoun County appeared satisfied with existing conditions and he did not know whether Negroes of the county would want to serve on a jury; that it would be hard to get Negroes on a petit jury because of the right of challenge ... he had never considered Negroes for grand jury service; that it was a custom in Loudoun County, and so far as he knew in all the other counties of the State of Virginia, not to consider Negroes for any jury service in the state courts; and he had just followed the custom."[28]

Adrian told them he'd been sheriff for seven years and deputy sheriff for a decade before that, and that "he had never served [a writ summoning a person to jury duty] on a Negro, or known of such a writ to be served on a Negro ... and never remembered seeing a Negro serving on any jury; that one time years ago he remembered a question being raised in a criminal case where a Negro was on trial, about Negroes being excluded from the jury, but when the judge asked the Negro defendant if he wanted a Negro on his jury the defendant said no, so the trial proceeded with the panel of white jurors, and nothing was done about the matter; that they had been more or less expecting the question would be raised at some time; but that it was the existing custom not to put Negroes on any jury in Loudoun County; and this was a matter of common knowledge."[29]

Potential juror lists were drawn from lists of qualified taxpayers, which were segregated into a white list and a "colored" list, they said.

Some of the information Houston and Lovett had gathered was kept under wraps. In a confidential memorandum to the NAACP, they detailed other conversations they had had while in Leesburg. Verdie Robinson, an African American who ran a barbershop for whites in Leesburg, told them that practically all African Americans in town depended directly upon whites for their living, and it would be hard to get them to sponsor an unpopular movement. Robinson and others in the shop said they questioned the lack of fingerprint evidence and "expressed opinion that case looked like inside job."[30]

L. McWashington, who Houston and Lovett said had formerly been active in NAACP circles in the area, told them that General Jackson had said he saw Crawford the day before the murders and "after that no effort was made to discover whether any one else had any connection with the crime." McWashington said a Negro maid who had worked in the Ilsley home told him she had found a map of the house and of roads leading out of Middleburg in the bed of "a nephew of Mrs. Ilsley," but she did not want her name connected with the case.[31]

Among the questions being asked by skeptics of Crawford's guilt: why did Boeing not report the murders until after he'd walked all the way to the bank? Why had the men who'd come onto the Ilsley property that morning—the garbage man, the furnace man, and the milkman—failed to report the broken windows? Why the discrepancies between Boeing's and the other men's accounts of the milk delivery and other details of the cottage's condition? Why had Boeing hidden himself away from investigators for so long?

Houston's advice to the NAACP legal team was clear: the case must "be built up most carefully," on a solid legal and constitutional foundation, with an eye on appealing it, eventually, to the United States Supreme Court. "Particular emphasis should be laid on what seems to have been the course of conduct: to fasten the crime on one particular suspect, rather than impartially to investigate all the circumstances of the crime and deduce the suspect there from." He didn't believe anecdotes from McWashington and others would be of much help.[32]

Loudoun County officials described Houston and Lovett as "courteous and well qualified as lawyers," according to the *Loudoun Times-Mirror*. And, after the lawyers noted that no African American's name appeared on the lists of potential jurors, they were informed by county officials "that there had been no request by colored people of the county that their names be placed upon either the list of felony jurors of grand jury jurors."

"The opinion was expressed that colored people in Loudoun are entirely satisfied with conditions as they are and felt that they could at all times obtain justice at the hands of white jurors," the newspaper opined.

At 10 p.m. that Friday, Houston wrote to White that

> It strikes me more and more that here is something big if properly handled in Boston.
>
> If you can establish the principle that the Federal court will restrain the rendition of a Negro charged with crime in State A from State B where he is located, in case the indictment on which he stands charged was returned by a grand jury from which Negroes were excluded pursuant to a systematic practice of the state officers having charge of selecting the grand jury, then you have gone the greatest distance yet toward breaking up discrimination against Negroes on the juries of the South — because in such case every Negro who feels he is about to be indicted and who can get away from the South will beat it North and the South will be unable to get him back unless and until it abandons its practice of excluding Negroes from grand jury service. If they once get on the grand jury (which hears the county's secrets), it will be easy to get them on the petit jury.
>
> It seems to me then that you ought to bring the whole pressure of the legal department to see that the federal question is properly raised at once, and pressed to the utmost at Boston; taking care to get all possible facts about discrimination on the record ... it did not shape up so important to me when I first began to work on the case; but the farther I get into it the more I see the possibilities.

Days later, Houston sent a four-page letter to White, elaborating on the case and its wider implications.

> We all know that there was grave suspicion in official circles concerning the part the brother played in the case, and that certain interests seemed especially anxious to shield the brother from examination. A lot of things point to an attitude on the part of certain investigations to fasten the crime to Crawford, rather than to make a real impartial, thorough search of the evidence and clues to determine the person to be suspected. Would an intelligent Negro (the type of man whom the judge stated he selected for his grand juries from the white list) have permitted the authorities to load the crime on Crawford when there were so many glaring facts concerning the brother's relation to the case left unexplained?
>
> I think the case can be the means of breaking up discrimination against Negroes on juries in Virginia. It can also be the means of breaking up a certain feudalism on the part of the landed gentry, if General Mitchell is given a severe grilling and the case concerning the brother's participation is vigorously pushed. And when you realize that Mrs. Ilsley belonged to the social set which includes the wealthy sportsmen from all over the East, you can see that the case has certain implications affecting the entire Atlantic seaboard.
>
> I have a hunch that if you step out of the case, the ILD will take it over. Crawford is a member of the unskilled laboring class, destitute of funds and out of work. The case has certain elements of persecution by members of the idle capitalistic class. And to my mind it seems made to order for the ILD. So having entered the fight, you will have to decide how far you are going to follow it.

Houston's specialty was civil, not criminal law and, while he was willing to assist with Crawford's defense, "I would prefer not to have the responsibility for the case." Still, if White determined that he was the man for the case, "I am willing to go the limit in the case — and if necessary take full responsibility for trying it. We owe it to Crawford and to ourselves to see that this case is fought to the limit." He would not accept payment, beyond reimbursement for expenses.

On March 11, White sent a telegram to Houston's Howard University office, thanking him for his work in Loudoun County — "superb work, unbounded gratitude" — and then he sat down to write a letter to Houston.

"You raise the most important point yet brought up in the suggestion that winning the Crawford case on the base of exclusion of Negroes from federal juries will establish the North as an asylum for Negroes accused of crime. For such action would do more than anything else I know to force the South to toe the mark."

Publicly, Wilson held back the constitutional question — could blacks be tried if only whites were allowed to serve on juries — and spoke publicly only of concerns about mob violence.

"The more we get into this Crawford case, the bigger and more important it becomes," White wrote to Spingarn. "Aside from the principle involved in saving Crawford and, more important, establishing of the legal principle that Negroes will not be returned to demanding states in which Negroes are barred from juries, there is the psychological effect of our establishing this principle in the Crawford case prior to the time of final adjudication of the Scottsboro case."

Houston told White that he would testify at the Boston hearings, but needed to know if the NAACP would pay the expenses for he and Lovett to make the trip. They planned to drive to Boston, thus saving rail fare.

"We most certainly will authorize expenses of the trip to Boston and we do so with an expression of infinite gratitude to you and Mr. Lovett for your willingness to render us this great service only at the cost of actual expenses," White wrote back to Houston. "Privately, it is my opinion that your services will be the margin between complete victory and something less in this cause celibre."

On March 18 Wilson wrote to White to tell him that Federal Court Judge James Arnold Lowell, who would preside over Crawford's extradition hearings in Boston, had told him he would consider the federal question of excluding Negroes from service on juries. Wilson also said Crawford had given him information that morning "that strongly indicates that the brother of Mrs. Ilsley had opportunity, motive and immediate financial inducement to get rid of his sister."

And Wilson worried that the NAACP might drop the case or remove he and Allen from it. "If that is so, I should like to inform Mr. Allen at once in a spirit of fair play. I may be mistaken about this," Wilson wrote. "For two months I have devoted some part of every day and every night to the Crawford case, having in mind the greater question of rights to the 650,000 Negroes in Virginia."

Despite Houston's work on the case in Virginia and the fact that he was coming north for the March 24 hearing, White did his best to reassure Wilson that the NAACP had no intention of pulling him from the case in favor of the Howard dean.

"Let me say to you as unequivocally and as strongly as I can that there is not the slightest likelihood of our losing interest in the Crawford case or that we want to relieve you and Mr. Allen ... it is a great achievement on your part to have gained assurance that Judge Lowell will consider the federal question of the exclusion of Negroes from jury duty in Virginia."[33]

In papers filed in Boston March 21, Wilson and Allen argued that Crawford's detention was in violation of the Constitution because the warrant was based on the Loudoun County grand jury's indictment, which was "null and void, and was procured in a manner which denies to your petitioner rights guaranteed to him by the Constitution of the United States," because blacks had not been considered for jury service.

"There exists in Loudoun County and the State of Virginia against colored people, members of the Negro race, generally, and against the petitioner particularly, an unreasonable race or color prejudice, which will make it impossible for him to obtain that fair and impartial jury of the vicinage, guaranteed to him by the Constitution of the United States and that will deny to him to due process of law and the fair and impartial trial which are of right his under the fourteenth amendment to the United States Constitution."

Wilson and Allen also sent White a copy of a power of attorney they had convinced Crawford to sign that day. The document would simplify Wilson's legal wrangling on Crawford's behalf, and stymied other groups who were attempting to insinuate themselves into the case. It was an important weapon in the NAACP's continuing skirmishes with communist groups.

"I have no doubt of the effort of the communists being made to get in on the case here," Wilson said. The power of attorney guaranteed that "nobody can see Crawford without my permission."[34]

White was in agreement about communist tactics. "It is a fixed policy of the communists now to try to horn in on every case the Association enters and try to gain control of it and, unfortunately, some colored people are not wise enough to see what they are letting themselves in for," he told Wilson.[35]

Crawford told Houston and Lovett that the first time Galleher had seen him after his arrest, an assistant warden had forced him to leave his cell, even though he had said he didn't want to see anyone. Crawford's cellmate, Herbert Finch, had told Crawford that he didn't have to leave his cell if he didn't want to.

"This evidence tends to show that the first conference between Galleher and Crawford, during which Crawford was supposed to have confessed, had its inception in a state of duress," according to the NAACP attorneys. "The law is plain that when duress had once been set in motion it voids a confession unless the duress has come to an end prior to taking the confession."[36]

Houston recommended that they find Finch to get his statement, and those of anyone else who may have been in the cell. "As I view the case with the information now available, it will be impossible to convict Crawford without the alleged confession. The objective facts, apart from the confession, do not link Crawford up with the crime sufficient to prove his guilt beyond a reasonable doubt. Therefore the circumstances surrounding Galleher's interviews with Crawford should be minutely scrutinized from every possible angle."[37]

White urged Allen to hire an investigator to find Finch. But months later the NAACP team would still be trying to track him down.

Wilson wasn't as optimistic as Houston. He did not appreciate Houston's presence in Boston. "Apparently jealous of prerogatives," Houston told White in a March 23 telegram.

Wilson wanted White to personally investigate in Middleburg so that he could be called to testify, an effort to block "the dead certainty of Crawford's conviction if tried in Loudoun County by a jury of white men and the possibility, always present when a Negro is suspected of crime, of a lynching bee." Wilson suggested a series of questions for White to pose to people in Loudoun County — is there discrimination in Loudoun County rail stations? Are blacks treated equitably at Middleburg and Virginia hotels, restaurants, cafes, stores, banks, post offices, racetracks?

White responded in a March 23 letter in which he said he was rearranging his schedule to be able to make the trip to Loudoun County — and, at the same time, he tried to soothe things between Houston and Wilson.

"Wasn't it a heartening thing that Messrs. Houston, Lovett and Marshall should have been willing to make the sacrifice of time and money to help in this case? It must have been most helpful to you and Mr. Allen, busy as you both are, to have the assistance of these able young lawyers to run down the facts and the details of the law. It must have also been encouraging to you who have battled so long to have this tangible evidence of the rightness of the cause when such men are willing to make great sacrifices in a vitally important case of this sort."

But tensions between Wilson and NAACP officials in New York remained high. Wilson worried that the Association, eager to garner public sympathy for Crawford's case, would release too much information.

"I don't try my cases in the newspapers," Wilson wrote to Wilkins.

> I have at heart the situation of this poor boy Crawford, and not as keen on making propaganda out of it as might be. If it comes to the attention of the court that prosecuting the Crawford case is merely incidental to NAACP propaganda, we will be out of court with a rush and Crawford will go back to Virginia. On the whole, I think it better to be wary of newspapers.

If you have a fool killer in your office, set him to work on the person who had published in your news letter this week that we are going to put the District Attorney from Virginia on the witness stand.

Why don't you tell them the whole case and be done with it? I am out of patience with this sort of thing.

Wilkins was no less terse in his response:

I overlooked your obvious discourtesy to me when I was in Boston last month to speak for the Branch, on the grounds that you were an eccentric old gentleman who perhaps felt that his years and long service to the Association made it unnecessary for him to be courteous. I do not see that it is necessary, however, for anyone, no matter how eccentric, especially a lawyer and one who has been exposed for so long to the supposedly refining atmosphere in Boston, to set down an uncivil letter. There is really no excuse for the kind of language you used in your letter and we can obviate the recurrence of it, in the event you cannot find more pleasant expressions, by simply agreeing not to write to each other.

In order to continue his work in Virginia, Houston needed Wilson to provide him with a power of attorney for Crawford. But Wilson, still chafing at Houston's inclusion on the NAACP legal team, and with his own power of attorney from Crawford already on record, dragged his feet.

"I have written Mr. Wilson twice about the letter of instructions and photostat copy of power of attorney, but have not heard from him. Failure to receive the letter of instructions and photostat copy of the power of attorney kept me from going up in the country [to Leesburg] Saturday," Houston said.[38] White pressed Wilson for the documents, and asked him to have a photograph taken of Crawford, "not too dressed up, but looking respectable," that could be distributed to the press. "There is one which is being used in the colored press, taken when Crawford was dressed in badly rumpled, nondescript clothing, with a rope tied around his waist in lieu of a belt."[39]

Houston wanted to find African Americans in Loudoun who were qualified to serve on grand juries and depose them on their willingness to serve on grand juries. Researching state code, Houston concluded "that a person cannot by tried in Virginia for a felony except upon an indictment; that a single grand jury being disqualified renders the indictment void. If that be so, then Virginia cannot proceed on an indictment founded in a violation of the Constitution in excluding qualified grand jurors because of race; and so far as the particular indictment is concerned, Crawford is illegally detained." Attorney Samuel Leibowitz had produced "qualified Negroes" to show grand and petit jury discrimination in the Scottsboro Boys case, Houston told Wilson.[40]

Allen didn't think it was a good idea to have the "qualified" African Americans testify at the hearing, telling White "that the admission by Judge [Alexander] in the stipulation that it is his opinion there are Negroes properly qualified is sufficient; and that bringing up witnesses might tend to weaken the strength of the judge's admission."[41]

Houston agreed with White, and told Allen so by telephone, and then in a letter.

"It is not perhaps good legal ethics to consider the public reaction and especially that of the press to a case, but one of the chief values of the Crawford case is that it offers us such a perfect opportunity to focus attention upon the violation of the constitutional rights of the Negro in the southern states and particularly with regard to the exclusion of Negroes from juries," Houston wrote.

"In the Scottsboro cases this has been exposed to the gaze of the civilized world. The Crawford case offers us an unparalleled opportunity to do this under even more ideal conditions and in an atmosphere which will do untold good for the eight or nine million Negroes who live in states where such rights are denied them. It is also of advantage to the Association as the Communists are working night and day trying to convince Negroes that we are a timorous, impotent organization and that the only hope of the Negro lies in revolution."

Loudoun prosecutors were also preparing to argue the legality of the Southern tradition of excluding blacks from juries. Galleher had already contacted Alabama Attorney General Thomas E. Knight, the chief prosecutor in the Scottsboro Boys trials, asking his advice.

Houston and Lovett planned to take Verdie Robinson, whose father and grandfather "have run the best white barber shop in Leesburg," to testify in Boston. Robinson was "a Negro who can discuss the qualified Negroes of Loudoun County ... he knows both white and colored in the county," Houston told White. He described Robinson as "a Howard graduate, intelligent although somewhat diffident. But he is getting more force the farther into the case he gets."[42]

Houston, Lovett and Robinson went to Leesburg April 21, checking on white grand jurors and looking through taxpayer lists for qualified blacks. "We located one [white grand juror] as a clerk in a Sanitary chain grocery store, and another as a general mechanic working for the public utility in Leesburg ... [and] located at least eight names of Negroes with qualifications equal or superior to the two white grand jurors. We also got some names of Middleburg Negroes with equal or superior qualifications ... Robinson knows all these people personally: both white and colored."[43]

Leesburg's courthouse lawn, once home to a stable, a jail, outhouses, a public whipping post, pillory and stocks—and, until the end of the Civil War and passage of the 13th Amendment in 1865, slave auctions—was a typical southern town green, with a few large chestnut trees, a monument to the county's sons who had died in the Great War, and the Confederate monument erected more than 20 years earlier. The grounds were surrounded by a spike-topped black iron fence, which could be breached only through four pivoting gates.

The adjacent Leesburg Inn had been built the same year as the latest incarnation of the courthouse. The hotel was a large building by the standards of rural Virginia in the early 1900s, three stories tall, with wide verandas off of most of the rooms. It was heated by steam, lighted by electricity and had a large staff of cooks and waiters who served meals seven days a week.

As they crossed the courthouse lawn, Robinson pointed out that on the World War I memorial to "Our Glorious Dead," the names of African Americans "appear at the foot of the list, with a line separating their names from the names of the white sons," Houston said. "Even unto death!"[44]

White sent Boardman a check for $25, "just a small expression of our appreciation to you for the fine work you did on the Crawford case."[45] But the NAACP's financial woes, exacerbated by a nationwide bank holiday declared by Roosevelt on March 6, were hampering the association's ability to defend Crawford. The legal team wanted to return Boardman to Boston to testify at the upcoming extradition hearing, but couldn't figure out how to pay for the trip from New York.

"I shall take up at once with the Legal Committee the matter of Miss Boardman being present on the twenty-fourth," White wrote to Wilson on March 8. "By that time the bank moratorium ought to be lifted. If we are put on scrip, however, I don't know how we will get her beyond the New York state line." FDR's bank holiday ended on March 13.

Wilkins arranged to have *Pittsburgh Courier* chief editorial writer George Schuyler travel to Boston to cover the extradition hearings, and to have Schuyler's stories distributed to the press.

White sent a special delivery letter to Wilson on April 22 in which he said he and Wilkins "talked it over this morning [and] we both felt that we would not have Miss Boardman come up to Boston, as we are sending Mr. George S. Schuyler who is to do a special feature story for the colored press." Schuyler was advanced $35. Boardman didn't make the trip to Boston for the extradition hearing and returned to the NAACP her $25 advance.

Lowell presided over the final extradition hearing in Boston on the morning of April 24. Wilson and Allen represented Crawford, who was not in the courtroom for the hearing; Bacigalpuo represented Massachusetts.

Lowell was 64; born and bred in Newton, Massachusetts, "an aging, flashily-dressed eccentric," according to *Time* magazine. He had earned both his undergraduate and law degrees from Harvard and had run his own private practice for nearly 30 years before being nominated by President Warren Harding to the U.S. District Court in 1922. He had served as a state representative, as chairman of the Massachusetts Committee on Workmen's Compensation, as a member of the Massachusetts Board of Labor and Industries, as delegate to the Massachusetts Constitutional Convention of 1917-1918, and on the board of the Massachusetts Commission to Consolidate Laws. But he was also a controversial figure, whose habit of editorializing in front of jurors had caused decisions made in his courtroom to be overturned with unusual regularity. In 1932 he had been rebuked by the Supreme Court for telling a jury that a witness's nervous habit of wiping his hands during trial indicated that he was guilty.

According to a brief filed on Crawford's behalf, the exclusion of African Americans from jury duty by law was contrary to the express wording of the Fourteenth Amendment — and even if the law were fair on its face, a state would still be denying Fourteenth Amendment rights if it administered it unfairly. Virginia, according to Houston, was seeking Crawford under the Constitution and his rights were simultaneously being denied under it, "and you can't spit and whistle at the same time."[46]

In written testimony, Alexander said he had never known African Americans to be called for jury duty in Virginia's 26th District, which included Loudoun, Fauquier and Rappahannock counties. Alexander — who, as presiding judge, oversaw the compiling of grand jury lists in the district — said prospective jurors were selected from lists of qualified taxpayers. And while he was sure there were African Americans living in the district who were qualified to sit on petit and grand juries, none of their names had ever been placed on a jury list. Wilson and Allen submitted written interviews they had conducted with Russell and Adrian in which both of the officials also said that they had never known an African American to serve on a Loudoun County petit or grand jury.

Lowell stunned both Massachusetts and Loudoun County officials when he granted the NAACP request for a write of habeas corpus. He was as cantankerous as ever in announcing his decision:

> I say this whole thing is absolutely wrong. It goes against my Yankee common sense to have a case go on trial for two or three years and then have the whole thing thrown out by the Supreme Court.
> They say justice is blind, but justice should not be as blind as a bat. In this case it would be if a writ of habeas corpus were denied.
> Why should I send a negro back from Boston to Virginia, when I know and everybody knows that the Supreme Court will say that the trial is illegal? The only ones who would get any good out of it would be the lawyers. The whole thing is absolutely wrong.
> Governor Ely in signing the extradition papers was bound only by the question of whether the indictment from Virginia is in order. But why shouldn't I, sitting here in this court, have a different constitutional outlook from the governor, who sits on the case merely to see if the indictment satisfies the law in Virginia?
> I keep on good terms with Chief Justice Rugg of the Massachusetts Supreme Court, but I don't have to keep on good terms with the chief justice of Virginia, because I don't have to see him.
> I'd rather be wrong on my law than give my sanction to legal nonsense.[47]

Bacigalpuo backpedaled on behalf of the prosecution.

"Are we going to say that the State of Virginia does not uphold the laws of the United States?" Bacigalpuo asked.

"They have not done so when it comes to a question of putting Negroes on juries down there," Lowell said. "The whole thing to me is a piece of a stage play. The writ of habeas corpus is allowed." Bacigalpuo said the state would appeal the decision. Technically, Crawford had been freed, but he was ordered held at the Charles Street jail on $25,000 bond pending the continued legal action.

The NAACP team was jubilant; the South enraged.

"This case involves an entirely new approach to the question of negroes serving on juries in the South," a jubilant Walter White told reporters after the hearing. "It differs from the Scottsboro and other cases, in that those cases seek to set aside a verdict after conviction, whereas here our attorneys are attempting to establish that a state which bars negroes from grand and petit jury service in violation of the Fourteenth Amendment to the Constitution cannot demand the return of a Negro fugitive for trial because such a state has already illegally and unconstitutionally indicted the fugitive and denied him his rights even before his actual trial."[48]

White flashed the news to NAACP headquarters in Washington, where Wilkins, in turn, issued a fiery press release announcing the association's victory.

"The rich whites are pushing the prosecution of Crawford to the limit and the case is looked upon as a class affair," Wilkins wrote. "The common people of the vicinity express a belief that Crawford is not guilty and that the real murderer is being shielded. It is said that the middle and upper classes of the county may engineer his lynching if he is returned. The *Loudoun Times-Mirror*, mouthpiece of the wealthy gentry, continues the clamor for Crawford's conviction."

White sent a telegram to Allen and Wilson, congratulating them on their "superb victory" and suggesting that the NAACP Boston branch hold a mass meeting to celebrate and to raise much needed funds, including money to be sent to Alabama to help defend the Scottsboro Boys. "You have helped establish what may be most far reaching decision affecting Negro's Constitutional rights ever won," White wrote.

Wilson chafed at any hint of helping the IDL's Scottsboro case, and told White that Crawford's case was "of great importance to the colored people.

"I might suggest that instead of wasting all your ammunition on Scottsboro, you consider the proper presentation of the Crawford case to the higher court," Wilson said. "Your appeal to us to raise money for Scottsboro is in the face of a strong feeling here that the NAACP, not even in a generous gesture, ought to be allied with the Communists. I have put your request before our Executive Committee and they feel that the Boston Branch ought to put its efforts into the Crawford case."[49]

Allen called for restraint until after a final court decision in the case. "There has been ... a good deal of unfortunate publicity in regard to the statements made by the judge, and it has apparently aroused considerable feeling in Virginia and perhaps more or less throughout the South.

"This is unfortunate, because it may react against us when the case comes up before the Circuit Court of Appeals. It is, therefore, most important that nothing should be said by any of us which will cause any additional resentment. It [sic] will be time enough for us to talk when we get a final decision in the Supreme Court of the United States. Until then the less said by us, the better."[50]

On Tuesday morning, with a victory in his pocket, Wilson was planning longer term. "Our remaining job is to hold what we have got, and we must not quit while fording the stream....

"I have just seen Crawford and he tells me to say to the NAACP that he is deeply grateful for its work in backing him, and says that he hopes to live long enough to show to the world that he had no part in the death of Mrs. Ilsley, who was to him a generous friend and a very kind employer. He was over come with emotion and could hardly express himself, but I am sure that he appreciates what has been done for him," Wilson said in a letter to White.

White offered his greatest congratulations and thanks not to the Boston lawers, but to Houston.

"Without you, we could never have won, for you pushed back the horizon for us and caused us to see the profound implication of the case," he told Houston. "It may well develop that this is the most far-reaching decision affecting the Negro's constitutional rights which has ever been won, and I am perhaps happiest because three young Negro lawyers played the decisive part in the victory. Thanks again and again."[51]

EIGHT

Leesburg Prepares for a Trial

Across the South the condemnation of Lowell's decision was harsh and nearly universal. In Richmond, Attorney General John Saunders expressed "amazement"[1] at the decision. Crandall Mackey, a former Arlington County Commonwealth's Attorney, suggested that an "indignation meeting" be held in Leesburg and offered to be its keynote speaker.[2] The offices of Virginia's congressional delegation were flooded with telegrams from angry constituents.

On Tuesday morning Congressman Martin Dies, a Democrat from Texas, introduced a resolution asking that the Federal judgeship held by Lowell be abolished. According to the Dies resolution, Lowell "has displayed a venom and a prejudice unparalleled in the judicial history of this or any other country, and has arrogated to himself the powers of dictatorship, and ruthlessly trampled upon the laws of the nation, and has had the effrontery to attempt to justify his shocking conduct by asserting that the fact that negroes do no serve on juries in Virginia renders any trial in that state illegal."

In a vituperative speech on the House floor the next day, Democratic Congressman Howard W. Smith of Virginia demanded that Lowell be impeached. He introduced a resolution appropriating $5,000 to the House Judiciary Committee to investigate Lowell.

"There is a strong sentiment in the House for action against the Massachusetts judge," Smith said. "Under Judge Lowell's theory, no woman as well as no negro could be extradited to Virginia, because neither serve on juries in the state. There is no law, however, to prevent either from serving and likewise no one has an inalienable right to serve on juries."[3]

Smith laid out seven charges against Lowell, including abuse of power, violation of his oath and using "his judicial position for the unlawful purpose of casting aspersions upon and attempting to bring disrepute upon the administration of law in the Commonwealth of Virginia and various other States in this Union." Any judge is impeachable who is either "so ignorant of the laws as to amount to flagrant incompetency, or who knowing the law deliberately, willfully and knowingly, in direct contravention of the Constitution and well-established precedent and authorities of the court of last resort, release on the world a self-confessed murderer of the most vicious type," Smith said.

There were opposing voices in the House, including Republican Robert Luce of Massachusetts. Luce and Lowell were friends; they had served together in the Massachusetts legislature and the state's constitutional convention. "I testify that he is a man of exceptional intelligence; that he is a man of perfect probity; that he is a man with the highest regard for justice; that he has filled his office honorably; and that all suggestions that this episode is part of a career of malfeasance are absurd ... the only valid charge, the only charge with which any proof is presented is— and I deny that telegrams from disappointed litigants are proof— that in one instance, one instance in all his long and honorable career, he made a decision that has not satisfied the gentleman from Virginia," Luce said on the House floor on April 26.[4] If the House were to move forward with impeachment proceedings in the Crawford case, it would encourage a plague of similar requests from litigants dissatisfied with other judges, and would be bound to move forward with those requests as well, Luce said.

Moreover, Lowell's decision to not send an accused man into a jurisdiction "when it is believed he cannot get justice," was correct, Luce said.

"I am going to ask ever man here to ask himself this question," Luce said in the House. "If tomorrow Germany should ask President Roosevelt to extradite and send to Germany a Jew, would I vote to support the President if he did it?"

The House approved Smith's resolution by a 209–150 vote. Judiciary Committee Chairman Hatton W. Sumners, a Texas Democrat, said the committee would take up the issue before the end of the week. "Our first duty will be to determine the facts as to what actually transpired," Sumners said. "Up to the present, there doesn't seem to be any great controversy over the facts."[5]

The Bar Association of the City of Boston quickly passed a resolution condemning the attacks made on Lowell in the House of Representatives. "Whether his decision was right or wrong will be determined by a higher tribunal to which an appeal has been taken," the resolution said. "But in the meantime, he should be free from attack for performing his judicial duty honestly and in accordance with his best judgment."[6]

Lowell appeared unfazed by Smith's promise to have him removed from the bench. "I don't care what he said. I don't know what he said and I don't want to know," he told reporters.[7]

And Wilson was confident that Lowell's decision would stand. "I think the position of Judge Lowell is impregnable, and our care here is to proceed as to give no reason to the people at Washington to do further harm to him," he told Houston.[8]

In Leesburg, the *Loudoun Times-Mirror*, which generally touched on two or three topics on its weekly editorial page, devoted the April 27 editorial page in its entirety to Lowell's decision to release Crawford. Corbell's column, illuminated as he was by Galleher's inside knowledge of the extradition hearings, was obtuse, to say the least.

"If this newspaper understands correctly the ruling of Judge Lowell in the Federal District Court in Boston Monday ordering the release of George Crawford, it means that no negro may be tried by a jury on which a member of the colored race does not sit," the newspaper's editor wrote under the headline "AN AMAZING COURT RULING."

> By the same token, a Chinaman charged with crime may not be tried by a jury on which a Chinaman does not sit. Nor may a jury the panel of which does not include an Indian sit in judgment on an Indian indicted for crime. It is a preposterous ruling, which no good lawyer for one moment believes to be correct. Likewise, it is a ruling fraught with dangerous possibilities.
>
> Judge Lowell, in his comment from the bench, showed utter lack of knowledge of conditions in Virginia and Loudoun County. The law in Virginia does not prohibit the placing of negroes on juries and if the practice has been to call only white men for service it is because officials have exercised the discretion given them under the law. There is no obligation on judge or jury commissioners to select colored men for service on the juries.... The practice in Virginia, adhered to over a long period of years, has proved entirely satisfactorily to both white and colored people in Loudoun.
>
> There has been no racial feeling in Loudoun over the crime for which Crawford has been indicted. From the night of the commission of the foul deed there has been no difference in the attitude of white and colored people here in respect to the punishment of the criminal....
>
> Crawford may not be guilty. But it is Virginia's position, as a sovereign state, that the question of guilt or innocence of the man is a fact to be determined by a Virginia jury, in accordance with Virginia's established practice in trying persons accused of crimes. If Crawford be not guilty, a Loudoun jury will set him free, if he be proved guilty a Loudoun jury will mete out to him the punishment demanded by the black crime of which he stands accused. Crawford is assured of a fair trial in Loudoun.

On the front page of the same edition of the *Times-Mirror* was a short story under the headline "Negro Dances Here Banned by Council," with a few details about a dancehall in Leesburg that had been closed after complaints from white citizens about "disorder."

It had been a tough year for Billy Mitchell. His book *Skyways* had been taken off the market because it had not sold enough copies to cover the advance he had received from the publisher. He was working on another manuscript, warning of America's vulnerability to attack by a foreign power, but it was never published. He had also begun a one-man letter writing campaign to Congressmen and other public figures in which he accused the American aviation establishment of intentionally slowing aviation progress.

And he was frustrated by Loudoun County's inability to bring Crawford south. He believed the NAACP, "a communist organization financed to some extent from abroad," as taking too central a role in the case.[9]

When Corbell called Mitchell at his fishing camp in Maryland for his response to Lowell's decision, Mitchell — as usual — was not reluctant to vent his spleen. "Communistic elements and an unpatriotic federal judge" had combined to free Crawford from jail, according to Mitchell, who told Corbell that he and others in Middleburg had already suspected even before Lowell's decision that Communist groups were exerting influence on the court. Mitchell continued,

> There is only one way in which a member of the federal judiciary can be brought to account for his actions. That is by impeachment proceedings before Congress. I, therefore, had a conference with various friends of mine on the subject, and then requested Representative Howard W. Smith of Virginia, our Congressman, to be ready to introduce impeachment proceedings, provided Judge Lowell subverted justice to the wrong ends. This, Judge Smith has done.
>
> There has never been a more flagrant case where justice has been thwarted than in this one. Crawford is a man with a long criminal record. He is a great danger to any community and to the entire country. He has been regularly indicted by the grand jury of Loudoun County. The request for his extradition has been regularly made by the governor of Virginia. The request was granted by the governor of Massachusetts, but now, due to Communistic elements and an unpatriotic judge, justice has been thwarted.
>
> If proceedings of this kind are allowed to go on, it means that any person can avoid just punishment if he can prove that he has colored blood, Indian blood, Chinese blood, or any other blood in his system that is different from that of the jury.
>
> This proceeding should lead to a constitutional amendment which would make it mandatory for a criminal that has been regularly indicted by a grand jury to be turned over to the state requesting it at once. The foolish, impractical and dangerous system of extradition between the states is merely a hangover from Colonial days and will lead to endless trouble in the future unless done away with.[10]

Mitchell fired off a letter to Governor Pollard, concluding that "if decisions such as this are allowed to stand, it means that no negro can be tried by a jury in Virginia, unless negroes constitute a part of the jury. Therefore, negroes apparently will be able to commit any crime they desire with impunity."[11] At Smith's suggestion, Mitchell sent a flurry of similar letters to his powerful circle of friends in Wisconsin and elsewhere, asking them to demand that congress impeach Lowell.

"This is a disgraceful proceeding," he told Fitzhugh Lee, his old commanding officer from his days serving in the infantry. "Not only the people of Virginia, but the people of every state should take an interest in having that fellow impeached. Our congressman has already drawn articles of impeachment against him, which have been presented to the House and have a fair chance of passage.

"I think everyone who is interested in this state should use his influence, particularly with the congressmen in the north, to have them vote for the impeachment of this judge. He has a bad record behind him, in addition to this case."[12]

To John Cudahy, a hunting and fishing comrade who FDR would soon appoint as ambassador to Poland, Mitchell was more blunt. "This fellow Lowell is perfectly worthless as a judge. He appears to be influenced by anybody who comes around him, particularly communists or negroes ... for any right thinking American to condone such a performance as Judge Lowell put up is incomprehensible."[13]

Mitchell would tell his sister, Katherine, that Lowell should be extradited to Virginia and "strung up" with Crawford.[14]

White, fearing the lingering influence that Mitchell had on public opinion — and despite Allen's call for calm — suggested that Wilkins issue a press release attacking "the choleric outbursts" of Mitchell and others who had spoken out against Lowell's decision. "It is amusing almost to the point of ridiculousness for Congressman Martin Dies of Texas to ask Congress to abolish Judge Lowell's office" in light of Texas' reticence to grant African American's their Constitutional rights, White wrote.[15]

"As for Congressman Smith of Virginia and his attempt to secure impeachment of Judge Lowell for upholding the law, his action is anarchy of the worst sort. Decent people, white and colored, will denounce the attempts of these two Congressmen to lynch a courageous and intelligent jurist for upholding the finest traditions of the law."

White also sent a telegram to United Press International in response to Mitchell's claim of a communist hand in NAACP actions. "Would be most grateful if United Press dispatches would state that Crawford case from beginning has been handled exclusively by National Association for Advancement of Colored People, which is not communist, but which strives for just enforcement Federal Constitution without discrimination because of race or color."

Spingarn, his law partner, Charles Studin, Houston, Wilkins and White met in Spingarn's Washington office on April 27. The rumors about Paul Boeing were on their agenda. "It was agreed that Miss Helen Boardman or other investigator should be sent to Rockville, Maryland, 14 miles out of Washington, to investigate the condition of the body of Mina Buckner, Mrs. Ilsley's maid, by inquiry of the family undertaker and others as to the reported mutilation of her breasts and other parts of her body indicating that a sexually perverted person had killed her," according to an internal NAACP memorandum.

On April 28 Houston passed along to White a mysterious tidbit about Roy Seaton. About two weeks earlier, Seaton "got a call from a Washington detective office and responded by coming down to Washington for an interview with the detective agency," Houston wrote.

"The agent represented that he was working in the interest of Crawford and attempted to get out of Mr. Seaton what Mr. Seaton knew about the case ... the person who contacted me does not know the name of the agent with whom Seaton talked. He promised to get me this information, but so far has failed to do so."

"What you say about Seaton is very interesting," White wrote in his response to Houston the next day. "I think I told you about Boeing's brother who came to see me and said they had hired Burns' Detective Agency.

"I wonder if this is a trick to get Seaton and some others who have told us the truth to give them information."

White still had not heard anything from Seaton when he wrote to Houston on the topic again May 9.

The notoriety of the Crawford case nationally was overshadowed by the trials of the Scottsboro Boys. Eight of the nine defendants there had been convicted and scheduled for execution in Alabama's electric chair. The ILD appealed the convictions to the Alabama Supreme Court, which upheld all but one of the lower court's rulings. The ILD's arguments — that the defense was inadequate and hadn't had time to prepare for the cases, that angry crowds in Scottsboro had intimidated the jurors, and that Alabama's exclusion of blacks from juries was unconstitutional — were scheduled to go before the United States Supreme Court in October.

"Remembering the recent attack on the Southern jury system by defense counsel in the Scottsboro case, and the somewhat less recent action of Governor Moore of New Jersey in refusing to extradite Robert E. Burns to Georgia, because of the allegedly inhuman treatment he would receive on a chain gang there, the South is doing some soul-searching," *New York Times* correspondent Virginia Dabney wrote from Richmond on April 30. Recent events had put the Southern penal and jury systems "sharply into the spotlight," according to Dabney. "It may be that we are about to witness substantial changes in both of them as a result of the recent episodes."

"Failure to call negroes for jury service in the South will produce more and more complications as time goes on," the *Richmond News Leader* said. "The second trial of the Scottsboro case probably has marked an epoch in this respect. Increasingly, it will be contended that white juries are prejudiced against negro prisoners in cases involving alleged crimes against white women. This, in turn, may increase the difficulties of extraditing negroes who escape into Northern states. To avoid this, the fair and prudent course, in our opinion, is to remove the cause of complaint by using negro jurors on occasion."

Lowell's decision in the Crawford case "has already had one extra-legal effect," *The Nation* said on May 10. "The discrimination suffered by the Southern Negro, not merely socially and economically, but before the law, has been more widely publicized than in any other single episode in a generation."

In a responding letter to the editor, White wrote that "it is not difficult to see how far-reaching this decision may be, nor how profound its influence may be in bringing about the end of flagrant and notorious denial to negroes in the South of their unconstitutional rights." He also appealed for contributions to help continue the legal struggle. Money was tighter than ever. The NAACP in May was forced to let some employees go and trimmed the salaries of others by a third.

The total cost to defend Crawford so far had been only $471.11, thanks in large part to the five lawyers involved in the case all contributing their time, and accepting only reimbursement for their expenses. In a May 4 memo to Wilkins, White suggested that the financial information be released to the press, which might then compare the NAACP's frugality to the thousands of dollars being spent on the Scottsboro case, and "emphasize again the economical way in which we not only fight but win cases."

"I did not have a friend in this town, and when that lawyer from Virginia came to the jail he put words on my mouth and said I confessed," Crawford was quoted in a subsequent NAACP press release. "I did not confess, but if it had not been for the NAACP, I guess I would have been back in Virginia, and maybe sentenced to death by now. I didn't kill Mrs. Ilsley. I was here in Boston when it happened. I don't know about all those law points brought up in court by Mr. Allen and Mr. Wilson, but I know I am innocent. I sure thank the NAACP and Mr. Allen and Mr. Wilson." White drafted an appeal to readers of *The Nation* to send checks to the NAACP's New York headquarters. "The association is fighting this case against very great odds, not only because our investigations strongly indicate Crawford's innocence and establish firm grounds for belief that an attempt is being made to make him the scapegoat to protect another person, but particularly because of the fundamental principle which affirmation by the United States Supreme Court of Judge Lowell's decision will establish. Unfortunately, unless we are able to secure help there is a grave possibility that we shall not be able to make the fight as it should be made." And he, Houston and Lovett drove across the Virginia countryside to drum up support for the NAACP and its defense of Crawford.

Though Houston had done virtually all of the legal work in Virginia, he was still not officially part of Crawford's defense team. White was working to change that, despite the tension it was creating between Houston and the NAACP attorneys in Boston. On May 1, he asked Spingarn to write personal letters to Allen "and tactfully suggest to him" that Houston and Lovett be invited to serve as associated counsel on the case.[16]

"Butler Wilson is bitterly opposed to this because he does not want anyone else to come in, thus lessening his own glory," White told Spingarn. Houston and Allen had a long talk when Allen passed through Washington on May 5. Allen was "not enthusiastic about having any counsel of record except himself and Mr. Wilson," Houston told White. "The matter is unimportant; let it drop."[17]

And while Houston wasn't the counsel of record in the case and had not made an appearance in a Boston courtroom on Crawford's behalf, he was more often than not the public face of the defense team — to the point that *Newsweek*, in its review of the case, sang his praises above those of Allen and Wilson. "I am sorry I cannot accept the laurels tendered in your article," Houston wrote to *Newsweek*'s editor. He and Lovett "are unofficially associated with the case. We obtained the evidence of grand jury discrimination in Virginia [and] were present at the argument before Judge Lowell, but took no part in it." Houston closed his letter — a copy of which he sent to Russell in Leesburg — with praise for "the professional courtesies" he, Allen and Lovett had received at the hands of authorities in Virginia. "Such candor and professional courtesies lead me to have new faith in the administration of justice in that section of Virginia," Houston said.

Separately from his work on the Crawford case, Houston had filed a complaint in Alexandria about the jury system there. An all-white jury was set to hear three cases in which African Americans were to be tried for murder, assault and manslaughter.

"Judge Lowell's great service was his publicizing of the long-standing injustice in the South in the exclusion of Negroes from juries, and already extra-legal effects of his decision may be noted," *The Nation* reported at the end of June. "Attorneys for a Negro held in Alexandria, Virginia, for manslaughter after an automobile accident advised the judge, William P. Woolls of the Corporation Court, that they expected to raise the question of unconstitutional discrimination as in the Crawford case (in a contiguous Virginia county), since no Negro had been called to the grand jury which would consider the charge. To Judge Wooll's great credit, without waiting for more formal procedure, he called a new grand jury with a Negro in the panel, and further ordered the names of seven colored men to be placed in the grand jury of forty-eight. Moreover, the clerk of his court shortly after announced that the names of twenty colored persons in Alexandria would be added by the jury commissioners to the regular jury list of approximately three hundred."

Later that summer the *New York Times* reported that judges John L. Ingram and Ernest Howells had ruled that for the first time since the turn of the century African Americans could serve on grand juries when the Criminal Court in Richmond convened its October term. "The decision to resume the custom abandoned thirty years ago was reached by the two judges in a discussion of the case of George Crawford," according to the *Times*.

"Even if the Circuit Court is upheld, and Crawford is sent back, the action in Richmond indicates a civilized attitude toward outside criticism quite different from the hysteria which prevailed in Alabama during the Scottsboro trials," *The Nation* said.

But there was still resistance to segregated juries in Virginia. Willford Gilman, a farmer from Ashland was fined $10 for contempt of court when he refused to serve on a grand jury with two African Americans in Hanover County Circuit Court.

On May 23, Allen and Wilson, representing Crawford, and Bacigalpuo and fellow Massachusetts Assistant Attorney General George B. Lourie, representing the state, stood before the United States Circuit Court of Appeals in Boston. Allen and Wilson argued that Lowell had acted within his discretion and was justified in his decision because Loudoun County did not place African Americans on its juries. Bacigalpuo and Lourie asked the court to overturn Lowell's decision, arguing that validity of indictments could not be attacked in habeas corpus proceedings for interstate extradition. That was an issue to be raised at trial, they said. After more than four hours of argument in a crowded courtroom, Federal judges George H. Bingham, Scott Wilson and James M. Morton, Jr. took the case under advisement. No decision was expected until June 15.

On May 29, Lowell received a stiff dose of criticism from the U.S. Supreme Court for his actions in another criminal case. Angelo Quercia, who had been convicted in Lowell's court of violating the Harrison Narcotic Act, had appealed the conviction, saying Lowell had exceeded the bounds of fair comment when he told the jury of Quercia's testimony, "I think that every single word that man said, except when he agreed with the government's testimony, was a lie." Lowell "did not analyze the evidence, he added to it, and he based his instructions upon his own addition," the court said.

On June 11, 1933, Houston dictated a memorandum on the significance of the Crawford case.

First, the case raised the question of the limitation of state power under the Constitution. "The power to return a fugitive from one state to another lies wholly within the Constitution, and when one state requests the return of an alleged fugitive it invokes the Constitution," Houston said. The memo continued,

> The Crawford case raises the question whether a state can openly violate one section of the Constitution while appealing to another section of the Constitution to make that violation effective ... the position of the NAACP is that a state cannot appeal to and nullify the Constitution at the same time ... this question has never been passed upon by the United States Supreme Court on the particular combination of facts present in the Crawford case, and is a Constitutional case of first impression in the Federal courts....
> The NAACP does not contend that Crawford should not be returned to stand trial in Virginia on a *lawful* indictment. Its position simply is that Virginia cannot invoke the Constitution to return Crawford to answer an unlawful, unconstitutional indictment. At any time Virginia can empanel a grand jury agreeable to the 14th Amendment, and on the basis of the indictment returned by that grand jury make demand for Crawford's return. It could have done that before Judge Lowell's decision or at any time since, or still at any time in the future.

The case had also taken on the fundamental question of the independence of the Federal judiciary, because of Smith's call for Lowell's impeachment.

The impeachment was made based on newspaper reports of Lowell's decision, Houston said — newspaper reports that "were garbled and incorrect." Smith had said that Lowell "insinuated that Crawford could not get a fair trial in Virginia and would not even give the Commonwealth Attorney from Virginia the opportunity of presenting his argument.

"These statements were wholly untrue. Judge Lowell stated he had no doubt Crawford could get a fair trial in Virginia, but that a legal trial could not be founded upon an unconstitutional indictment." As for Galleher, he had not argued the case in Boston, Houston said — Bacigalpuo had.

If Lowell could be impeached based on inaccurate newspaper reports, then other Federal judges could be impeached for affirming Lowell's decision, or for any other politically unpopular decision, Houston said.

"All of them will be working under the shadow of the disapproval of a temporary Congressional majority. The independence of the American judiciary will be gone so far as the Federal courts are concerned."

Finally, Houston believed that the Crawford case, if ever tried in Virginia, "would expose the whole feudalistic system of the absentee landlord of the fox-hunting section of Virginia." Evidence appeared to indicate not only that Crawford was innocent, but also "that the authorities are shielding someone who would appear to have considerable knowledge of the crime."

And the case had broader implications, Houston said. "Due process of law, to be due process of law, must know neither race, color or previous condition of servitude. An actual abuse of justice against the Negro is a threatened abuse of justice against every white citizen of the United States."

On Thursday, June 15, the Circuit Court of Appeals for the First Circuit reversed Lowell's decision and ordered him to have Crawford turned over to Massachusetts State Police for extradition to Virginia.

In its order, the court referenced several previous interstate rendition cases, including *Drew v. Thaw*, in which Harry Thaw had been indicted by a New York grand jury after he had escaped from the Matteawan State Hospital for the criminally insane and fled to New Hampshire. The governor of New York had requested extradition. Like Crawford, Thaw had applied for a writ of habeas corpus and the District Court had ordered that he be freed. The Supreme Court eventually reversed the District Court decision, saying that "the constitutionally required surrender is not to be interfered with by the summary process of habeas corpus upon speculations as to what ought to be the result of a trial in the place where the Constitution provides for its taking place."

As to whether Virginia discriminated against African Americans, the court found that it had previously been established "that the discrimination exercised by the state officers of Virginia in making up the lists and drawings of the grand jurors by whom Crawford was indicted, was an infringement of his rights guaranteed by the Fourteenth Amendment." But did that discrimination render the indictment void?

"There are a number of cases in which the question has been considered and, as we understand them, they all point to the conclusion that the matter in question is an irregularity of a kind that must be availed of at the trial in the state court where the indictment is found; that it is an irregularity that may be and is waived, if the person on trial does not seasonably and in the modes provided by law raise the question in that court. In other words, that it does not render the indictment void or defeat the jurisdiction of the court in which the indictment is returned...." The NAACP would have to challenge Loudoun's jury selection process in Leesburg, at Crawford's murder trial. Crawford was remanded to custody for execution of Governor Ely's warrant for extradition, but would continue to be held in Boston pending the appeal. Allen said the defense team planned to appeal the decision to the United States Supreme Court.

Galleher told the *Times-Mirror* that his office was prepared to expedite the trial when Crawford was sent to Leesburg, and he would ask judge Alexander to convene a special term in the event the court was not in session when Crawford came South.

"The prisoner, Mr. Galleher emphasized, is assured of a fair trial before a Loudoun jury, with every legal right to which he is entitled carefully safeguarded," according to the *Times-Mirror*.

On June 19, the House of Representatives voted another $3,000 to defray expenses for the Judiciary Committee's investigation of impeachment charges against Lowell. The resolution, which was introduced by Smith, was approved 188–159. Congressman Oscar Stanton De Priest (R-IL)—the first African American elected to Congress in the 20th century—was among those opposing the resolution.

Behind the scenes, the NAACP team was still trying to figure out what had really happened at the Middleburg cottage. In June they got wind of a story, which, if proven true, would set the state's case on its ear. The Virginia woman who had sent the anonymous letter to the *Amsterdam News* claiming that Paul Boeing had admitted to the murders was "a white woman of Virginia who now lives in New York and who recently visited relatives near Middleburg," according to White.[18] The editor of the *Amsterdam News* "has recently come into possession of a note which he thinks was written by the same person, and he has asked for the return of the letter which you have in order that he may compare the handwriting," White wrote to Wilson.

On June 21, White wrote to some sympathetic Loudouners—Mack Taylor, John Moten and William Hall—asking for their help in tracking down the anonymous woman or evidence to back up her story. While in Middleburg, the tipster had learned that Paul Boeing "was recently or is now critically ill in a hospital near Leesburg," White wrote. "Thinking that he was about to die, according to our informant, the brother confessed to the nurses that it was he who murdered his sister and her maid."[19] White asked each of the men to respond confidentially with any information they could provide.

No evidence to back up the story was ever found. The woman who wrote the letter was never heard from again. But Paul Boeing's reputation in some quarters of Middleburg kept him on the NAACP's short list of potential suspects.

Belief in Crawford's case, and support for White's choice of the case as the one with which to challenge the South's jury discrimination tradition, was hardly universal. Felix Franfurter, a Harvard Law School professor and a member of the NAACP Legal Committee, told White that he had "the very gravest doubts" about the path White had chosen. "I was quite confident that Judge Lowell would be reversed by the [Circuit Court of Appeals], and I should think the chances are pretty slim of any other result in the Supreme Court.

"I am extremely doubtful of the wisdom of raising the question regarding jury discrimination on habeas corpus from a warrant on state extradition." An adverse decision in the fight against jury discrimination "is greatly to be avoided," he said. "The way to raise it is the direct way, namely, in case discrimination is exercised either by law or in practice in the state of trial."[20]

There were others who felt that Crawford would do better in a Virginia courtroom if he were represented by Southern lawyers. June P. Guild, an attorney, social worker and teacher at the African American Virginia Union College, told American Civil Liberties Union Director Roger Baldwin that Crawford's legal team should include "a Negro and a white woman lawyer"—and she volunteered herself. She also recommended that the ACLU be involved "to offset the prejudices against the NAACP as an organization of colored people."[21]

On June 24, White dictated a letter to be sent to Crawford. With it he included a carton of Lucky Strike cigarettes. "This note comes to bid you be of good cheer and to assure you that we shall do everything possible to prevent your being returned," White said. "We shall appeal your case to the United States Supreme Court and in the event that Court affirms the verdict of the Circuit Court of Appeals, we shall defend you in Virginia."

A week later, Crawford, sitting in cell 32 of the Charles Street Jail, sat down to write White a letter. Crawford's handwriting was neat and legible, but he had the spelling and grammar of an uneducated man. He had received the letter and cigarettes White had sent to him, and "was more then glade to get them as I dont have enny one to come to see me." Crawford told White he hoped they could meet soon to discuss his case.

"I was bond in the south. My poor mother and father died while I was small. I had one sister and God taken here from me so you cin see I have had a hard time in this worild," Crawford wrote. "I left the south because the white people dun all they could to keep me in prisern. I left the South and come north now it look like they wornt to put me to deth."

White had a typed copy of the letter made; the language and spelling were corrected and the revised letter was issued in an NAACP press release.

In August, the ILD took up the case of three African American teenagers who had been accused in June of raping and killing an 18-year-old white woman in Tuscaloosa, Alabama. A judge ordered the men be represented by local lawyers and had the ILD attorneys escorted out of town by National Guardsmen. The accused and deputies who were escorting them to Birmingham were ambushed by a mob that shot all three teenagers. One of them survived, and it quickly became clear that the sheriff and his men had done little to protect the prisoners. There was some evidence indicating that they had been only too eager to hand them over to the civilian firing squad. The sheriff would later blame interference from the ILD as the cause of the murders, which were protested all the way to the Roosevelt administration — with no apparent effect — by the ILD, the ACLU, and the NAACP, led by Houston. No indictments were handed down in Alabama, and federal authorities did not pursue the case.

On August 31 Crawford's lawyers asked the United States Supreme Court to decide if Massachusetts had to extradite Crawford to Virginia for trial. "The course of reasoning upon which the Circuit Court of Appeals for the First Circuit reached its conclusion, vacating the order of the District Court, was predicated upon unwarranted assumptions and assertions and was rested upon decisions which do not support the conclusion of the Court," they said.[22]

The correct determination of the case by the Supreme Court "has become a matter of grave public concern and, by reason of the resolution presented in the Congress of the United States to impeach the judge of the District of Massachusetts because of his decision in this case, such determination by the highest tribunal is desired ... the importance of the issues to be determined is evidenced by the fact that since the resolution of impeachment was introduced in the Congress, Negroes have been included in the lists for jury service in three states where previously they had been uniformly excluded ... that such discrimination is customary in the State of Virginia, so that it has become a matter of common knowledge, is admitted by the officers of that state."

In September, Lowell's problems continued to deepen when charges were filed with the Congressional subcommittee claiming that he had acted inappropriately during cases involving the shipment of poisonous ginger extract from Massachusetts to western states.

The Supreme Court denied review of the Crawford case on Monday, October 16. The NAACP released a statement in which it said it was "naturally disappointed that the Court did not take into account all the social and economic implications in this matter. The fight for Crawford has not, however, been without concrete results. Four states [including Virginia] have put Negroes on juries for the first time in thirty years since Judge Lowell's decision." That was good news for African Americans, but could dull the sharpness of the NAACP's defense of Crawford.

On the same day, the ILD announced that there had been 13 lynchings in the United States since the first of August. In most cases, police knew members of the lynch mobs and their names were made public, but none were convicted of crimes, according to the ILD.

Tracked down in Boston by reporters, Lowell refused to comment on the Supreme Court's decision. "Boston harbor looks unusually beautiful right now, probably because of the peculiar slant of the sun on the water," was the judge's only response to their questions.[23]

White considered applying to the Supreme Court for a re-hearing.

"Should a re-hearing be denied, we will go with Crawford to Virginia and defend him there, raising, of course, immediately the question of Crawford being indicted by a jury from which Negroes were illegally excluded," White said. "Investigation by the NAACP has convinced us of Crawford's innocence and that he is being used as a scapegoat for a crime committed by whites. We are in this fight to the finish."[24]

But, in a special delivery letter to Houston on October 17 — sent after a 10:30 a.m. meeting with Wilkins and Spingarn — White admitted that none of them believed applying for a re-hearing would be successful. "It would be simply a means of getting more time for raising money, making investigations and gaining more publicity on the issues involved in the Crawford case," he said.

He also made it clear that they wanted Houston to take over the case as it moved south.

"I am instructed to authorize you to proceed with the investigation and select an investigator ... above all else we want you as chief counsel and trust that nothing whatsoever will prevent your being in full charge," White told Houston.

Houston went to Leesburg that day and met with Judge Alexander. Galleher was telling his friends at the *Times-Mirror* that Crawford might be arraigned and tried by November 15 but, according to Alexander, the trial would be in December, using the original, disputed indictment.

Houston told the *Times-Mirror* that Crawford's defense would probably revolve around the testimony of the same witnesses who had appeared in Boston saying Crawford had been there, and not in Middleburg, at the time of the murders. The NAACP would provide defense attorneys — probably not Allen or Wilson — for Crawford's trial, and the ILD would play no part in the proceedings.

Houston felt unequal to the task of heading Crawford's defense, but he and Allen had come to an agreement: "Massachusetts council inadvisable at trial," Houston said in a letter to White. "The men here feel if Crawford could be defended by all Negro counsel it would mark a turning point in the legal history of the Negro in this country." But still he hesitated to commit himself, because he felt he would have to set aside his Howard responsibilities—and Howard officials had already reminded him that they were the ones paying his salary and had "first claim on my services."

On October 20, White wrote to Wilson and Allen in Boston, frantic that they finally get Crawford to sign a general power of attorney to Houston. The signature would make Houston's efforts in Leesburg easier; White was also trying to block communists from getting Crawford to sign the case over to them:

> Confidentially, the Communists are trying to seize the case and unless this power of attorney is sent to Mr. Houston there is very real danger that all that has been fought for and won in the case to date may be lost ... I wish also that you would both see Crawford before he leaves and emphasize to him the necessity of his not listening to anyone else and sticking to the NAACP. We will continue our fight for him to the bitter end but we cannot be further bothered by interference by the communists if they are able to get to Crawford and to persuade him to risk his neck in their hands.

Within days, the worries of lynching, dismissed by so many Virginians as an outdated Northern bias, seemed once again all too real to the NAACP. As Loudoun prepared for a trial and authorities cleared the way for Crawford to be sent south, a mob estimated at 3,000 took over the streets of Princess Anne, Maryland, about 120 miles east of Leesburg, to lynch an African American man who had been accused of assaulting a white woman.

NINE

Taking Sides

On Monday, October 16, 1933, near the village of Monokin in Maryland's rural Eastern Shore, 71-year-old Mary Denston was raped by an African American man. Denston, the wife of a farmer from Somerset County, told Sheriff Luther Daugherty that she had been walking to her daughter's home when the man had grabbed her and ripped at her clothes until a passing state road employee heard her cries and chased her assailant away. She had not known the man who attacked her, Denston told Daugherty, but she was sure she would recognize him if she saw him again.

More than 500 citizens joined county and state police in a search for 24-year-old George Armwood, an African American who had been in trouble in the area before, and was assumed to be the man who had attacked Denston. Maryland State Police found Armwood that evening at Beaver Dam, near Snow Hill, Maryland. They arrested him and a white man, John Richardson, who they said had given Armwood a ride from the site of the attack to Beaver Dam. Worried about potential violence from the crowds that had grown during the day in Princess Anne, Snow Hill and Salisbury, they drove Armwood away from the Eastern Shore, to Baltimore.

At about 10 p.m. on Tuesday, 25 Maryland State Police traveled with Armwood to Princess Anne for a preliminary hearing. Authorities in Baltimore told newspapers that Armwood had confessed to attacking Denston. Somerset County State's Attorney John B. Robins said he would recall the county's grand and petit juries to address the case and would seek the death penalty in the case. Robins and Somerset County Judge Robert F. Duer assured Maryland Governor Albert Cabell Ritchie that there was no danger of a lynching. Later, Ritchie would say he had offered to have Armwood returned to Baltimore after rumors of impending mob violence, but had decided against it after talking to Somerset County officials.

"The responsibility for Armwood's being at Princess Anne tonight rests squarely on the shoulders of Judge Duer and State's Attorney Robins," Ritchie said in a statement to reporters.

On Wednesday, word got out that Armwood had been secreted into the Somerset County jail, and a mob began to gather in the town square. Over the course of the day the crowd swelled to an estimated 3,000 townsmen, farmers, their wives and children. They demanded that the Maryland State Police detail that had been sent to protect Armwood release him to them. The police called Ritchie's office in Baltimore, asking for reinforcements, who arrived late in the afternoon brandishing revolvers, billy clubs and tear gas. Ritchie also directed the local American Legion post to guard the prisoner, but the post's commander, E.C. Young, refused.

"I have no authority as commander of this Legion to call out its members as a military unit or for police duty," Young said. "I am willing as a legionnaire to protect the townspeople and their property. However, I have no desire personally, as a citizen, as a legionnaire or as a commander of a Legion post to engage in a police duty for the protection of a negro charged with such an atrocious crime. The laws of our organization forbid such use."[1]

Duer, who lived about a half mile away, came to the jail and asked the crowd to disperse. He would oversee a grand jury hearing of the charges against Armwood the following Monday, and justice would be handed down in a special session of his court beginning just three days later, he told them. He was jeered by the mob.

As the evening wore on, the crowd grew more restless. Police called for them to disperse. When they would not, police fired tear gas into the mob, which initially retreated, but at about 9 p.m. they finally stormed the jail, throwing bricks and stones that injured eight police officers. They rigged together a battering ram out of wood from a nearby lumberyard, forced their way through the outer jailhouse door and were let through a second by someone inside the jail. They dragged Armwood out of his cell and were cheered by the huge crowd on the courthouse lawn as they brought him, bloodied and confused, out of the jail.

There is no record of the police pursuing the crowd in an attempt to rescue Armwood from the lynch mob. Police did, however, take Richardson from the jail — he had been ignored by the mob — and drove him back to Baltimore.

Armwood's clothes were ripped from him, a rope was tied around his neck, the other end attached to the rear bumper of a car that pulled him through the town. The mob tormented Armwood as they proceeded through the town, screaming and spitting at him, throwing rocks and slashing at him with knives. The crowd cheered a young boy when he leapt forward to cut off one of Armwood's ears.

The mob herded Armwood to Duer's house, where they intended to hang him. There were no trees large enough for the deed in the judge's yard. Instead they unhitched the rope from the car's bumper, threw it over the branch of a large oak tree in a neighbor's yard, and hoisted Armwood's already lifeless body above them. A short time later they cut the body down and dragged it back to the public square, where it was doused with gasoline and lit on fire.

In addition to murdering Armwood, the mob had injured a total of 13 Maryland State Troopers during the melee at Princess Anne.

The next morning, Houston fired off an angry telegram to Ritchie.

"Unless Maryland is determined on relentless prosecution of mob and all State officials concerned in the Armwood lynching, Negroes would prefer to be spared the farce of the usual fake investigation, and to leave the shame of Maryland naked before the world," Houston wrote.

On the same day the Student Council at Howard University sent a more restrained letter to President Roosevelt, calling for an end to lynching.

"Because of this unconcerned attitude by our National Government, the promulgators of mob violence have become bolder and are slowly marching upon our National Capital, for the last episode of this horrible drama occurred within less than 100 miles of Washington," the Howard students wrote. "We are calling to your attention the lynching of George Armwood.... Since the inauguration of the New Deal, mobs have continued to ply their trade and to take the law in their hands. Only last night, they received direct sanction for their dastardly deeds from a local commander of the American Legion.

Ritchie ordered the state's Attorney General, William Preston Lane, to investigate the lynching, and ordered Maryland State Police Commissioner Charles Gaither to send four officers to Princess Anne to open an inquiry there. Ritchie sent a telegram to Duer and Robins, demanding that they commit Somerset County's police to the apprehension of members of the lynch mob. Somerset County's acting coroner, Edgar James, empaneled a jury in preparation for an inquest.

Police told reporters they had names of seven or eight of the 3,000-member lynch mob, but there were no immediate arrests.

In Baltimore, the ILD led a protest against Armwood's lynching and the impending hanging of Euel Lee, an African American who was scheduled to be executed on October 27 for the murders of a white former employer and his family in Taylortown, Maryland.

"It looks to me as if this country is headed toward race riots worse than it has ever known," Houston wrote to Dr. Will W. Alexander, executive director of the Commission on Interracial Cooperation. "The first thing some mob is going to try to lynch a Negro in an urban community, and then there is going to be plenty trouble. The surface of Negro life is calm, but there are deep swift currents running underneath."

Houston and NAACP attorney Leon Ransom, themselves veterans and Legionnaires, contacted commanders of several American Legion posts, asking that they "take vigorous and persistent action and not let up until you have obtained complete satisfaction from the American Legion itself castigating the attitude and expression of Commander Young and the L. Creston Beuchamp Post," who had stood aside during Armwood's lynching and were accused of protecting members of the lynch mob. The lynching "was one of the most revolting and atrocious lynchings which has ever stained the history of the United States," they wrote.[2] The NAACP, the National Urban League, the ILD and a host of African American groups called for action to be taken against members of the lynch mob and any officials who had failed to stop them. ILD attorney Bernard Ades announced that he was prepared to appeal the case to United States Attorney General Stille Cummings if the state failed in its investigation and prosecution of the case.

But members of the mob weren't easy to track down, despite the fact that some of them — including William Denston, the rape victim's son and a policeman at Lower Merion Township, near Philadelphia — admitted their roles in the lynching in newspaper interviews. At a coroner's inquest held in Princess Anne less than a week after the lynching, all 21 witnesses called to testify — including Somerset Sheriff Luther Daughterty — said they hadn't recognized anyone in the crowd of 3,000 who had marched through their village and dragged Armwood to his death. They were all strangers, they said.

"I looked right in the faces of some of that mob and I didn't recognize a single soul," Daughterty said. "Not a single soul. I bet they were from down Virginia way."[3]

On October 23, in the wake of the Armwood lynching, White sent letters to Pollard, Alexander, Galleher and Adrian asking for "full protection" for Crawford when he was returned to Virginia, including whatever time he would spend in Leesburg to be arraigned and tried.

"We, of course, know that the possibility of a lynching or other form of violence is remote," White wrote. He continued,

> We are making this request, however, because of the fact that officials at Princess Anne, Maryland, last week also thought a lynching impossible and, failing to take the proper precautions, permitted one of the most ghastly lynchings in American history to occur.
>
> We also are making this request because of the statement made by General William D. Mitchell to one of our investigators— that had Crawford been apprehended at the time of the murder of Mrs. Ilsley, Crawford undoubtedly would have been burned at the stake.
>
> There is great likelihood that a number of curiosity seekers will gather when Crawford is returned and at the arraignment and the trial. Frequently a pacific crowd has been transferred into a mob. Ample precaution should be accorded and every step taken to prevent the gathering of any appreciable number of people. We feel certain that you will zealously guard the good name of Virginia by taking even what may seem to be extreme steps to prevent any disgrace in the form of violence to the State of Virginia.

On October 24, Wilson wrote a letter to White saying he "saw Crawford Saturday and found him very much agitated and in no condition to act deliberately about his affairs." Crawford signed the power of attorney for Houston that day.

In every communication with White, Wilson pushed to remain involved in the case, suggesting that the power of attorney to Houston be limited to the Leesburg trial, leaving he and Allen to take up what he considered to be inevitable Supreme Court arguments.

"I am afraid we are going to have trouble with Wilson," White wrote to Spingarn. "He obviously does not want to get out of the case and wants to have his name still connected with it in the event there is a lot of publicity and especially if the case should go back to the United States Supreme Court on the jury question."

"The case is likely to be badly messed up unless Wilson and Allen are cleanly and completely severed from it.... Wilson told me over the telephone this morning that Crawford had sent [a] letter to him with the notation, 'I want J. Wilson Allen and Butler R. Wilson to be my attorneys.'"

Late in the afternoon of the day that Crawford signed the power of attorney, Lowell ordered him turned over to Virginia officials. Crawford was turned over to Massachusetts Police Lieutenant Frank Hale for extradition to Virginia. He was to be jailed in Alexandria, rather than in the Leesburg jail, though Galleher and other Loudoun County officials continued to insist that no trouble was expected there.

In Leesburg, Houston filed a motion to quash the grand jury's indictments of Crawford. In selecting the potential jury list, Alexander had not considered African Americans, "solely on account of their race and color, [and] it is a custom in Loudoun County to use white men exclusively for grand jury service and exclude qualified Negroes solely on account of their race and color," according to Houston's affidavit. The grand jury that indicted Crawford "was composed exclusively of white male citizens, to the great prejudices and detriment of the defendant George Crawford, who is a Negro, a person of the colored race and of African descent."

On Saturday, October 28, Adrian and Cooley brought Crawford south from Massachusetts. When their train arrived at Union Station at 8:10 a.m., the trio, joined by Galleher and surrounded by Washington DC police officers, walked to a large black car. The were escorted by Virginia State Police for the 20-minute drive to the jailhouse in Alexandria, where they were met by Alexandria City police. Crawford, who was kept in chains for the entire trip, would be held at the Alexandria jail for the duration of his trial.

That same morning, Bertie DeNeal was taken into custody as a material witness. On Galleher's order, Adrian took her to the Loudoun County jail, where she was ordered held until the trial on $2,500 bond.

The *New York Times* reported that "Commonwealth's Attorney Galleher is giving serious consideration" to calling a new grand jury, this time to include at least one African American, to re-indict Crawford, in an effort to sidestep the NAACP defense team's objections and lessen the chances of the case being overturned on appeal. Days later, unnamed "court officials"—almost certainly Galleher—denied it, according to the *Loudoun Times-Mirror*. "It was explained that jury lists were made up by jury commissioners, appointed by the court, and that the filing of any vacancies thereon was a matter resting exclusively with the commissioners, over whom the court lacked authority. The list as at present made up contains the name of no colored person," the *Times-Mirror* reported.

Judge Alexander asked Governor Pollard to remove him from the case because he could be called as a witness during hearings on the motion to quash, which attacked Alexander's action in drawing the grand jury that had indicted Crawford. Pollard designated Circuit Court Judge James L. McLemore of Suffolk, Virginia, to sit for the Crawford trial in Alexander's place.

Where Alexander was an immaculate and modern man, McLemore had a more traditional — some in Leesburg would say 19th century — appearance. He had a lazy eye, large ears that stuck straight out from the sides of his head, and gray hair parted down the middle and shaved off on the sides. He was considered a legal genius; a soft-spoken, thoughtful man who had at one time been a candidate for the Supreme Court and was one of the best-known judges in the state. Dabney wrote to White that he "need have no concern about the selection of Judge McLemore. He is a former member of our temporary special court of appeals and is one of the wisest, kindest and fairest of jurists, essentially a human being in every impulse and with all a very good lawyer ... in my judgment, you could not have had a better substitute for Judge Alexander. Evidently, the Governor chose with the utmost care." And while it was not widely known at the time, he was a member of the Virginia Commission on Interracial Cooperation. "This absolutely must not be talked about, but it might help you to have this information," NAACP Field Secretary in Richmond Daisy E. Lampkin told White.

Douglas Freeman of the *Richmond News-Leader* had access to Virginia Governor Pollard, and he fed information he gained from the relationship back to White, acting as a behind-the-scenes liaison between the governor and the NAACP. On Nov. 4, he wrote to White to tell him "everything looks favorable for a fair hearing of Crawford in the best Virginia manner.

"The Governor has definitely decided that Judge McLemore is to hear both cases, and simply as a precautionary measure, he has ordered a strong detachment of some ten men of the Virginia Motor Police to Leesburg, ostensibly to handle traffic. This he did confidentially, at the instance of Judge Alexander, who said that he wanted to have men inconspicuously present who could be counted on to meet any emergency."

McLemore was due in Leesburg Monday, November 6, to hear arguments on Houston's motion to quash the indictment against Crawford. Galleher might also be called to testify at the hearing about the confession he said Crawford had given him in Boston, so Frank M. Wray, the Commonwealth's Attorney of Clarke County, was retained by Middleburg's elite to assist the prosecution team. Wray, a former commander in the state's American Legion, had dark hair and eyes, a sharp nose, and was self-conscious about balding. He was commonly addressed by the honorific "captain" from his days in the American Legion.

On October 30 Dabney wrote a letter to White recounting a conversation he said he'd had with "a well known citizen of Leesburg, one whom I think you probably met while there last week." According to Dabney the man — "not a 'poor white,' and I don't think he is more prejudiced against Negroes than the average citizen of Loudoun" — had predicted the trial would run smoothly "if the defense isn't damn fool enough to bring colored lawyers in there. If they do that there may be trouble ... if a Negro lawyer gets to cross questioning a white witness, particularly a white woman, I don't know what might happen."

To White, the identity of the speaker was obvious: it was "unquestionably Galleher," he wrote in a letter to NAACP attorneys Lovett, Ransom and James Tyson. The *Times-Mirror* had reported that Houston had "indicated that efforts were being made to retain an outstanding white lawyer in Virginia as chief counsel for Crawford." That was not the case, and White was sure Galleher had been the one who had handed that information to his friends at the newspaper, in an effort to stampede public opinion and the NAACP.

While the Commonwealth's Attorney was generally "courteous" in pre-trial discussions, White predicted in an October 31 letter to Ludwell Denny that Galleher was "likely to be rather nasty during the trial." Galleher threw the NAACP team the first curveball of the Leesburg proceedings when he instructed that only Houston — and no other attorneys — be allowed to interview Crawford at the Alexandria jail. Houston, who had traveled to Birmingham, Alabama, under the expectation that other members of the NAACP defense team would be able to proceed with the case in his absence — complained that the prosecutor had handicapped their preparations. Galleher told the *Washington Post* that a simple misunderstanding had kept Ransom and Tyler from seeing their client in his cell. When he had asked Crawford who his attorney was, he had named only Houston.

"For obvious reasons it is unwise to permit a flock of lawyers and others whom we do not know to have access to the prisoner," Galleher said. "The accredited counsel of the prisoner will be allowed to see him and as we saw it the best method to determine the identity of his accredited counsel was to ask the prisoner, which we did. We have no intention of embarrassing the defense in its preparation and it seems to me that it is greatly to the interest of the defense that we take the utmost precautions."

Dabney also told White that "it is impossible for any jury to be drawn in Virginia which will not have on it at least one or more crackers ... you will inevitably run up against the kind of White man in which resentment against the Negro grows in direct proportion to the ability and intelligence of the Negro."

But White and Houston were more convinced than ever that Crawford's case gave them a great opportunity to present an all-black legal team in a southern court to argue a case that had gathered national attention.

"Up to that time Negro lawyers, particularly in the South, were seldom employed even by their own people, on the grounds that they lacked, among other things, experience," White would say, adding,

> But these same lawyers could not obtain experience for reasons of nonemployment. An increasing number of brilliant lawyers like Charlie Houston himself were graduating from first-class Northern law schools. These men were needed in the South particularly, as well as in Northern cities, to handle the many thousands of cases of individual litigation or issues affecting the basic rights of Negroes and other minorities. At the same time we were experiencing difficulty in obtaining the services of top white lawyers because of the bitter feeling surrounding the Crawford case. We decided that the die must be cast sometime soon on the issue of the use of Negro lawyers in important cases. We knew that for many years to come there would be certain types of cases in which there would be an advantage in having a white lawyer in preference to a Negro attorney, but our real objective was to hasten the time when an attorney's color in a court of law would be of no importance and where the only criterion would be his ability.[4]

The NAACP in New York received a rambling letter, filled with misspellings (sometimes calling Ilsley "Ellsby") from another anonymous tipster in Fargo, who accused the Mellon family of involvement in the murders.

The anonymous writer said the whole Ilsley family "is surrounded avensious [sic] cunning ... may he [sic] some insanity in forefathers, etc. they are all quite peculiar class of people." According to the letter, one of Ilsley's brothers had lost $60,000 in a Wisconsin pecan factory and ended up in "the poorhouse." Ilsley's father had been treated by a doctor in Fargo for a "nervous strain." The letter probably had more to do with the unpopularity of Andrew Mellon, who had serve as Secretary of the Treasury under three administrations and had recently been appointed Ambassador to the United Kingdom, than with any actual evidence related to the Middleburg murders.

The hearing on the motion to quash the indictment on the ground that Negroes were illegally excluded from the grand jury that indicted Crawford was scheduled to be held Monday, November 6 in Leesburg. On November 1, White wrote to seven African American newspapers—the *Richmond Planet*, *Pittsburgh Courier*, *Chicago Defender*, *Philadelphia Tribune*, *Washington Tribune*, Baltimore *Afro-American* and *Norfolk Journal and Guide*, as well as the Chicago-based Associated Negro Press, the Associated Press, the Scripps-Howard newspapers and the *New York Times*—asking them to cover the arguments.

White was plagued by worries about communist influence on the case. He sent a clipping cut from the *Daily Worker* to Freeman at the *Richmond News-Leader,* which White said demonstrated "the kind of continued bombardment the NAACP receives because we are not trying to overthrow the American government, but fighting for justice under the American form of law ... an absolutely fair trial, and more, must be given to Crawford in order that the Communists may not again have ammunition with which to attack America; also so that Hitler may not be able to use this in Europe."

With only a few days remaining until hearings began in Leesburg, there were still suggestions from many quarters that Crawford's legal team include — possibly even be headed by — white attorneys. Some attorneys offered their services to White; more were recommended by the *Journal and Guide* and others. An all-black legal team was deemed a mistake by many of those advising White.

"I think you can rest assured that if you and Dean Houston choose your White counsel wisely you can count on a perfectly uneventful hearing, both of the motion to quash and on the indictment itself," Freeman told White. Dabney said he had "become still more convinced that the appearance of a Negro lawyer in the case might have a bad effect on the jury. I talked with a prominent attorney here yesterday who would not himself object to the participation of a Negro attorney, if he were on the jury, but who said he felt convinced that it would result in Crawford's electrocution. He said others had expressed the same view to him."[5] And Lampkin said Commission on Interracial Cooperation secretary Reynolds had recommended placing a white attorney on the NAACP legal team.

White asked Denny to check the background of John S. Barbour, one of the white attorneys that had been recommended to him. Just after lunch on November 1 Denny sent a telegram to White: "Our information is that Barbour is unprejudiced high type and probably best reputation as lawyer in that section. Probably would not be influenced by popular pressure. Do not know his specific attitude on racial question or this case." Others recommended included Bank of Leesburg president E.E. Garrett and General Assembly members Aubrey Weaver of Front Royal and R. Gray Williams of Winchester. White listened to the advice, and thought of adding a white Virginia lawyer to the Crawford legal team. But in the end he stuck with Houston and the other African Americans making their way to Leesburg. The NAACP legal team defending Crawford would be exclusively black.

The ILD, which had finally managed to force the NAACP out of the Scottsboro case, made it known that it felt a united front, some kind of cooperative effort with the NAACP, was the best strategy for Crawford's trial. White had no interest in a deal.

On Friday, November 3, Houston filed a series of documents at the Loudoun County Courthouse in preparation for the upcoming hearing on his motion to quash.

In his Plea in Abatement, Houston declared that all of the members of the grand jury that indicted Crawford were white, despite the fact that there were in Loudoun County numerous African Americans who were qualified to sit on juries. Such was Alexander's faith in the county's white landowners that he had placed the names of 34 of them on grand jury lists multiple times since 1929.

"But in selecting the grand jury list aforesaid the judge did unlawfully exclude, and did refuse, fail and omit to consider all and/or any qualified Negroes, members of the colored race and of African descent, solely on account of their color and race," Houston said, and "it had long been and still is the custom in Loudoun County to use white men exclusively for grand jury service; and the judge in selecting said grand jury list followed said custom." The defense team asserted "that by the unlawful exclusion of all qualified Negroes from the grand jury list and, in consequence, from the venire and the grand jury itself, the defendant herein, a Negro, has been greatly prejudiced, and has been denied due process and the equal protection of the laws in violation of the Constitution of the United States and the law of the land."

Houston also filed a pair of petitions listing the names of dozens of African Americans who owned property in Loudoun County. He hoped to use the titles and tax receipts for their properties to prove that there were African Americans qualified to sit on juries in the county. In addition, Houston requested copies of court documents filed in relation to Alexander's selection of the February, 1932 grand jury.

Juries in Loudoun County were created by selecting qualified men from the taxpayer rolls, which were separated into "white" and "colored" lists. According to Houston, the "custom in Loudoun County to use white men exclusively for grand jury service and exclude qualified Negroes solely on account of their race and color" was an unlawful policy perpetuating a caste system found throughout the south.[6]

"We have subpoenaed 45 Negroes and we are ready to subpoena that many more if they are necessary to prove our case," Houston told *The Washington Post*. And he was prepared to subpoena white men too, "as a basis of comparison with the Negroes as to their availability for grand jury service." Prosecutors would call a dozen of their own witnesses.

The next day — Saturday, November 4 — Galleher filed a response to Houston's motions, denying that in selecting the grand jury Alexander and he had denied Crawford equal protection. Galleher denied that the process "unlawfully excluded" African Americans, and denied "that there were numerous Negroes, if any, in the said Loudoun County, fully qualified for said grand jury service."

Houston would be joined by Lovett and assisted by Marshall for the Nov. 6 hearing. If the case went to trial Tyson and Ransom would join them. They would be forced to commute daily from Washington for court appearances in Leesburg. The all-black NAACP legal team, along with reporters covering the trial for the *Afro-American* and other black newspapers, were denied rooms by Leesburg innkeepers. At the same time, McLemore and white members of the press were staying at the Leesburg Inn next to the courthouse.

William Preston Lane concluded his investigation of the Armwood murder and called on Somerset County State's Attorney John Robins to arrest nine men identified as having participated in the lynching. But Robins told Lane that he believed another mob would gather to free the men if they were locked up in the jail in Princess Anne. "If the sheriff should endeavor to take them to Baltimore City for safe keeping, I doubt seriously if it could be done without serious trouble," Robins said.[7]

"The fact that Mr. Robins does not agree to my position and that he has so far not made any arrests does not necessarily mean that he will not," Lane would say. "I can't go down there and dictate to him, though. The matter is up to him."[8]

But Ritchie was determined to bring at least a few members of the lynch mob to trial. In the early morning hours of November 28 as many as 300 armed members of the Fifth Regiment of the Maryland National Guard, under the command of Adjutant General Milton A. Reckord, stormed into Somerset County. Four area men — including druggist William H. Thompson, who had served on the jury of the coroner's inquest into Armwood's lynching — were rousted from their beds and taken to the Salisbury armory.

The guardsmen had shut down the telephone exchange in Princess Anne to keep news of the arrests from spreading through the village, but word got out and a crowd estimated at 3,000 took to the streets of Salisbury, demanding that the prisoners be released. Photographs published in the *New York Times* showed the guardsmen holding back the angry mob outside the Salisbury Armory; bayonets were drawn and tear gas was fired during an hours-long confrontation in the streets of the town. The crowd jeered the guardsmen, cursed Ritchie, and threatened to lynch Lane. At one point a fire truck was called to the scene and firefighters sympathetic to the home crowd turned its hose on the guardsmen.

Lane had planned to take the prisoners to Princess Anne for a preliminary hearing but, with thousands of angry men storming about the armory, instead ordered the troops and their prisoners to retreat to Baltimore. With weapons drawn they boarded the trucks they'd come in and roared out of town under a hail of rocks and angry catcalls.

The crowd wasn't calmed by their departure, turning on out-of-town journalists who had been following the sensational case. Reporters were chased through the streets; a cameraman was beaten and his equipment destroyed; three cars were burned and, along with a newsreel sound truck, shoved into the Wicomico River. Five hundred angry men chased a group of reporters through the halls of the seven-story Wicomico Hotel, billed as "the finest hotel on Maryland's eastern shore." The hotel manager, who shuttled the reporters from floor to floor and room to room in an effort to avoid violence, assured the men that the crowd meant to do no more than give them "a good beating."

"I don't think it would be any worse than that," a *Washington Daily News* reporter said the manager had told them. Eventually the reporters were able to slip out of the hotel and into taxis that waited to secret them out of town.

On the same day the riots were going on in Salisbury, Steve Hopkins, the superintendent of the Somerset County Almshouse, reported that someone had dug up Armwood's grave and apparently taken the dead man's remains.

Ritchie abandoned his efforts to have prosecutors pursue action against the men accused in the Armwood lynching. Robins would have to prosecute that case, and any others resulting from the subsequent riots, on his own. The four men who had been arrested were released by a three-judge panel — including Duer — that said the state had made the arrests without issuing warrants or producing witnesses.

"A few minutes later, the horns and sirens on automobiles parked outside the building shrieked as in a Fourth of July celebration," the *New York Times* reported.

Crawford, dressed in a plain gray suit, was placed in chains at the Alexandria jail and driven to Leesburg in a four-car convoy, guarded by 25 police officers armed with rifles, clubs and tear gas to appear at his first hearing in Leesburg on November 6. A contingent of Virginia State Police, under command of Captain T.K. Sexton and armed with riot guns and tear gas cans, were assigned to guard all of the courthouse doors during the hearings. Governor Pollard had also sent Brigadier General Gardner W. Waller, head of Virginia's state militia — and an old friend of Billy Mitchell's — to observe the proceedings. The courtroom was filled beyond capacity and more people milled about on the courthouse lawn.

Crawford, described by the *Loudoun Times-Mirror* as "a short, stocky negro," was at first held in the courthouse's jury room, where he sat quietly, smoking cigarettes. He appeared nervous as he entered the crowded courtroom. Seated beside Houston at the defense table, he showed "the pallor of long confinement [and] has been well cared for during his imprisonment in Massachusetts," the newspaper said. "He appeared well fed. He was well dressed, cleanly shaved and had recently been given a hair cut ... he sat in his chair, his feet barely touched the floor."

In his testimony, Judge Alexander testified that he had made up the grand jury list in the Crawford case exactly as he had always made up jury lists — by culling names from the county's tax list.

"Did you or did you not consider the Negro population?" Houston inquired.

"I considered the population as a whole," Alexander responded. "I didn't know whether they were white or colored." He knew personally all of those selected to be on the grand jury, and considered them "a little above the average," with reputations for honesty, intelligence and reliability.

Alexander said his practice was to call for grand jury service only those citizens he knew through personal knowledge to be qualified as grand jurors. Men who served on grand juries should be of more than average intelligence, good repute and be substantial citizens within the community, he said. There might be African Americans who met the statutory qualifications to serve on juries—but he did not know any himself, Alexander said. Wray, who represented the prosecution with Galleher, reminded the court that African Americans were serving on juries in some Virginia courts.

Houston called more than a dozen African Americans to testify, asking each about their education, how much property they owned, how much they paid in taxes each year, all in an effort to demonstrate that there were black men qualified to serve on the county's juries.

The prosecution called only one of its witnesses, H.C. Rogers, supervisor of the Mt. Gilead District, who offered "expert testimony" on the qualifications needed to be a grand juror in Loudoun County. Houston objected to Rogers' qualifications as an expert in the field; McLemore sustained the objection and the prosecution rested without having any of its witnesses testify on the record.

"All the testimony here today shows there have been no Negroes on grand juries or trial juries in Virginia, so their deliberate exclusion must be admitted by the Commonwealth," Houston said in his conclusion. "Public policy in Virginia is that Negroes are not to serve on juries." Alexander "has been revolving around a closed circle—a wheel excluding all Negroes. In other words, a caste system is prevalent in Virginia and the South."

Galleher disagreed.

"The Commonwealth denies Negroes were excluded, denies there are Negroes in Loudoun County qualified for grand jury service and denies the Constitutional rights of negroes were invaded," he said. "Judge Alexander selected an intelligent class of people he thought would measure up to the requirements of law."

And Wray argued that Houston's entire premise was moot.

"No man can demand a mixed jury. If that contention be true—the contention that Negroes are entitled to mixed juries—than foreigners could not obtain fair play unless granted mixed juries. The same principle would apply to persons under 21 and to women because they are excluded from jury service and if on trial would be in the hands of juries among whom they were not represented."

McLemore said he would hand down his decision the following day.

As Crawford was taken from the courthouse, a large crowd pressed around him. "I felt a little concerned," Houston would say later, but there was no violence.[9]

"Every man, white and black, in Loudoun knows that no matter what the negro's qualifications may be, he is excluded from jury service because he is a black man," Houston said. "Why all this fight, unless deep down there is something solid that makes Southern courts exclude negroes?"[10]

On Tuesday morning, McLemore told Houston he was denying the motion to quash. The defense team had not proved that Alexander had excluded African Americans from the grand jury because of their race, McLemore said.

"I think that we have all followed the general custom of trying to select for grand jury service men of more than ordinary intelligence," McLemore said.

I am satisfied there are colored men in Loudoun competent to serve on grand juries, but the question raised here is that by not having colored men on the grand jury list this indictment is illegal. There is, in the light of Judge Alexander's testimony, no legal basis for such contentions. The matter is too well settled in law for discussion here. There is but one question here, and that is did judge Alexander exclude negroes from the list because of their race or color. It was his duty and responsibility to decide who fulfills the qualifications set forth in the statute. There is no evidence that he has excluded negroes because of their race and color.

McLemore overruled Houston's motions and the plea in abatement.

"The only evidence I have as to whether the judge did select the grand jury list in the light of those conditions and prerequisites 'laid down by law' is his testimony," McLemore said. He continued,

I state from memory. I have not the evidence written out. I think the Judge said he made out that list from men he knew, and thought possessed the qualities that would entitle them to serve as grand jurors in a way that would be reasonably acceptable to the State. I think he said also in making up the list the question of color or race did not enter his mind. I have no reason to doubt the Judge in his testimony and if that is true — if his testimony is true — then surely it must be admitted that he did not exclude them because of race or color. In order to exclude you must have some purpose. You must have a consciousness that you have got to decide between one or the other, and if you did not have in mind that question at all but selected from the list of citizens presented to you, 48 persons that you thought measured up to those requirements, without regard to or having in mind the fact that it was a colored man or a white man, of course it would have been no violation of the statute.

It is not for me to say what the future course of this state will be in the light of agitation and discussion which has been brought about by this particular case. That is a matter that will have to be met, and I have no doubt that it will be met in a way that will satisfy all parties.

Houston asked the judge to rule on his contention that Alexander had adhered to Loudoun's social system, which effectively blocked African Americans from jury lists.

"I respectfully request a ruling on testimony that Judge Alexander picked the grand jury from his personal acquaintances," Houston said. "Your honor should say something about the caste system existing in Virginia. Inside the circle are white people. Outside are black people. Black people cannot get inside."

McLemore appeared irritated by Houston's implication.

"If I have any doubts, I always leaned toward the colored man. I carry no feelings myself. We're perfectly conscious that the social caste is well marked in Virginia. I have nothing to add to my decision." He complimented all of the attorneys for "their very able manner" in presenting their arguments and for "courtesies shown one another and the court." He also praised the spectators. "I never saw a more orderly assembly of people. There was no particular interest in this case shown than in any other murder case. There has been absolutely an absence of anything like excitement. I have seen nothing to create a suspicion that the people of this county might resort to violence."

McLemore scheduled December 12 as the first day of Crawford's trial for the murder of Agnes Ilsley. Houston entered Crawford's plea: not guilty. A second trial, for Buckner's murder, would come some time in January.

Police guards again had to force their way through a large crowd as they left the rear entrance of the courthouse and hustled Crawford to a car waiting on the street near the Post Office. "Crawford nervously shifted his glance from side to side," according to the *Times-Mirror*, but "there was no hostile demonstration." The car, with Crawford inside surrounded by police officers, and with state police cars escorting it, sped away down Market Street, past the pauper's graveyard on the edge of town and back to the safety of the Alexandria jail.

On the courthouse steps, Houston was approached by a group of newspaper reporters, including one from the *Richmond News Leader*. Would the NAACP legal team seek a change of venue? No, Houston said — "the fact that Crawford might get a fair trial in some other county in Virginia would not mean anything; but that he could get a fair trial in Loudoun County would demonstrate to the world that there are places in the South where a Negro can get a fair trial no matter what crime he is charged with." Houston told the reporters that he wanted the trial to be conducted in such a way as to serve as a model for other cases involving potential racial antagonisms. Loudoun County and Virginia's justice system would be on trial as much as Crawford would, and the case would stay in Leesburg if the NAACP had to cram it down the county's throat, he said.

"Every present circumstance leads us to believe that Crawford can and will obtain a fair trial in Loudoun County. It is not our intention to move for change of venue when the trial begins. We are now convinced that the Commonwealth of Virginia will offer to the country an entirely new picture of Southern justice toward the Negro."

Whether he believed it or not isn't clear, but at the very least Houston was doing what he could to soothe Loudoun County residents— including those who would eventually serve on the jury for Crawford's murder trials— who had been incensed by Lowell and others during the extradition hearings.

But the *Richmond News Leader*'s November 8 story about the motion to quash quoted Houston as saying "We are going to cram this case down Loudoun County's throat." Taken out of context, it was exactly the kind of thing that could undo Houston's efforts to pour oil on the waters in Northern Virginia, and he sat down to write the newspaper and its readers an explanation of sorts.

"Since the South has many things to answer for, it may interest you to know that in this case my associates and I have received every professional courtesy at the hands of the county officials and the attorneys for the Commonwealth," Houston wrote. "We have traveled all over the county making our investigations and have yet to encounter the first unpleasant incident." The hearing on the motion to quash "was as full and as fair as it could be."

Troopers had been in force around the courthouse during the hearing, something Houston hoped would eventually not be needed at the trials of African Americans any more than at the trials of whites, but "in view of the recent atrocious lynching of George Armwood in Maryland, I must ask that Crawford's guard be continued and all vigilance exercised, still, I have not seen the first hostile demonstration toward him, although I have heard one or two idle rumors of threats."

On November 14 Pollard wrote to White that he had been "disappointed" to read Houston's words in the Richmond newspaper. The implication had been criticism against Virginia authorities, Pollard said. "I am deeply interested in maintaining friendly racial relations," the Governor said.

White quickly responded with a copy of Houston's letter to the newspaper and some soothing words, and Houston followed up with his own conciliatory letter to Pollard. "My associates and I appreciate all that your office has done," Houston wrote. "We regret, and I am sure you regret, the social atmosphere which compels the presence of a large body of state troopers as a wise precautionary measure."

Looking to encourage his embattled lead attorney, White wrote to N.A. Norrell at the *Richmond Planet* about Houston's "brilliant showing" in Leesburg: "White and colored folks alike felt that we would make a serious mistake to follow any other course than continue with our present counsel and I am in one hundred per cent agreement with them."

Alexander "was not nearly as frank on the stand as he was in the clerk's office when we got the stipulation," Houston told Allen and Wilson. "He was shifty and evasive; but in substance we got out of him everything but the admission expressly that he had followed custom [of placing only whites on juries]."

"The court found the exclusion of Negroes, that there were qualified Negroes, that there was a caste system, but refused to find that Negroes had been excluded solely on account of race on the ground that to exclude one had to bear in mind and consider, to pass judgment upon, and that since Judge Alexander did not consider Negroes in selecting the grand jury, did not have Negroes in mind, he did not work a constitutional discrimination although uniformly he had selected white men only," he said.

Houston also laid out plans to "break up the perfunctory performances in the South of sticking one lone Negro on a jury list simply to dodge the Constitutional question." Houston said "the petit jury point is going to be more subtle and far reaching than the grand jury question. Judge McLemore advised Galleher to add some Negroes to the trial jury list; but our point is that you cannot validate a bad list by adding a few Negroes on the end. If a Negro has a right to be considered for a single position on the list, he has a right to be considered for *every* position."[11]

The NAACP was scrambling to raise the money needed to defend Crawford. "It will take money to fight this case properly," White told a crowd gathered at the Nineteenth Street Baptist Church in Washington. "There is a tremendous amount of investigation to be done and many services have to be paid for before we even go to trial. Mr. Houston and his associates are glad to give their services without fee, because of the importance of this case to colored people everywhere. The NAACP needs, then, a fund for expenses in the case, not a real defense fund. Even so, the amount needed is large."[12]

White was pushing NAACP chapters to call for more contributions to pay for costs associated with the case — Houston suggested a December donation drive under the slogan "Make a Christmas Gift for Freedom" — and their efforts, combined with the case's notoriety, were paying off. White began reimbursing the legal team's expenses on a more timely basis, even sending Houston $100 in advance "as a contingent fund against which to draw in covering expenses of investigations, transcript, etc."[13]

"Money is beginning to come in for the Crawford case and we are racking our brains to think of all the possibilities for raising money," White said.[14] Wilkins begged the legal team for a story that would keep public's attention focused on the case.

"If we cannot release pretty soon some 'blood and thunder' sensation, involving Crawford's personal welfare, the danger to his life, or some such angle, I am afraid the publicity will peter out so far as raising money is concerned," Wilkins said.[15]

Among those electing not to make a financial contribution was the ACLU, which decided "no issue of civil liberties" had been raised in the case, "save the exclusion of negroes from the grand jury [and] that has already been raised in court proceedings." The ACLU Board "does not care to pay old bills and they see no issue in the present trial to justify a contribution," ACLU founder Roger Baldwin told White.

More money was coming in, but the NAACP's financial situation was still tight. Included in Houston's itemized expenses were costs for telegrams, stamps, stenographic services and gasoline for his car trips to Leesburg. He had bought new shoes and shirts, as well as tobacco and matches, and provided a few dollars of pocket money for Crawford.

White Loudouners saw no need for such fundraisers. The owner of Dunn's Department Store in Leesburg told customers that "too much money has been spent on that nigger already."[16]

The Virginia National Guard was also preparing for the Leesburg trial. "I am informed that the Negroes Protective Association is distributing literature in Loudoun County, intimating that the authorities were covering up a white person who was really the perpetrator of this deed," Waller wrote to Mitchell on November 24. "Can you tell me to what extent this circulation has been effected?"[17] Whether Waller had evidence that the NPA, which had made little news since being formed in Richmond in 1897, had truly resurfaced in Leesburg, or he had mistaken the NAACP for the NPA, is unclear. In any case, Mitchell could have assured Waller that Crawford was the only man Loudoun County authorities ever considered a suspect in the murders of Ilsley and Buckner.

With a trial date finally set, the Western Union Telegraph Company rented a building on King Street in Leesburg and announced that six telegraphers and a dozen tables would be available there for out of town reporters covering the trial. Western Union also hired runners to carry messages from reporters who would be seated at reserved tables in the courtroom to the temporary telegraph office.

Those reporters and other outsiders were only seeking to overturn a long held Southern "custom"— the exclusion of African Americans from juries— according to a November 9 editorial in the *Loudoun Times-Mirror*.

"The news value of the Crawford trial for the big metropolitan newspapers and the national press associations lies in the constitutional question involved," the newspaper opined, adding

> Had Crawford been arrested in Virginia his trial would now be but a memory. His apprehension in another state made it possible for his attorneys to raise in the Federal courts during extradition proceedings the question of constitutionality of the indictment returned against him here.
>
> Crawford's guilt or innocence is of small moment to the daily newspapers, outside of those in Virginia. His trial is to be the vehicle for focusing public attention on a custom that has prevailed in the South since Reconstruction days and which was followed prior to that tragic era. There was a change during the regime of the scalawag and carpetbagger when the South, temporarily, lost control of her own destiny. To upset the prevailing custom here is the object, and clearly defined purpose of Crawford's attorneys. That is the reason the case is being given wide publicity. If it were a mere murder trial a paragraph or two would suffice for the outside daily newspapers.
>
> Competent lawyers who have studied the case are agreed that the constitutional question involves one of grave moment and transcending importance to Virginia and the South. The Crawford defense contends that the accused colored man was deprived of his constitutional rights because of the fact that no colored man sat on the grand jury that indicted him, and that the name of no colored resident appeared upon the list from the grand jury was drawn [sic]. It is contended that repeated failure of the court to summons colored men for grand jury service constitutes discrimination within the meaning of the Fourteenth Amendment to the federal constitution. A ruling by the Supreme Court of the United States, sustaining the point would, it is pointed out, make it mandatory upon judges of trial courts to place qualified colored men on grand jury lists, and even on the lists from

which trial juries are selected.... The hope of Crawford's attorneys, clearly, is to get the case before the United States Supreme Court, in the expectation of obtaining from the tribunal a ruling establishing a precedent they think will change conditions in the South.

On November 11, Houston wrote to Freeman at the *Richmond News-Leader* about the continuing calls for a white attorney to sit at the defense table during Crawford's trial. Frustrated by his own internal debate and the flood of advice about whether or not to take on white associate counsel, Houston said he had become "enmeshed in my own propaganda."

"As Mr. Ransom and I are both teaching at the Law School it would be impossible for us to explain to the Negro bar our bringing on white counsel," Houston said. "You may not know the pressure on us in this regard, but if we brought in white counsel our usefulness here would be at an end."

And Houston had Crawford's well being to consider as well. "My colleagues feel that he will stand as good chance with us as with white counsel; that interracial counsel are likely to develop discord and that would be worse than all Negro counsel ... I am trying to see whether this case can be lifted above racial prejudices either at the bar or at the counsel table."

Even allies were lobbying for a white lawyer to be added to the NAACP defense team. The Commission on Interracial Cooperation's L.R. Reynolds wrote that "it would strengthen the case immeasurably if you had the prestige of an outstanding white attorney born and reared and educated here in Virginia ... I recognize that what I am saying might be of doubtful value in the face of the very satisfactory handling of the case by Negro lawyers alone." *The Nation* said in a November 22 editorial that three cases—Crawford's murder trial, the Scottsboro Boys case and the murder trial of Athos Terzani in New York City— would test American justice, "especially in regard to its capacity to triumph over race or class prejudice."

"Virginia and Alabama have reacted in opposite ways to national public opinion in regard to their administration of justice," according to *The Nation*. While the hunt for Crawford and the extradition battle waged in Boston had led many to believe that Virginia would railroad Crawford to the electric chair, "Virginia appears to have responded to national apprehension about her justice by an intelligent and humane effort to give Crawford equality before the law and to prosecute him in such a way that the outside world cannot do other than credit Virginians with fair play. It was first thought possible that the indictment proceedings might be reopened and a new grand jury assembled which would include Negroes. This has been denied by Judge McLemore, but — what is more important — it has been decided that Negroes shall be included in the panel for the trial jury before which Crawford is to be brought on December 12."

But *The Nation* had it wrong. There were no plans for African Americans to appear in the jury box in Leesburg.

On November 15, Russell wrote to McLemore — now back in his office at the Circuit Court in Suffolk, Virginia — asking for guidance in the drawing of a jury for Crawford's trial. He suggested calling 54 potential jurors.

"I think certainly there should be a larger number of jurors, more than the usual twenty, and I am quite willing to accept your judgment for fifty-four, fifty of whom are to be summoned by the sheriff," McLemore responded on Saturday. "Of course I do not know how far and how general a discussion of this case has gone, and therefore do not know what may be expected in an effort to get the necessary panel...." The jury commissioners "would save a good deal of trouble if they included some dozen or more negroes in this list, provided they can find that number of eligibles. I cannot suggest that to them of course, but I believe it would be the part of wisdom, if they can't see it that way to do so, and this should be done, if at all, before the list of jurors is drawn for this trial of this case."[18]

That same day, Russell entered an order requiring jury commissioners Samuel Luck, C.A. Whaley and John W. Thompson to meet at his office to supplement their list of potential jurors to as many as 300 names. The original list they had compiled "is insufficient for the panel to be selected in the trial of *Commonwealth of Virginia vs. George Crawford*," according to the order.

McLemore would eventually order that 104 names be drawn for the jury list. When Loudoun's jury commissioners fulfilled the requirements of the order, the resulting list included the names of 104 white Loudoun men.

And Houston had made it clear he would accept no whites at the defense table, either. The battle for an integrated jury system would be fought and decided by purely segregated forces.

White and Houston gathered no encouragement from their pretrial interviews with white officials. Houston paid $5 for Seaton's train ticket from Loudoun to Howard, but found the magistrate unreliable. A mutual acquaintance at the Justice Department, James E. Amos, knew Ben Gunner, head of the detective agency Ilsley had visited the day before her death, "but because of trouble he has had with the Burns Agency (apparently everybody hates them) he has not spoken to Burns men for eight years." Amos and Gunner were, in fact, "mortal enemies," White told Houston.[19]

On November 23, Houston filed documents with the Circuit Court summoning Alexander, Russell, Adrian, current and past jury commissioners Luck, Whaley, Thompson, Frazier, V.B. Harding, G. Shirley Carter, G. Hampton Virts and A.P. McGeath, and twenty African Americans from the county to testify at Crawford's trial. The implication was clear: Houston would continue to argue against the exclusion of African Americans from Loudoun County jurors.

"To exclude qualified Negroes from petit juries solely on the grounds of race and color constitutes just as much discrimination as their exclusion from grand juries," Houston said.[20]

Two weeks before the trial was scheduled to begin, Galleher announced another addition to the prosecution team: State Senator Cecil Connor. Silver-haired and thin lipped, Connor had spent his life working as a prosecutor in courtrooms across Virginia's rough and tumble northern tier. He was tough, confident, aggressive, and in control of any room he entered. He had been born in the tiny hamlet of Philomont in western Loudoun, educated in the county's schools and, like Galleher, had taught in them for a short time as well. He studied at Washington and Lee University, where he earned his law degree in 1896, was admitted to the Virginia State Bar in 1898 and began practicing law in Leesburg that year, in the offices of J.B. McCabe and J.R.H. Alexander, Sr. He had been a witness to the lynching of Charles Craven and, at first, had refused to testify at the coroner's inquest. But, after being threatened with contempt of court, he said that every man in Leesburg, with the exception of three men already identified, had tried to prevent the lynching.

Connor was an active Democrat, joining a Westmoreland Davis Club and representing Leesburg at the 1932 State Democratic Convention in Richmond. He served on the board of trustees of the State Teacher's College of Virginia, was on the board of directors of the People's National Bank and was instrumental in the formation of the Loudoun County Chamber of Commerce. He had been Commonwealth's Attorney in Loudoun from 1912 until the spring of 1927, when he resigned to take his State Senate seat. And in 1928, despite his reluctance at the Craven inquiry, Connor had been one of the authors of an anti-lynching bill that was eventually passed by the General Assembly.

Like Wray, Connor had been convinced by private citizens to join the government's legal team. "Connor's services had been proffered ... by a group of citizens," Galleher told the *Loudoun Times-Mirror*.

The prosecution team Galleher had assembled had years of experience together, and with Loudoun County judges. Judge Alexander's father had been one of the partners in the first law firm to hire Connor. When he had resigned as Commonwealth's Attorney to run for the General Assembly, Alexander had been appointed to replace him. Alexander was appointed to the Circuit Court by Governor Byrd in 1929. As Circuit Court judge, he had picked Galleher to be the new Commonwealth's Attorney.

Surrounded by his family at his home in Chestnut Hill, Massachusetts, Judge Lowell died on Thanksgiving Day, 1933. He had been diagnosed with erysipelas less than two weeks earlier and had developed pneumonia two days before his death. Antagonism toward him and his decision in Crawford's case did not immediately die with him.

Houston and the other members of the NAACP legal team would have no more luck finding rooms in Loudoun during Crawford's trial than they had during the November hearings. The Leesburg Inn remained closed to them, and White wrote to both Pollard and Freeman on December 4 that African Americans in the county had exhibited "considerable reluctance" to house the NAACP team.

"We can well understand the reluctance of these local colored people, who will have to stay there after we shall have gone. I wonder if any pressure is being brought to bear on them locally or if any quiet threats are being made."

Some thought was being given to holding night sessions during the trial, which would have forced the black attorneys and reporters covering the case to find places to stay in Loudoun or make the two hour commute to Washington each night and back again early each morning. And Crawford would have to be housed at the Leesburg jail, something he and Houston thought an unwise temptation of violent fate.

On December 6 Freeman responded to White. "I am unable to see what may be the reason for the attitude of the colored people of Leesburg, unless it is that they are timid about receiving strangers whose presence might arouse antagonism," Freeman wrote. "I have no idea they have been told to decline hospitality to the visiting lawyers and observers. That would not be in accordance with the spirit of the people of Loudoun. They might fight, but they will always fight above board."

And, Freeman said, some people in Leesburg believed that White was white. Freeman suggested "a brief article in the Leesburg paper that you have colored blood. This could be done as a simple news story, remarking the fact that you were one of the few known persons of colored blood who had blue eyes. If you have no objections to this, I shall be glad to arrange it." White agreed to the idea.

That evening, in a speech before the Federal Council of Churches of Christ in America in Washington, President Roosevelt made news when he called lynching "a vile form of collective murder."

"We know that it is murder, and a deliberate and definite disobedience of the commandment 'thou shalt not kill.' We do not excuse those in high places or in low who condone lynch law," Roosevelt said. "But a thinking America goes further. It seeks a government of its own that will be sufficiently strong to protect the prisoner and at the same time to crystallize a public opinion so clear that government of all kinds will be compelled to practice a more certain justice.

"The judicial function of government is the protection of the individual and of the community through quick and certain justice. That function in many places has fallen into a state of disrepair. It must be a part of our programme to reestablish it."

Speaking at the 19th Street Baptist Church in Washington days before the trial was due to begin, Houston said African Americans should come out to Leesburg to support Crawford, even if they risked getting their "heads cracked."[21]

He was misquoted in Loudoun as saying African Americans should come to Leesburg "to crack some heads."[22]

"Word from Washington was that a large delegation of colored people from the capital would come here for the trial, negro leaders having advised them to be present," the *Loudoun Times-Mirror* reported.

What no one outside of the NAACP team knew on the eve of the trial was that Crawford's alibi had collapsed. In early November, with rumors swirling across the county of a cover-up and the possibility that Paul Boeing had, in fact, killed his sister, the NAACP legal team had decided that it had to root out as much of the truth as possible from someone other than Crawford, who seemed always to transform his story to conform too much to the wishes of his audience. It was a decision that would cripple their plans for Crawford's defense and supply a wealth of ammunition to their post-trial critics.

Immediately after the Motions to Quash hearing, Houston told McLemore and Galleher about rumors the NAACP had heard about Boeing's involvement in the murders. Houston said the defense would be obligated to raise the issue in court if it could be substantiated, but he felt it was distasteful to do so without evidence. He proposed that the Commonwealth permit him to interview witnesses with prosecuting attorneys present, to either clear Boeing or find more substantial evidence of his guilt. McLemore and Galleher agreed.

"I would not permit Crawford to be sacrificed to cover Paul B[oeing] if he were guilty," Houston said. "The judge agreed with me.

"So it looks as if a lot of the sensational may be taken out of the trial; and for this I am glad because it is a tough thing to accuse a man of murdering his own sister even if he is a nut. However, we are going to run down every clue and if the dirt is there it is going to be brought out."[23]

With Adrian at his side, Houston interviewed DeNeal at the Leesburg jail, where she was being held as a material witness. Her story was inconsistent with Crawford's alibi. She said Crawford had left Boston with her in December 1931 and they had separated upon arrival in Washington. She said she had spent the day with him on December 26 in Jack Skinner's stable and had received a letter from him shortly after New Year's Day, postmarked from Richmond. She said "a dark skinned colored boy" came to her Middleburg house the day of the murders with a note from Crawford asking for food.[24]

When confronted with DeNeal's story in his cell at the Alexandria jail, Crawford admitted his Boston alibi had been a lie. He had stayed at Pat Harrison's Richmond home; he and Charles Johnson stayed at Lessie Hedgepath's row house at 1616 Third Street in Washington after the murders and had left some clothes there. Houston went to Hedgepath's home and retrieved the clothes—a fact he would not reveal publicly until long after Crawford's trial. But any fantasies of Boeing's guilt or Crawford's innocence had evaporated. Houston's goal now was simply to keep Crawford out of Virginia's electric chair.

TEN

The Trial

"Loudoun has never, nor has Virginia, since the dark era of Reconstruction, witnessed a trial of graver consequences to the South than that for which the stage has been set here," the *Loudoun Times-Mirror* announced in its final issue before the trial began.

McLemore gaveled the trial open at 10 a.m. on Tuesday, December 12, 1933. The courtroom was packed with whites and blacks sitting side by side on the wooden benches on both the main floor and the small balcony running along the back of the room. Three tables had been set up for reporters. Troopers stood at the entrance, wearing riot helmets and black windbreakers over their blue uniforms, tear gas guns ready for any trouble from the crowd.

In choosing the jury, men were excused for medical conditions and because of their farmer's hours; one said he was used to rising at 5 a.m. and going to bed no later than 8:30 p.m. Some men were able to avoid sitting in the jury box with the help of letters from doctors.

Herman Piggott was confined to his house in Hamilton and "is unable to attend to any kind of business," Dr. W.D. Sydnor wrote to the court. Gibson, who kept up his Leesburg practice and was on the staff of Loudoun Hospital in addition to acting as county coroner, wrote letters advising McLemore that E. Neville Bradfield should be excused because his wife was expected to deliver a baby any day; Josephus Carr was suffering from repeated bouts of lumbago; and J.C. Downey "will explain to you the situation of his family and condition of wife. Any statement that he makes will be true — and trust you will give it consideration."

Houston asked the potential jurors if any of them belonged "to any organization the obligations of which are binding upon you to feel that the Negro is an inferior being and is not entitled to the same rights and privileges which any other member of society is entitled to." None of them responded.

Did any of them belong to the Ku Klux Klan? None responded.

Would they be unable to give impartial treatment to evidence in a case in which a Negro was charged with killing a white woman? None responded.

Would they have any problem giving equal credence to testimony delivered by both white and African American witnesses? None responded.

Twenty men were culled from the larger group of venire men. Eight names would be stricken from that list the following morning.

McLemore released them all to go home, warning them not to discuss the case with anyone. "Report anybody to the court tomorrow who attempts to talk to you about it," he told them.

After a short break, the court was reconvened to hear an NAACP motion to quash the list of potential jurors. According to the motion, the venire panel drawn by Loudoun County's jury commissioners should be thrown out "by reason of the unlawful exclusion of all qualified Negroes." Crawford, "a Negro, has been greatly prejudiced and has been denied due process and the equal protection of the law in violation of the Constitution of the United States and the law of the land."

Houston called the current jury commissioners, who had drawn the 300-man venire list, to testify. C.A. Whaley and Samuel Luck, a neighbor of the Ilsley's and father of Middleburg mayor William Jordan Luck, said discrimination had not been involved in the process. "Why were not Negroes selected?" Houston asked Whaley.

"We found none we thought suitable," Whaley said.

African American contractors Isaac and Lucian Allen had built Luck's house, but he maintained that neither they nor any other black men in the county met the standards for honesty and intelligence needed to serve on juries.

"Did they show intelligence in building your house?" Houston asked Luck. "Yes."

"Were they honest as business men?"

"Yes," Luck said.

"Were they fair-minded?

"They seemed to be."

"Aren't they all of the statutory requirements?"

"Yes, but they did not come up to the full standards."

"What are your standards?"

"Well, I'm not certain, but they have to be intelligent," Luck said.

Thompson was a night watchman who had worked "as a farmer, on bridges—most anything I can find to do." White found him to be of "obviously limited education and mentality." When asked to read from a list of voters the name of any African American whom he knew and had considered placing on the jury for Crawford's trial, Thompson hesitated for some time. He held the paper at arm's length and had to squint, moving his lips as he read. "Judge McLemore showed his disgust by getting up from the bench and pacing the floor back of the dais as the commissioner failed to give any reply," according to the *Afro-American.* "The prosecutor was plainly embarrassed.

"Finally Commonwealth Attorney Galleher went to the commissioner's aide and discovered that he had been reading, or attempting to read, the white names. When the proper section was given him he called off the name of a colored man whom he knew, but the name was not on the tax list. The second man whom he said he knew had been dead for several years."

All three jury commissioners testified that they had not discriminated against African Americans in selecting the venire. Everyone on the tax list, regardless of their race, was considered for the jury if the commissioners considered them qualified for jury duty — but there were no Negroes on the list whom they considered qualified.

In the end, McLemore denied Houston's motion to quash the venire.

"I would certainly not be frank if I said this question is free from difficulty; I think it is not," McLemore said in rendering his decision from the bench.

> The question of selecting juries is one that is giving concern to courts and to the legislatures over a very wide range of territory and time. I believe it has always been one of the objectives of the legislature and certainly of the courts towards that goal that would mete justice to all men. I can hardly conceive of a court with any other conception.
>
> I am also conscious of the fact it is most difficult to do; that we have to deal with human nature as we find it, with its weaknesses, and when we complicate them many times with political influences and color influences, racial influences, we find it difficult sometimes to hold the scale even and administer justice with a perfect hand. No act of man is perfect so we have to strive as near as possible when we attain unto that approach to equal justice, and that is certainly, I believe, the object of the courts of today — certainly those I have some knowledge of.
>
> I know myself it is the one thing I want to do in this particular case, see that justice is meted with a perfect hand. I can hardly hope to accomplish my purpose, but I aspire to do that which I think most nearly approaches it, and I am asking for the helpful assistance of the bar and others connected with administration of justice here to aid me in that objective.
>
> There are three jury commissioners in the county; there are six districts, as pointed out. We must not forget the fact that the three jury commissioners, unless they are unusual men having very broad range of acquaintanceship, cannot know all the people in the county. I suspect you would hardly find three men, unless in some way entangled in politics, that would know half the people in the county, so we are forced to use men that must of necessity select some men that they don't personally know. I assume, being human — they are, and we all are — they get the best judgment on them they can. I am not ready to believe jury commissioners or others in those responsible positions are going to perjure themselves and make up a roll they think is going to convict or acquit, but try to select good men. It follows, of course, in selecting one hundred or so men, they necessarily exclude maybe one thousand or more, so this question of selection should not be confounded with the thought of excluding in one sense; to exclude all others when you select a small company that must serve as juries, but to say exclude them purposely, to give preference to those you select, is not a fair statement.
>
> I do not know how the jury commissioners selected this list; I never saw either of them before in my life. They impress me as honest, good men ... they tell me they know very few colored people in their respective districts and perhaps less

number in those districts they do not live in, so it is a violent presumption to say because they do not know, they have excluded him because of race or color. They cannot do that. Of course they cannot. If that is done, and proven to be done, proceedings would be void.

But I think it would be just as wrong to say, if you are going to presume they are doing that because they have not selected in their judgment and in the exercise of their judgment and in the exercise of their discretion men —colored men — they did not know, or those they know whom they thought not equal to some white man they knew about, and therefore did not put them on, would be an opinion I don't think the court ought to indulge.

And, as I say, the question is troublesome. It seems to me with the evidence before me, if I am to adhere to my rule in the case of the grand jury as it is in this case, is even stronger than that which was brought before the court at the other hearing in this matter I see no reason to change my ruling and I will, therefore, have to overrule the motion at this time.

The jury commissioners' selections would stand.

McLemore would receive "abusive and vituperative telegrams from Negro organizations" for the decision. "Judge McLemore was unperturbed by their receipt," the *Times-Mirror* would report. Among the telegrams was a missive from the ILD in Richmond. "Your denial of the rights of Negroes to serve on the Crawford jury is part of the special oppression of the Negro nation," the communist group said.

The jury empaneled by McLemore was a cross section of white Loudoun: a banker, a few clerks, farmers, and storeowners. In a community as small as Loudouns', many of their names were already known to those packed into the courtroom and had been placed on jury lists in the past: George R. Hess, Charles E. Spring, T.J. Smallwood, C.T. Wortman, E.F. James, R.M. Legard, Roy D. George, H.C. Thompson, W.W. Wine, S.W. Blocker, Walter M. Everhart and George B. Menefee.

A guard of 25 Virginia State Police, led by Motor Vehicle Commissioner Frazier and accompanied by Virginia State Police Captain Sexton, escorted Crawford from the Alexandria jail to the courthouse in Leesburg for the first day of testimony on Wednesday, December 13. "The police were heavily armed, being equipped with sub-machine guns, riot guns, gas bombs and masks and revolvers," the *Loudoun Times-Mirror* reported. "They surrounded the prisoner, with guns ready for instant action, as the negro, handcuffed, was removed from the car in which he was brought here to the clerk's office, and later to the courtroom."

McLemore had made it clear that he would not allow the case to become the kind of spectacle the county had witnessed at Ilsley's funeral. Reporters would have access to the courtroom, but photographers would not be allowed in the building. The courtroom's 300-person seating limit would not be exceeded. But on the first day, spectators began arriving at the courthouse long before the trial was scheduled to begin. H.L. Rodeffer had driven down from Lovettsville, 15 miles north of Leesburg, to be the first person into the courtroom. The Hitts were there early, as was Julia Whiting, Winifred Maddux, Mildred Russell and Mrs. Dixon Plaster. The women of Middleburg, including Edith Kennedy Sands and Eugenia Fairfax, were driven by their chauffeurs to the courthouse. All of the benches were filled; the balcony was packed; people were standing at the back of the room and in the stairwell. A dozen reporters sat at the tables that had been reserved for them. Russell wore a new blue flannel suit; White sat unnoticed on a bench behind Houston, taking notes and eavesdropping on the people sitting around him.

"Crawford sat alone, unguarded, and virtually ignored, behind his counsel," reporter Frank Getty wrote in the *Washington Post*. "He is a smallish negro, with long, powerful arms and a shuffling gait, a not unintelligent face, aquiline nose, furrowed forehead and close-cropped hair."

"Only when he was being identified by witnesses did Crawford, slouched for the most part in his chair, the most inconspicuous person in the crowded courtroom, take any interest in the proceedings. When he was pointed out by witnesses ... the chunky, furrow-browed negro beamed good-naturedly, and was restrained with difficulty from popping to his feet and bowing....."

The NAACP team was a curiosity to many in the room. "Here he comes now—he ain't black and he ain't white," a white spectator said as Houston entered the courtroom, according to a reporter from the *Afro-American*. "I can stand a thoroughbred nigger, but I can't stand these mongrels." White also noted the "mongrel" comment.

Not included in the list of witnesses—for either the prosecution or the defense—was Roy Seaton, despite the prominent role he had played in the early days of the investigation and the inflammatory statements he had made about Crawford being railroaded to the electric chair. "It developed, however, that Seaton has disappeared from his usual haunts in Middleburg and was nowhere to be found," the *Times-Mirror* reported. Galleher "maintained silence when questioned as to the whereabouts of the former magistrate. It was ascertained from other sources, however, that Seaton had left Middleburg for a visit several days ago and that he had later returned to pack up his effects and take his departure for an unannounced destination.

"The *Times-Mirror* had a report that he was in Washington, and had been seen in the vicinity of Howard University, school for colored students in the city, the law school of which Charles H. Houston, chief counsel for Crawford is dean." Seaton had been interviewed by Houston at Howard, and had stayed for a time at a boarding house on 13th Street in Northwest Washington. But he did not appear in Leesburg during Crawford's trial and, despite his deep ties to Middleburg, wouldn't be seen in Loudoun County again.

McLemore's first order of business was to address newspaper articles, including one that had appeared in that morning's *Washington Herald*, which forecast racial tension and violence in Leesburg:

My attention has been directed to articles appearing in one of the papers circulating around this territory in connection with the trial of this case or in reference to the trial of this case, more particularly the town. I am surprised that such an article should be in the paper. It seems to me that the man who wrote it could have been employed much better at something else. The only purpose it can have is to make a little more difficult the duty and effort on the part of the law of this state to conduct this trial properly. It has already been rendered difficult enough by reason of the magnifying of many matters that were not worthy of that publicity.

I cannot imagine the good people of this county giving themselves over to any sort of incendiary remarks or statements that would bring disrespect upon the county and shame and disgrace upon its name in the trial of this case, which is simply the trial of a man for murder to determine whether he is guilty, the same as in any other case of murder. There is no county that has a personnel of higher order than here. The same rules and the same principle that are found in all murder cases are involved here. The same kind of evidence will be introduced, and no doubt there will be the same conduct on the part of counsel in attempting to prove on the one hand that the accused is guilty, if he is, and on the other hand to see than he be freed if he is not guilty ... the Commonwealth and the counsel have the same rights in the court room, and if they conduct themselves properly, I have no doubt they will be treated exactly like the white people.

I see nothing to justify the article which I have before me. I see nothing to justify any improper criticism ... I want to admonish you to give no consideration to anything that tends to stir up feeling in the trial of this case ... I admonish you to use that same real toleration and conservatism and common sense which has been prevalent in this case up to now.

Crawford could be found innocent of the charges against him, McLemore told the jury, or he could be found guilty of murder in the first degree — and sentenced to 20 years in prison, life in prison, or death in Virginia's electric chair — or guilty of either voluntary or involuntary manslaughter.

In his opening statement, Galleher laid out a timeline of Crawford's movements in the weeks leading up to the Middleburg murders, telling the jury that Crawford had been seen in town within just a few hours of the murders. Ilsley's body was "nude from the breast down" and had been "beaten all over her breast" in addition to her skull fracture, Galleher said. Witnesses would testify that they had seen Crawford write the note to Nokes that was later found in Ilsley's car, according to the prosecutor.

Galleher called on the jury to find Crawford guilty and to "mete out a punishment commensurate with the nature of this heinous crime."

Houston, in his first chance to speak to the jury, waived the defense's opening statement.

The prosecution's first witness was Homer Spitler. Questioned by Connor, the doctor said that when he arrived at the cottage on the morning of the murders, Seaton and Henry Frost were already there. Glass "was shattered above the knob" in the back door. He found Ilsley lying inside her room. "She was dead. Both eyes were very much swollen. She had wounds on her head and bruises over her body. She was lying over on her body, her right knee flexed. The room was in a rather disturbed condition ... the body, of course, was covered with blood from head to foot. There was blood on the floor. There was blood on the head. There was blood on the walls."

Buckner's body was lying on her cot, with her right foot on the floor, and she was holding her false teeth in one hand.

"I think that Mrs. Buckner never moved after she was hit this smashing blow, but Mrs. Ilsley, I am confident, thrashed around in her own blood for some time before she died ... Mrs. Buckner had a cut in her forehead, at the base of her skull, her head, and a smashing blow involving almost the whole of her face." He thought she had been standing when she was hit and fell back on the bed. Ilsley had died from "concussion and hemorrhage combined — shock." Despite Ilsley's semi-nude state, there was no "sex element" to the crime, Spitler said. He thought Ilsley had been attacked first.

One man could have killed both women, he thought, and both women may have been killed with the same instrument, though he had not been able to determine what the murder weapon was.

Gibson was the prosecution's second witness. Checking notes he had taken the day of the murders, he testified that he had arrived at the cottage at about 10 a.m., having driven down from Leesburg with Galleher and Adrian. It was his impression that Ilsley had come home, undressed, thrown down the bed and laid down on top of the bedclothes to read when she was attacked. "The book that she was reading was opened and covered with blood," he testified. Her brain could be seen where her skull had been fractured, just behind her left ear, and several other wounds and bruises marked her head and face.

Hunter had been called to perform autopsies on the women and to determine if they had been raped, Gibson said. "I am not capable of doing that sort of work." Hunter arrived at the cottage in the late afternoon, some time between 4 and 5 p.m.

"There is one thing I failed to mention," Gibson said at the end of his testimony. "There was a bootjack standing in the room. I never saw but two of them in my life. My grandfather had the other. I don't know where it is, but I would give anything to have it. But this bootjack was there, and it was covered with blood ... this bootjack is iron. This bootjack was made like a big bug — a big iron bug — and they come out and have little feet on the side."

Under cross-examination, Gibson told Houston that he believed Ilsley "was killed with that bootjack." He did not know what became of the bootjack since he last saw it, on the day of the murder. He had examined it in Ilsley's room and said there had been hair and blood on it.

Did the prosecution have the bootjack, Houston asked? They said they did not. Adrian said the Sheriff's Office did not have it either.

Gibson's testimony about the murder scene was particularly harrowing.

"The front of her skull was completely crushed in ... now, her brains were on the ceiling. There was blood all over the washstand and all over the ceiling. There was blood on the washstand and it was very evident that somebody had washed their hands. There was blood on the towel ... Mrs. Buckner was killed so quick she never knew what hit her. The other woman struggled and rolled all over the room."

The testimony of pathologist Oscar Hunter, and the acceptance or rejection of it by the jury, was "the turning point of the case," according to White. Hunter, who had been on the staff of George Washington University Hospital and worked with Sibley Memorial Hospital, Montgomery Hospital and the coroner's office of the District of Columbia, in addition to his own private practice, testified that he had arrived in Middleburg at 5:30 p.m. the day of the murders. There was evidence that Ilsley "had put up a terrific struggle," he said. When he had examined Ilsley's body, he had found "two little crinkly hairs. Microscopic examination of these showed distinct melanotic pigment in the basal layers of the skin — that is, the bottom layers of the skin. These hairs were not the same structure as Mrs. Ilsley's hair. From the fact that the skin was pigmented and the hair was of a crinkly character, we concluded definitely that this was Negro skin and Negro hair."

Ilsley may have lived as long as an hour after she was attacked, dying some time between 1 and 3 a.m. She had been killed with a blunt instrument of some kind, Hunter said. He had not seen the bootjack.

Henry Frost, who lived about four miles from Middleburg, told the court that he had arrived at the Ilsley cottage with Seaton at five minutes after nine the morning of the murders. Under cross-examination by Houston, he said Paul Boeing came into the cottage while he was there. "I think to get some wearing apparel — some clothes. Of course, I can't swear to that...." Boeing went into one of the other rooms in the house. "...I couldn't say just what he did in the other room." Boeing did not go into the room where his sister's body lay, Frost said.

Billy Mitchell — white-haired, ruddy-faced, dressed in a gray suit — testified that he'd last seen Ilsley alive at the Hitt's party at about 11:45 p.m. Winifred Maddux left the Hitt's with Ilsley, he said. The next morning, Mitchell said, he prepared to go fox hunting, changed his mind, and was changing out of his riding clothes when Frost arrived with news of the murders. Mitchell said he sent his "manager" to the cottage while he finished changing, and then followed, arriving at the Ilsley's about 9:20 a.m. He went into the cottage.

Mitchell said he saw an iron beetle bootjack, about 13 inches long, in Ilsley's room.

"It had a long body, a round head, two tentacles that projected to the front to where the foot was inserted for the purpose of taking off the boot, and there were three legs on each side, made of iron, on which it stood, the front ones being higher than the rear ones to hold the bootjack up. I would say it weighed around five pounds." There was blood on the bootjack when he saw it, Mitchell said.

Under cross-examination by Houston, Mitchell said he had been in the manor house days after the murders. "The last time I saw the bootjack, it was in Mrs. Ilsley's house on the second floor — on the second floor, Mrs. Ilsley's large house."

The courtroom was silent when Galleher called Paul Boeing to the witness stand for what was to be the emotional centerpiece of the prosecution's case against Crawford. Houston was now convinced that Boeing had played no part in the murders, but there were many in the courtroom, and around the country, who remained suspicious. "Spectators leaned forward to catch every word of Boeing's testimony ... a pin falling to the floor could have been heard as Boeing testified" the *Times-Mirror* reported.

Boeing was "dapper, high strung, aesthetic," according to Frank Getty, while Crawford was "squat" and "ill favored." They nodded and smiled at each other as Boeing approached the stand.

Boeing had been out of the area, living in New York and Minneapolis, since the murders. Though he was not on trial, had not been charged with any crime and was appearing only as a witness for the prosecution, Boeing brought an attorney to the trial. Flynn Andrews, a lawyer based in New York, sat at the prosecution's table during Boeing's testimony.

Boeing was "a dapper young man, typical scion of a wealthy family [who] appeared extremely nervous when he was called to the stand," according to the *Afro-American*. "He is of dark complexion, with his hair brushed back in a glistening pompadour. His mannerisms were slightly effeminate ... he spoke in an extremely polished manner, picking each word deliberately." Getty said Boeing had tears in his eyes as he "told of his panic upon finding the murdered body of his sister." His voice was "soft, cultured, well modulated," according to White.

When Boeing identified Crawford from the stand, Crawford stood and bowed, much to Houston's chagrin. Boeing said he had met Crawford during a visit to Middleburg in May, 1931. Ilsley had been away from Middleburg during the summer of 1931; Boeing said he had driven with her from Milwaukee to Middleburg that September. Crawford was gone by then and Holt had moved out of the cottage. Boeing said he stayed in Middleburg about a month, returning on November 1 and staying until shortly after the murders.

He had stayed in the cottage after dinner to read until about 11 p.m. that night, then went over to the big house, where he let out a puppy that was being housebroken. He came back for a glass of milk and a handful of crackers, and then, leaving lights on in the living room, the hall and on the front porch of the cottage, he returned to the manor house for the night. He stayed up until about 11:30 p.m. working on furniture designs.

When a banging shutter woke him during the night, he turned on a light and looked out at the cottage, but saw nothing unusual. He went back to bed.

The next morning he went to the cottage, wearing his pajamas, an overcoat and an old pair of Oxfords, to get some riding clothes. Most of his clothes were still at the cottage, he said.

"I went through the kitchen, dining room, and down a corridor. The doors were open," and both women usually slept with their doors closed, Boeing testified. He saw Buckner's body first. "I looked to the left and saw what had happened there. I looked into the other room and saw my sister. I immediately went out. I was dazed and numb and wanted to find someone to tell what had happened."

He ran through the streets of the village, eventually returning with "someone," though he couldn't recall who it was. He went inside to get shoes and clothes. Hitt came and took him away to her house.

The mood in the courthouse was tense as Houston rose to cross-examine Boeing. There was some expectation that the black attorney would try to prove the white witness had played a role in his sister's murders, and no one knew what the town's reaction would be to that confrontation.

There was a crash at the back of the room and everyone jumped. A window had fallen shut, or someone had slipped on the steps leading up to the balcony.

Boeing told Houston that he had stayed in the manor house because "every time that either house had been unoccupied, it had been robbed — broken in to and robbed."

"Do you know whether Mrs. Ilsley went to Washington to consult detectives before she was murdered?" Houston asked.

"I do not know," Boeing testified.

"Was Mrs. Buckner hard of hearing?"

"Just a little."

"Was it such that she could not have overheard any commotion going on?"

"That I don't know."

"When did you last see Crawford?"

"About June 12, 1931."

"When you came back from Milwaukee in September, was Crawford there then?"

"No, he was not."

"Did Mrs. Ilsley ever have any disagreement with Crawford?"

"Not that I know."

"Did you hear anybody having any difficulty with Crawford?"

"I know very little about him."

The standoff between Houston and Boeing hadn't climaxed as many in the courtroom had expected. Some breathed sighs of relief. Reporters from the *Afro-American* were among those who remained puzzled by the turn of events.

Galleher continued to bring witnesses to the stand all through the day.

Winifred Maddux said Ilsley had driven her home from the Hitt party, dropping her off at Belray Farm, a thoroughbred horse farm her stepfather owned outside of Middleburg at either 11:30 p.m. or 12:30 a.m., she couldn't recall which.

Alexander Grayson testified that he owned a dog who "ain't bad, but he barks a lot," though it apparently did not bark during the night of the killings — and Grayson said he had not heard any other dogs barking during the night of the murders, either. When he went to tend the furnace the next morning, he found the garage doors open and the Ford sedan missing, but he told no one about it until after the bodies were found.

Harry Leonard said he had slept lightly the night of the murders and was up several times with a sick baby. The front porch light at the Ilsley cottage was on that night — it shone into his bedroom window. At 12:30 a.m. he saw Ilsley walk across her front porch and turn off the light as she entered the cottage. He had seen no one else, and nothing outside the house seemed unusual to him that night.

The prosecution's last witness of the day was Bertie DeNeal. Asked to identify Crawford, DeNeal, dressed in a blue tailored suit and wearing a black felt hat, stood up to point him out. "Both smiled broadly as they exchanged glances," according to the *Times-Mirror*. "Crawford leaned back in his chair to get a better look at his former paramour."

Questioned by Wray, DeNeal said she had left Middleburg and her family on September 5, 1931, taking a bus to Washington, where she met Crawford, who was using an alias — Charlie Smith. The two of them took a bus to Boston, where they got a room at Jenny Thompson's home at 37th and Claremont. A few days after Thanksgiving they left Thompson's, moving into Mary Fraction's in Boston. Crawford worked in a garage owned by Basil Hutchinson. They returned to Washington in December. Crawford stayed in the city, while DeNeal continued on to Middleburg.

On Christmas day — the day after the manor house was burglarized — Crawford had sent DeNeal a note from Jack Skinner's stable, asking her to bring him something to eat, she said. Early the next morning she went to the stable. Crawford was wearing his chauffeur's uniform and an overcoat. He told her he hadn't been able to work in Washington and was on his way to Warrenton to see a man who owed him money, then on to Richmond, where he hoped to get a job driving a truck at a packing house, where he had worked in the past.

In the first or early in the second week of January, 1932, she received a letter from Crawford postmarked from Richmond, saying he expected to start the truck driving job that Monday, and asking her to send him two dollars. She wrote back that she didn't have the money. She burned his letter and could not recall the address where Crawford had said he could be reached.

Just after noon on January 12, a man she did not know came to her door with a note from Crawford, asking that she send him some food. "It didn't say where he was at, where he wanted me to find him," DeNeal said. "It didn't say nothing." The man who brought her the note "was just a dark, brown-skinned man with just plain hair, dressed in very cheap clothes, a dark coat, and a kind of little lighter pants. He had a cap but no overcoat."

Weeks later, on March 10, she had received a package with a fur coat in it, sent to her by Crawford. She said Deputy Sheriff Paul Alexander came to get her and took her to the post office; he also loaned her money because the package had been sent COD, and she had opened the package at the post office. Alexander confiscated two letters that were addressed to her that he discovered in the coat. She and Alexander "went on the way from the post office on down the road and we read the letters," which were in Crawford's handwriting but were signed in Charles Smith's name. He wrote that he was in Boston and asked her not to tell anyone where he was.

Houston objected to DeNeal's testimony about the letters, saying they would have to be produced by the prosecution. The judge agreed. Wray said he would recall DeNeal to the stand the next day. Houston refused to cross-examine DeNeal until Wray was finished questioning her.

At 4:55 p.m., McLemore adjourned court for the day. White immediately issued a statement to reporters:

> I want to pay unstinted tribute to the superb fight for Crawford which Messrs. Houston, Lovett, Ransom and Tyson have waged.
> Legal and racial history has been made by these four able and courageous men. Negroes have rightly poured adulation at the feet of white lawyers like Darrow and Leibowitz who have defended Negroes.
> Let them now show equal appreciation to these lawyers of their own race, who have dared and fought. It took real courage to face this situation.
> And their handling of the case, brilliant to the superlative degree, has won for them the profound respect of everyone in the courtroom.

Surgery would keep fingerprint expert Fred Sandberg from testifying. Houston wanted to depose Sandburg, who was not able to commute by train — "his condition is such that he believes that a railroad journey would shake him up," Houston said — but McLemore said a deposition would not be admissible. "My impression is that in a criminal case you have got to confront the defendant with the witness. It is an irregular method of getting criminal evidence," the judge said. Houston was so desperate for the testimony that he offered to pay the cost of a private ambulance to bring Sandberg to Leesburg. But Sandberg, who Houston believed would have testified that Crawford's fingerprints had not been found at the murder scene, would not come to Leesburg.

By the time Houston and his team left Leesburg that night, a freezing rain was falling across Northern Virginia. All along the road to Washington, cars were abandoned in the icy conditions. It was slow going. The attorneys took a break to grab a bite to eat at a grocery store at Tysons Corner. The drive to Washington took five hours.

Conditions were even worse Thursday morning, forcing the NAACP legal team to take the train to Leesburg, and then walk several icy blocks to the courthouse. When court reconvened at 10 a.m., Galleher said he would wait to recall DeNeal to continue her testimony. Instead, he called another series of witnesses, this time to testify that Crawford had been near Middleburg when Ilsley and Buckner had been killed.

Buck Bland, who lived in The Plains, a village about eight miles south of Middleburg, had been training horses for Jack Skinner at his stable in Middleburg and was familiar with both DeNeal and Crawford. Bland and Skinner would occasionally see Crawford walking when they were riding. On Christmas morning, the day after the manor house was burglarized, Bland had given Crawford a ride in his car from The Plains to Skinner's stable. "He went upstairs in my room at the stable," Bland testified. He went home that night and when he came back the next morning, Crawford was still in his room. DeNeal came to Crawford there about 9 or 10 a.m. on December 26.

W.C. Pearson, a white filling station operator and prison guard, said he knew Crawford from his time at Camp Ten in New Baltimore, in Fauquier County, about 15 miles south of Middleburg. Pearson said he had been walking to work at his filling station in Gainesville, about 12 miles from Middleburg, before dawn on December 28, using a flashlight to find his way, when he saw Crawford on the opposite side of the road. He recognized Crawford by his distinctive pigeon-toed walk. Crawford was wearing his chauffeur's suit, an overcoat and a cap, Pearson said.

"What are you doing out this time of the morning?" he had asked. Crawford told him he worked for people in Middleburg who had taken him to Washington.

"What are you doing coming back this way?"

"I stopped to see somebody," Crawford said. Crawford said he had been held up and his car stolen, Pearson said.

"Come on back to the filling station, I'll catch you a ride," Pearson said.

There was no telephone service in Gainesville that early — the exchange wouldn't be powered up until later in the day — so they couldn't call anyone. They turned on the lights at the filling station, set down and waited. Eventually a car came down the Haymarket Road, heading toward Warrenton. Pearson went out, stopped the car and asked the driver, Lemuel Gray, to give Crawford a ride.

"Was Crawford always respectful in his dealings with you?" Houston asked on cross-examination.

"Yes, sir," Pearson said.

"And always with all of the other white people around there?"

"So far as I know."

Gray confirmed in his testimony that he had given Crawford a ride as far as Warrenton.

Herman Butler worked at William Skanker's farm in The Plains and testified that he had seen Crawford there on Christmas day. Pat Harrison, who worked in the Larison Brothers tobacco manufacturers factory in Richmond and was a shoemaker at night, said he had known Crawford since before the Great War. Crawford had stayed at his house in Richmond for about a week or ten days in late December 1931, leaving sometime in early January, he said. A letter addressed to Charlie Smith arrived at Harrison's home the same day Crawford left, Harrison testified. The letter, which he said had money in it from DeNeal to pay Harrison for Crawford's room, was later taken by detectives. Again Houston objected about testimony referring to the letters, which had yet to be introduced into evidence. This time Galleher responded by producing the letter, reading it to the jury and entering it into evidence as commonwealth's exhibit number five. It was addressed to Charlie Smith, postmarked January 7, 1932, and signed "Birtie." There was laughter in the courtroom "and Crawford appeared highly amused" as Galleher read the letter aloud, according to the *Washington Star*.

My Dear Little Dolings

I am tryin to get my self to getter to write you jest a few line to let you hear from me I am not at all well in health or mine I have been jest all to pieces sence I have been parlin from I jest can not do any thing at all I do hope you air getin a long all right I gess you had be gain to think that I had for getin you but I will never be able to do that I am glad to hear that you was staying with one of your old friend the children all send love to you I was so sorry to hear of your sister death was she the one was at Worenton Va well I find this old thing jest the same or worst have told all kind of lies about me and you [inelg] away to getter but that will be all right have not hear any one called your name but him and I told you that I would send you some money if I could I have not got any for myself he have not give me cent and I would ask this one to save his life I hope it will be so we can soon be together now write juest as soon as you can I will write more next time if it will so I could I would come down there right soon I am hope to hear from soon I have so much to do and all the time worry about you so you the best you can until I see I hope it wont be ling now I will write to you real soon be a good boy until I see you form one will all way love you.

B.A. Coleman, Deputy City Seargent in Lynchburg, was previously Seargent with the State Convict Road force. He had known Crawford since January 1926, when Crawford had served time at his camp. He was the guard Crawford had been credited with saving, earning him a commuted sentence from Governor Byrd in 1926. Coleman testified that he'd last seen Crawford January 8 or January 9, 1932, "approximately four or five days" before he heard of the murders and, in fact, days before the murders occurred. Crawford had shown up at Coleman's Lynchburg home, where he got lunch and they talked about people they both knew in Middleburg. Coleman loaned Crawford $4 for bus fare to Richmond. Crawford, who was wearing his chauffeur's uniform, gave him a watch as security. Coleman still had the watch, which he displayed in the courtroom. He had replaced the original strap, which he said looked like it was meant to be worn by a woman.

Coleman also discounted Crawford's role in saving his life when he was attacked in 1929.

"I don't know as he saved my life," he said under cross-examination by Houston. "...He carried me from the camp up to the doctor's ... I think he tied a towel around my head and that one of the doctors said afterwards it might have had some tendency to save my life. I don't know."

Herndon farmer Robert Hughes testified that he met two men on the road the Sunday evening before the murders. He had been on horseback going to see a friend in Herndon; they were both on foot. "Hey buddy, do you know a place where we can spend the night?" asked one of the men, who identified himself as George Crawford. Hughes told them that they might find a room with Hammond Nokes, who lived about a quarter mile down the road. They followed him there.

When they got there, Nokes answered the door. Three or four other men, including his nephew, Rastus Nokes, Joe Hill and Alfred "Jiggs" Hall, were also there. Hughes said he left Crawford and the other man there, but saw them walking up the road near his place a few miles away the next day.

Hammond "Annie" Nokes had a colorful handkerchief protruding from his left cuff when he was called to the stand to testify. He was "a home recluse and ex–war veteran who has masqueraded as a woman since the war," according to the *Afro-American*. He worked in a laundry, drove a big car and, on the day of his testimony, wore a "red Clara Bow wig over a dark brown face from which protruded a closely-cropped beard. 'She' talks in a husky masculine voice, wears a green gown, beads, silk hose and women's galoshes, smiles coyly at the men in the courtroom.

"Her bosom and hips were padded *à la* Mae West. Sometimes the breast pads fall down to her stomach. Court authorities compel her to use the male restrooms in spite of feminine attire."

Nokes testified that he had fixed something to eat for Crawford and a second, taller man when they came to his door, but paid little attention to them. He did not hear about the murders until Adrian had him come to Leesburg several days later.

Rastus Nokes testified that two men had come to the Herndon home together that night, but could only describe one — Crawford. The two left Nokes' house before 9 a.m. Monday, saying that they were going to Middleburg. He said that he and Joe Hill had been at the garage, putting a wheel hub on a car, when Crawford came out of the house, asked for the Nokes' address, wrote it down in a small notebook, said goodbye and left with his partner. "He said he was going to send Hammond some money for the breakfast he had," Nokes testified.

Despite the significance of the testimony delivered by Hammond and Rastus Nokes, both Houston and Galleher seemed preoccupied by Hammond's sexuality.

"Is Hammond Nokes your aunt or your uncle?" Houston asked Rastus.

"Aunt," Rastus said.

"Your aunt?"

"Yes."

"I see."

There were titters in the courtroom as Galleher continued with a similar line of questions.

"Do you know whether Hammond Nokes is a man or a woman? Do you know of your own knowledge?"

"I don't know," Rastus said.

"You don't know?"

"No."

"Has he ever been regarded down there as a man wearing women's clothes?" Galleher asked.

"What is that?"

"Have you heard persons speaking of him as a man in women's clothing?"

"Yes, I heard people speak of it."

"You heard that spoken about it?"

"Yes, sir," Nokes said.

"Was that discussed when George Crawford stayed there?"

"No, sir," Nokes said.

A series of prosecution witnesses testified that they'd seen Crawford in the days before the murders, making his way ever closer to Middleburg. Most said that he had been traveling with another man. Few of them were cross-examined by Houston.

Elijah Gray, a horse trainer in Middleburg, said he had seen Crawford outside DeNeal's house on Christmas Eve, the night liquor had been stolen from the Ilsley manor house. "He jumped over the fence. He acted funny ... I jumped out of the car. He tells me he was George Crawford ... he tells me he was trying to get Bertie DeNeal's attention. He asked me if I would go into the house and tell her to come out, but I wouldn't do it. Then he tried to sell me a bottle of whiskey. I don't remember whether it was a quart or a pint that he wanted to sell. I told him I didn't drink.

"He wanted to borrow a dollar from me. I didn't have the money to spare."

Oscar L. Kitts said that he had seen Crawford in front of the Sanitary Grocery Company in Middleburg between 10 and 11 p.m. on January 12, just hours before Ilsley and Buckner were killed. "He acted like he was sort of afraid. He slipped around and dodged in between the Middleburg New York Café and Mr. Preston's garage and went in an alley." On cross examination, Houston was able to point out that Kitts hadn't come forward with his testimony until just three weeks prior to the Leesburg trial, nearly two years after the murders.

Prosecution witness J.H. Taylor, a handwriting and fingerprint expert "in charge of the Navy Identification Office, Navy Department," testified. At 9 a.m. just the day before he testified, Galleher's office had given Taylor several writing examples, including the note found in Ilsley's car and addressed to "Mr. Noke, Box 87, Herndon Village."

"I am to the conclusion that they are all written by the same person," he said.

Prosecution witness Ezra M.W. Costs was a watchman at the Colliflower Coal Company. His dog "made a fuss" sometime between 4 and 5 a.m. the morning of the murders when a Ford sedan with Virginia tags pulled into the coal yard on the Virginia side of the Highway Bridge. Two black men, one shorter than the other, got out of the car and walked up on to the bridge. They passed within 20 feet of him, Costs testified, and he could see them clearly by the electric lights in the coal yard. The shorter man, who had "a peculiar walk," had been driving, he said. Costs reported the car to authorities the next day, after hearing about the murders.

Finally, the prosecution recalled DeNeal to the stand.

Wray handed her a letter that she said she had written to Crawford while he was in Richmond.

"Why did you address him as Charles Smith in Richmond, Bertie?"

"That is what he told me to put on," DeNeal said quietly.

"Speak a little louder, please," McLemore told her.

"That is the way he handled the address, and that is the way I sent it," DeNeal said.

"Did he request you to address the letter like that?" Wray asked her.

"Yes sir, that is the way he told me to address it."

Wray introduced into evidence two other letters that had been found in the coat Crawford had sent to DeNeal. They were signed "Charles Smith."

Wray asked DeNeal whose handwriting was on the notes. There was a long pause before DeNeal swallowed and said, faintly, "George Crawford."

Wray introduced another letter, this one addressed to DeNeal from Mrs. Ethel Lacy's clothing store in Greenwood Park in Boston.

> You know Mr. Smith the Man uster to Wash. My Window Why I saw him the other day he told me he was Work in Linn Mass But you could send his Mail to My Brother flat at
>
> 1066 tremont St
> Boston Mass–
>
> and he Would send it to him for he see him every day I have a job for you $15 dollar a week.

Also read into evidence was a letter sent to DeNeal from "Chairl Smith," at the Tremont Street address on March 20, 1931.

My dear Berter just a line from the one that love you so I am Worry to deth a bout you truly hope this leeter Will find you Well and also the children I have a nice coat for you I will send it in a few days I would like to know When his you coming Back to me I have every thing Ready for you rite and send me all the news when you rite send your mail to 1066 tremont St in Boston But I am not work in Boston at all I am work in Linny Mass Plese don't say anything a bout me are mencher any thing a bout me at all just rite Chairl Smith and I will get it and if anyboyd want to know who Chairl Smith just tell them any thing if you want to come Why let me know at once I will send you the money and allsorkies Mildred own fer me. I am getting a longe find you Rember Mrs. Rich the lady took use to chuch that night my she died last Wenday Give my best love and Regard to the children honny I miss you ever so much Rite at once and let me know his you coming to me Ruth Reed send Best love to you and told me to tell you to come back home. Well that all the news from you Belove one

On the reverse side of the letter was a separate note:

Mrs Mary fraction Lost here sister the other day. You know who I am talke a bout She live at 806 Sferinge St.

It had been a busy morning. At 12:50 p.m., McLemore recessed court for lunch until 2 p.m.

Crawford was chewing a toothpick when he returned to the courtroom that afternoon. DeNeal once again returned to the stand, this time to be cross-examined by Houston.

She said she and Crawford had become friendly after she went to work for Holt, and when they went to Boston they lived as man and wife. "I went away because I wanted to get a job to work," she said. "I could not get no work around here ... when I went I paid my own way."

"Did you have your husband's consent to go away?" Houston asked.

"No sir, I did not."

She had decided to leave Boston after one of her daughters had written to her, asking her to come back home. She had no money for the trip, but was able to get a train ticket through some sort of public assistance, and her husband sent her $12. She gave some of the money to Crawford and they each bought a train ticket to Washington.

She said the Christmas Day note from Crawford was brought to her by an acquaintance named Tootie Williams—not the mysterious Charlie Johnson. Despite having left the state with Crawford—a violation of the Mann Act—and staying in touch with him for months after, she had managed to keep him from coming between her and her husband.

"My husband didn't know anything about it," she testified.

"You mean your husband didn't know you were off with Crawford?" Houston asked.

"No sir, he did not."

"You kept it from your husband?"

"Sure," DeNeal said.

When called to testify, D.C. Sands brought with him to the witness chair a bootjack that he said was the same one he had seen in Ilsley's bedroom, and which some investigators believed to be the murder weapon.

"Did you see this bootjack while it was in the room?" Galleher asked him on the stand.

"Yes sir," Sands answered.

"Was it just as it is now?"

"It had more blood at that time that it has now ... stains on the inside there that I think are blood." Sands said the bootjack and all the contents of the cottage had been taken to the manor house in the days after the murders. "That is where I got the bootjack," he said. John Boeing would testify that he had given the bootjack to Sands days after the murders, when he and his wife had found it while sorting through Agnes's things.

Houston wanted clarification — was the prosecution introducing the bootjack into evidence as the murder weapon?

"If the prosecution is going to claim that this is the death weapon, I am perfectly willing to let it go in," Houston said. "If they do not, I do not know what the materiality of it is ... is it introduced as the death weapon upon the basis of Doctor Gibson? If so, I am perfectly willing for it to go in."

The prosecution team wanted it introduced into evidence, but was not prepared to call it the murder weapon, Conner said.

"The reason we brought it mainly is because the eminent counsel for the defense indicated at one time to the Commonwealth that it was the remote inference — not a charge or implication — that the Commonwealth might be concealing something, which the bootjack was referred to by Doctor Gibson.

"It seems that for some reason or other the authorities in charge overlooked this implement that was in the room of the death chamber," Conner said. "We will introduce it for the information of the jury." But Houston wasn't prepared to let anything be entered into evidence under such vague circumstances.

"I submit that if they are going to bring in anything that might have been used as the weapon, you could bring in lamps, golf sticks and so forth," Houston said. "The only question I want to know is, what is it introduced as? Is it introduced for the purpose of showing the means or is it not?"

"It is certainly for the purpose of showing the possibility," Conner said.

"I think the purpose of introducing it is qualified," McLemore said. "Something else may or may not have been used. It is for the jury to determine whether, from the evidence in the case, it was used."

Houston entered an exception. "At the present time I do not think it is sufficiently traced to be allowed into evidence," he said. McLemore overruled the motion.

"I will leave it to the jury."

Galleher wanted to recall Paul Boeing to the stand to identify the watch Coleman had said Crawford had given to him, to bolster all of the testimony indicating that Crawford had been near Middleburg when the murders were committed, but Houston objected. "The question is not whether he was in Middleburg in December. The question is whether he is the person guilty of the Ilsley charge on January 12," Houston said. McLemore agreed with Houston, and Boeing was excused.

"I can't see, gentlemen, how that is material evidence in this case. It can have only one effect, and that would be prejudicial," McLemore said.

But Galleher's parade of witnesses continued through the day. Robert Hutchins, a special investigator for the federal Bureau of Narcotics, said Crawford was using the alias William Harris when they had met at Iona Dougherty's boarding house on North Hampton Street in Boston on October 15, 1932. Hutchins testified that Crawford and another man, James Proctor, came to see Dougherty that day. They got into an argument over money that Crawford claimed Dougherty owed him. Crawford said he would kill Dougherty "and got up and backed away from the table with his hands shoved in his pockets," Hutchins said.

"He told her he would kill her. He said that he had killed two white women in the state of Virginia, but he didn't state where. He knew that he had killed a negro woman in Massachusetts," Hutchins testified.

Crawford and Proctor returned to the boarding house on October 20, and the same argument flared up. This time, Dougherty's daughter went to call the police. Hutchins and Proctor physically pulled Crawford out of the house and into the street, where Crawford again boasted about previous murders, Hutchins said.

"He made a statement about two white women killed in the state of Virginia and the woman in Massachusetts ... after we got in the street he mentioned a name of Crawford," Hutchins said. "He said, 'read about me. It is Crawford.' We knew him by the name of Harris." At the time, Hutchins was not aware of the Middleburg murders, he said, but one day Dougherty showed him Crawford's picture in a newspaper article about the search for Ilsley's killer.

"She said 'here is this man Harris, which had a room at my house. He is a bad man. His name is George Crawford.'"

On cross-examination, Houston delved into Hutchins background, honing in on his military service. Hutchins said he had been a Captain in Company A of the 367th Infantry, 92nd Division, at Fort Benjamin Harrison, Indiana, in 1917 and had served with the 367th, an African American company, throughout World War I.

Detective Murphy testified that he had found Crawford's note to Nokes between the seats of Ilsley's car when he searched it at the Colliflower Coal Yard on the evening of January 13. There had been plenty of blood at the scene, but none was found in the car, he said.

"I think Mrs. Ilsley put up a terrible battle for her life," Murphy said. Houston asked if he thought the killer would have had blood on his clothes.

"I can answer that question but I don't want to deal into it too long. I might state this but, evidently — I don't know how to prove it — the parties that committed this crime did wash their hands in the sink in one of the rooms later, in my judgment."

With Galleher's witness list nearly exhausted, McLemore had the jury taken out of the courtroom while the NAACP and Commonwealth argued the admissibility of the Boston confession statement.

Inmates at the Charles Street jail in Boston only had to see those people they agreed to see, according to the testimony of James Morris, a deputy sheriff at the jail. Crawford had agreed to see Galleher, he said. The interview did not take place in Crawford's cell, but in a special, soundproof room made of glass on the second floor of the jail. A guard had stayed outside the room during the interview. At some point, Galleher had asked Morris, who was a notary public, to come into the room to administer the oath to Crawford. Stenographer Harold Kraus was also in the room. Morris had asked Crawford if he was making his statement of his own free will; Crawford said he was. Morris left the room after administering the oath and wasn't there to hear the actual confession, but he was back the next morning when Galleher brought a copy of the confession for Crawford to sign.

"Well, do you want to talk with him?" Morris had asked Crawford in his jail cell.

"I am not going to talk with him and not sign it," Crawford said.

According to Kraus, Galleher "positively" did not threaten Crawford or offer him inducement to confess. "Just about the time he was to make the confession, he broke out in tears." Everything that had been said in the room was in the transcript, Kraus said — there were no breaks not indicated in the transcript. Crawford had gone from repeated denials to a complete confession with no more inducement than Galleher's prodding, as reflected in the printed transcript.

It was late, a few minutes after 5 p.m., but the prosecution still had two more witnesses. The roads were treacherous and it was already dark outside of the courtroom.

"I understand that a car is coming in which we can go back home," Houston said. "I would not like to be marooned here." McLemore agreed to proceed another 30 minutes.

Edward J. Keating, a Lieutenant in Boston's Detective Bureau in Boston, said that he and Galleher had met with Crawford at the Charles Street jail at 3:30 p.m., after Galleher had obtained Crawford's confession statement. Crawford told them that Charlie Johnson lived at 1616 Third Street in Washington — the home of Lessie Hedgepath. Galleher, thinking Crawford was bluffing and hoping to break Crawford down, had told him no such address existed.

Court was adjourned at 5:30 p.m.

At 10:15 p.m., after a day of damning testimony and hours driving across Virginia's dark, icy roads, White sat down to write a letter to Wilkins.

> We're just back after another long, grueling day — the worst yet for the defense. It was mighty tense today — you could almost feel the electric waves.
> Berdie de Neal's drab story ... will put C. in the electric chair, if he goes there. She told Ralph Mathews [a reporter for Baltimore's *Afro-American* newspaper] today, though, that she still loved C....
> Crawford goes on stand tomorrow (Friday). Case will probably end Saturday. Verdict will probably be "guilty."

On Friday morning, the roads were again an icy hazard. White was up at 6 a.m. to catch a 7:40 a.m. train at Roslyn. Houston and the rest of the NAACP lawyers risked the trip to Leesburg by car. At one point their vehicle slid into a telephone pole.

At 10 a.m., with the jury still out of the room, Galleher took the stand to continue the hearing on the admissibility of the confession. He testified that he had sat opposite Crawford in the interview room at the Charles Street jail, and had told him that Coleman had said nice things about him. The attorney said he had slipped a newspaper clipping with a photograph of the cottage and Ilsley onto the table and left it there while he questioned Crawford. After about 30 minutes, he saw a change in Crawford: "About the time when I asked him if he remembered the cottage — if he knew the cottage — I at once observed a very changed expression upon his face ... his manner — and again, when I made the statement about Mr. Coleman, about what Mr. Coleman thought of him — was when I saw tears coming to his eyes. He was crying when I concluded my statement there and where the break is in his statement."

Houston moved to exclude the confession from evidence "upon clear grounds of inducement by threat or hope of reward." But Wray argued that "under the law this confession was voluntarily the expression of a free and untrammeled mind and ... the evidence overwhelmingly supports this point."

But despite the fact that Crawford had never signed the document and denied even having made the statement, McLemore allowed the confession to be entered into evidence.

"I think some of the statements made to the accused by Mr. Galleher were unhappy; they were capable of a double construction," McLemore said. "However, I have a very abiding conviction, in my own mind from reading the confession, that this man was not forced to tell this story."

The jury was brought into the courtroom. Morris, Kraus, Keating and

Galleher were called again and repeated their testimony, and the confession was read into the record. And, with that, Crawford's fate seemed to be sealed.

After a break for lunch, with Houston preparing to call witnesses for the defense and with the overflow audience crowding into the courtroom, McLemore again called for them all to restrain their emotions.

> We want all of you to come in and listen. I must insist that if your are coming in you keep quiet and not move around back and forth and move in and out. Those of you who cannot stay had better move out now, because you disturb our proceedings when you get up to go out, and you also disturb other people.
> The first consideration is the orderly conduct in this court. I am sure that you can aid us in this consideration. If these people here are going to stand, I do not object, provided they are going to be quiet and not talk to one another....
> I am very impressed with the conservativeness displayed by you people, both white and colored. You have done splendidly and I am sure your are going, if anything, to magnify that opinion of mine rather than dispense it.

The NAACP's defense took little time. Realizing that Crawford would be found guilty — and, in fact, *was* guilty — they were more interested in dodging a death sentence, and so painted a portrait of Crawford as a loyal, "respectful" black man who had accompanied, but had not assisted, the actual killer.

Several of the witnesses called by Houston brought into question the credibility of a single prosecution witness — Robert Hutchins, the narcotics agent who had said that Crawford boasted about killing two white women.

Victor Daly said that he had been in the 367th Infantry during World War I and said Hutchins had not been there. Lawrence Lee and Eugene Davidson provided very similar testimony. Conner objected, saying that impeaching that portion of Hutchins' testimony was pointless. "That is an entirely irrelevant, collateral matter," he said. Houston would later call Hutchins "one of the most contemptible persons" associated with the case, but was forced to agree with prosecutors that the only way to prove Hutchins' story false would be through a thorough search of War Department records, something none of them were prepared to postpone the case to pursue.

The defense rested its case before many in the courtroom thought it had truly begun. But White was insistent that the NAACP team had done the best job possible for Crawford.

"No four attorneys anywhere, of any color, could give a defendant any braver, more painstaking, more brilliant, or more scholarly defense than Messrs. Houston, Lovett, Ransom and Tyson," he told reporters when court adjourned. Privately, White was convinced that when the case was handed over to the jury the next morning, they would quickly find Crawford guilty and send him to the electric chair.

At 10 a.m. on Saturday, December 16, McLemore gave his final instructions to the jury, and then Galleher, Wray and Connor each in turn asked them to find Crawford guilty and sentence him to death.

"I realize, and I must tell you frankly, that it is not an easy thing for me to ask of you, and I am sure it is not an easy thing for you to take life," Connor told the jury. "But, gentlemen of the jury, it is not an easy thing to permit an innocent life to be taken without justification or excuse, as one was taken in the murder in this county on that night ... anyone who had a part in planning or committing this crime of murdering this refined lady in the privacy of her own home is beyond any reformation."

For the defense, Ransom reviewed key pieces of testimony, which he said contained discrepancies and contradictory statements, went over the instructions McLemore had given the jury, and thanked the prosecution attorneys for their "utmost courtesy." He left it to Houston to deliver the defense team's plea for Crawford's life.

Houston walked a thin line, coming as close as he dared to conceding Crawford's guilt in his effort to persuade the jury not to hand down a death penalty.

Crawford was a "homeless, hungry dog caught in a web of circumstances and led into crime by a stronger mind," Houston told the jury. But "you have seen how respectful he is. He may have been a thief when he was on the convict gang, but he is not a killer. We all know that he is not a killer type." And, despite what Virginia's law might say about the relative guilt of those who work in concert in committing murder, "not everyone guilty of first degree murder deserves the same penalty. There's a distinction between Crawford and the actual killer."

If they were to send Crawford to the electric chair, Houston told the jurors, they would kill with him any chance of tracking down the man who had actually murdered Agnes Boeing Ilsley.

"If you ever hope to catch Charlie Johnson and put him in the chair for this dastardly crime, there is only one man who can help you do it," Houston said. "If you ever hope to catch the man who really is guilty, don't wipe out George Crawford. If you do wipe him out, Charlie Johnson is gone forever. Although there are two honest women lying in their graves, the law does not say that you must take an eye for an eye and a tooth for a tooth, regardless of the degree of guilt of the accused. I submit that if you find George Crawford guilty, this is not a case for the supreme penalty....

"You see, at this stage of the proceedings I am not admitting his guilt. My task is to argue in case you find him guilty. I say that in case you find him guilty — not with the idea of turning him loose — you should consider that Crawford would not have been a party to a crime of violence if he had known of it....

"If you send this man to his death, there is no one who can testify against Charlie Johnson ... the only man living who had the activities of Charlie Johnson burned into his mind so that he could never forget him until he dies is George Crawford."

Before handing the case over to the jury, McLemore blunted Houston's argument, telling them that under Virginia law murder during a burglary constituted a first-degree crime; that an accomplice in a felony was due the same punishment as the man who committed the felony. As for the confession — which had been admitted into evidence during the trial but had never been signed by Crawford — jurors should give it just so much weight as they saw fit, McLemore said.

The jury retired to debate Crawford's fate shortly before 2 p.m.

With the benches still packed, Galleher and his prosecution team still seated at their table, McLemore still in his seat and all of the reporters still scratching out their notes, Houston stood to address the court. It was an exercise in courtesy, but it was also an attempt to reinforce the image of both Crawford and his NAACP defense team as respectful, respectable citizens, and a last chance to sway opinion about the future of African Americans in the Southern legal system.

"May I say that my associates and I, singly and in groups, have gone through every foot of this county at night and day, and we have yet to experience the first discourtesy," Houston said.

He was trying to exact as much good will as possible in preparation for the sentencing that would come after the inevitable guilty verdict, but he continued to plea for the placement of African Americans on Loudoun County juries.

"We can only hope to rise by convincing you that we are entitled to and are able to share in your institutions without endangering them ... when we settle questions like this, we do not want them settled as to a particular case ... ultimately, questions like this, to be satisfactorily settled, must rest on the acceptance of the community.

"We can not expect a change overnight. But if the question is treated with sincerity by both sides, we shall progress. We can not hope to rise by tearing down your institutions, we can only hope to convince you that we are entitled to share in them."

Houston's speech seemed to warm McLemore's heart, and he, too, addressed the open court.

"I came expecting to find instances of race prejudice," McLemore said. "But it never has been my privilege to try a contested case of this sort where the temper in the courtroom has been as splendid as it has been here. The people have been dignified and reserved. This case has been an oasis in the desert.

"It is most refreshing, gentlemen, and I say at the close of this case that I leave with the feeling that I have been caught with a new vision of what can be and what ought to be the atmosphere of every criminal trial."

McLemore even complemented the reporters who had covered the case.

He had met some of them socially at the Leesburg Inn where he and they had stayed during the trial.

At 3:45 p.m., the jury returned. The foreman, Hess, who had written the decision on a half sheet of yellow legal paper, handed the verdict to Russell. McLemore issued a final plea for calm in the courtroom.

"I just want to say to this assembly that I do not want demonstrations of approval or disapproval when the verdict is rendered. You would undo all of the things that I have said and believe about you if you forget yourselves, so I charge you to receive it in perfect quiet."

Crawford was told to stand. McLemore asked him if he wanted to say anything before hearing the verdict.

"No sir, I haven't anything to say," Crawford said.

Russell read the verdict.

"We the jury in the case of the Commonwealth of Virginia versus one George Crawford find the defendant guilty — as charged in the indictment — and fix his punishment as confinement in the penitentiary for the term of his natural life."

Three of the jurors — which three was never clear — had voted for the death penalty on the first ballot; nine voted for life in prison. The vote stayed the same on a second vote, and on a third. By the fourth ballot, the three hardliners had changed their minds.

McLemore formally sentenced Crawford as the jury recommended.

Houston entered motions to set aside the verdict and to send the case to a second trial. McLemore denied both motions. But Houston had successfully shepherded Crawford past the death chamber, a feat no one had imagined possible just a week earlier.

"Defense attorneys announced they would not appeal," Frank Getty reported in the *Washington Post*. "Actually, they were overjoyed." Houston and the other NAACP attorneys shook Crawford's hand, and the Virginia State Police guards escorted him from the courtroom.

"If there was any dissatisfaction, it was not voiced by the citizens who struggled to the exits to see the prisoner whisked away to jail at Alexandria and thence to Richmond," Getty wrote.

ELEVEN

Aftermath

Houston had understood from the beginning the significance of the Crawford trial, before even White had grasped it.

Years later, Houston would say the trial had been important for several reasons. It had been the first instance of an all-black legal team on a murder trial in Virginia, and had been an early link in the chain of NAACP legal challenges to institutionalized discrimination in the South. The NAACP's arguments in Leesburg against the exclusion of African Americans from juries had laid the groundwork for other challenges, which would bare fruit within months of the Crawford trial. More immediately, the NAACP defense team had kept Crawford from lynch mobs and the electric chair.

"We won it," Marshall would say. "If you got a Negro charged with killing a white person in Virginia and you got life imprisonment, then you've won. Normally they were hanging them in those days.[1]

The NAACP legal team had "demonstrated to the Virginia public that there are Negro lawyers in the country who can be courageous without being obsequious, lawyers who can make a fight without arousing racial antagonisms," according to Richmond's *News-Leader*. "That of itself gave the trial a certain educational value."

"It was some achievement to save Crawford's life when it was proven beyond a shadow of a doubt that he was guilty and that the confession he had made in Boston, before he entered the case, and which he then repudiated, was never the less a true confession," NAACP Field Secretary William Pickens wrote to the Associated Negro Press. The Scottsboro Boys case dragged on with no end in sight and, according to Pickens, the ILD was to blame. If the ILD had been in charge of Crawford's case, he wouldn't have been so fortunate, he said.

"If the Communist brethren had had the case, he would have got the chair, beyond a doubt ... take note: NAACP methods, with colored lawyers at that, saved a colored man who was clearly guilty, although the Communists with their methods seem unable to save nine Negroes, with the use of white lawyers who are supposed to have a better break with the courts, and although the nine Negroes are known by all the world to be innocent."

With the verdict and Crawford's sentence officially recorded, White spoke openly of Crawford's guilt.

"We were, of course, shocked to find shortly before going to trial that Crawford had not told us the truth," he told Freeman. "In a sense, however, the fact of his guilt under the law as an accomplice makes Virginia's assurance of a fair trial all the more significant ... it is probable that Dean Houston and I will shortly go to Richmond with Mr. Galleher to talk with Crawford to induce him if possible to aid in the apprehension of Johnson."[2]

White told Alexander Ector Orr Munsell, a Baltimore philanthropist who had helped finance Crawford's defense, that "an extraordinary thing happened when the prosecution opened its case by pointing out to the jury that every prisoner is innocent until proved beyond a shadow of a doubt to be guilty. In the speech of not one of the three prosecutors was there a single mention of race nor appeal to race prejudice:

> All in all, in the broader sense, it was more effective, in that Crawford was proved to be guilty, not of the actual murder but of having gone to the house with the murderer to commit a robbery. We found that he had not played fair with us and had not given us the full facts. This makes the life sentence instead of the death penalty all the more remarkable. Virginia certainly deserves credit in that here was a case of a man under the law guilty of the brutal murder of two white women, defended in the South by colored counsel and the atmosphere of tenseness and hostility at the beginning of the trial transformed by the attitude of the judge, the prosecution and of defense counsel into being almost a "love feast" by the time the jury's verdict was brought in.[3]

"The weight of conservative public opinion in the county supports the verdict," the *Loudoun Times-Mirror* said in its December 21 editorial. "In the light of the evidence and the instructions of the court, the jury returned what was, under all the circumstances, a proper verdict."

The Nation, too, saw Crawford's trial as a step forward for southern jurisprudence. It had been "marked by moderation and restraint on the part of the community, impartiality on the part of the presiding judge, and extremely able pleading by defense counsel," *The Nation* said. McLemore had ignored Houston's argument against all-white juries, "but in other parts of Virginia Negroes are actually serving on juries. In Hanover County Circuit Court, in that state, Judge Frederick W. Coleman lately imposed a $10 fine for contempt on a white farmer who refused to sit on a grand jury with a Negro. In Norfolk recently a jury of eleven white men served with a Negro foreman, and in Tennessee, North Carolina, and Kentucky Negroes are being included on jury panels, both for grand and petit juries."

By the middle of December, Houston had notified the court that Crawford was prepared to plead guilty for his part in Buckner's death if Virginia would agree not to call for the death penalty in that case. As part of the plea deal, Houston said he would drop plans to appeal the verdict in the Ilsley case based on the absence of African Americans in the venire, grand jury and petit jury, and said the NAACP team would do what it could to help the state track down Charley Johnson.

Days later, Galleher's up and coming status in the Democratic party and the notoriety he had achieved through the Crawford case earned him an appointment as Special Assistant Attorney General of the United States.

Perhaps out of sympathy for their loss, perhaps hoping to convert philosophical opponents, or perhaps simply in an effort to cash in on some of the wealthy contacts made during the Crawford case, White in early January sent NAACP literature to John and Paul Boeing and to Winifred Maddux. White wrote in a letter to Maddux:

> I had hoped I would have opportunity to meet and talk with you about the work of the Association which defended George Crawford in the recent trial at Leesburg. I wanted you to know something of the reasons why we were defending Crawford. It was in order to assure a fair trial incidentally, but primarily it was to raise once more the question of the constitutional right of Negroes to serve on grand and petit juries.
>
> Our activity on the jury issue in this case was responsible for the cities of Richmond, Norfolk, Fredericksburg and Alexandria, Virginia, calling Negroes for jury service for the first time (in some of these cities) in thirty years. We believe that the jury issue as raised in the Crawford case influenced the calling of Negroes for service in at least four other states.

But there were signs of dissension within the NAACP's ranks. At the annual NAACP business meeting in January, White's boast that Houston and the NAACP defense team had won a great victory was questioned by Martha Gruening, who, working in concert with Helen Boardman, repeated her criticisms in letters she began firing off to White and Houston.

"Because I am so closely connected and so deeply interested in the Crawford case, I am now frequently asked to explain the apparent failure of the defense," Boardman wrote in a January 15 letter to White. "As I have never understood the situation myself I am unable to make an adequate reply. It is extremely important that the facts in this case should be made quite clear. It is not merely the enemies but the friends of the Association that are questioning it and it is their support that is at stake."

She questioned the NAACP's statement that Crawford had lied to the legal team. She questioned the decision not to put on the stand some of the defense witnesses who had testified at the extradition hearing in Boston. She questioned the decision not to introduce Crawford's alibi defense at the murder trial. She questioned the credibility of DeNeal's testimony. She questioned Seaton's whereabouts and the defense's inability to keep Crawford's confession from being entered into evidence.

"Do you feel now that it was a mistake for us to defend Crawford?" she asked.

On January 18, White responded. Crawford had "fully and freely confessed" to Houston that everything in the confession was true, White said.

"I most certainly do not feel that it was a mistake for us to defend Crawford. As a matter of fact, I think the immediate results and those in the future will be all the sweeter because of the fact that there is no doubt of Crawford's guilt and to the further circumstance that the way in which the case was handled throughout gained important and far-reaching new ground."[4]

Boardman had not attended the Leesburg trial, but was still assigned by *The Crisis* to write a summarizing article. She sent a second copy of her January 15 letter to White and asked him in a handwritten note to again answer her questions. Her intent, she said, was to "write an article that will make the whole situation clear."

White wrote back to her to say he had sent her request on to Houston. "I am sure I don't know just what more I can say which will clear up the matter of the Crawford case in your mind."

On Thursday, January 25, from his office at Howard, Houston wrote to Russell about a recent visit he had made to Crawford's jail cell. "He is very anxious for you to have him transferred from the Henrico County Jail to the penitentiary. Inasmuch as we are not going to appeal the Ilsley case, and the time to file the bill of exceptions has expired, we will appreciate it if you will see that Crawford is transferred as soon as possible." Russell forwarded the note on to McLemore, asking him to sign an order for Crawford's transfer.

That same day in Princess Anne, Maryland, the Somerset County Grand Jury ended its special session without issuing any indictments in the lynching of George Armwood. The four men who had been arrested by Maryland National Guardsmen, five others who had been named as suspects in the case and every other member of the mob that had participated in Armwood's murder remained free.

On February 10, two days before his trial for Buckner's murder was due to start, Norfolk's African American newspaper, the *Journal and Guide*, published an article in which Crawford was quoted calling the charges against him "a frame-up." According to the *Journal and Guide* article, Crawford had told reporters during a jail cell interview that Galleher had fabricated the Boston confession and jailers had roughed him up in an effort to get him to sign the statement. Crawford also said he had never heard of Charlie Johnson, according to the *Journal and Guide*, and said Houston should have called the Boston witnesses to testify that he had been in Massachusetts when Ilsley was killed.

"George Crawford, principal in the celebrated case bearing his name, is not satisfied with the way his trial was conducted in Leesburg in December," the newspaper declared. He "chiefly objects to the failure of defense attorneys to call witnesses to his trial for murder, who had testified in his extradition hearing in Boston, establishing an alibi that he was not in Virginia at the time Mrs. Agnes Boeing Ilsley and her white maid, Mrs. Nina Buckner, were slain on the former's country estate.

"He regrets exceedingly that Butler R. Wilson, Boston attorney, was not present at Leesburg to offer testimony which would have benefited the defense in Crawford's opinion.

"He charges that he was manhandled because he refused to sign a confession at the insistence of Commonwealth Attorney John Galleher, of Loudoun County, Va.

"He does not think his trial was fair.

"He denies any guilt in connection with the two murders." And, in complete contradiction of the very theory that had convinced the Leesburg jury to set aside a death penalty, the *Journal and Guide* said Crawford "denies that he knows any man named Charlie Johnson, cited at this trial as the real slayer, whose arrest and conviction could never be effected if Crawford were put to death in the electric chair."

Judge Alexander, now returned to the bench in Leesburg, confronted Crawford with the *Journal and Guide* article in court on February 12. Crawford had moved himself back to within a step of the electric chair.

Crawford stood beside Houston as Alexander opened the proceedings in a nearly empty courtroom. But Houston, frustrated by Crawford's apparent attempt to torpedo his own case, had told Crawford he would have to explain the *Journal and Guide* interview to Alexander himself.

"Crawford, you are brought up here on this indictment charging you with the murder of Mrs. Mina Buckner, which you were formally arraigned upon and plead not guilty," Alexander said. "I am informed that you want to withdraw that plea and enter a plea of guilty. Is that correct?"

"Yes, sir," Crawford said.

"Now, in connection with that, there has been brought to my attention a newspaper interview published in the Norfolk *Journal and Guide*, on the tenth of February, in Norfolk, Virginia. Now this court doesn't want it to be said that any man that is brought here hasn't had, in every respect, a fair trial. This interview quotes you as saying that you did not have a fair trial on the Ilsley indictment, and that you could produce testimony, which would have cleared you of that charge, because you were not allowed to do so by your counsel."

"You mean the other charge?" Crawford asked.

"Yes, the Ilsley indictment," Alexander said. Crawford answered:

Those fellows came there to see me, but I did not talk with them about my case. They just came there and discussed it and started asking me how I come out in the trial. I asked who they were, and some of the fellows said that they were newspaper men. I didn't know them. They asked me if I thought I had a fair trial and I said that I left everything up to my lawyer. I asked them why they had come there and they still stayed a pretty good distance and when they had gone I asked who they was, and some of the other fellows told me they were newspaper men. I didn't know them.

"What the Court wants to know is whether or not your want to plead guilty or be put on trial," Alexander said.

"Yes sir. I plead guilty. I don't care to be put on trial."

"You understand that there has been no pressure brought to bear upon you, and that you are entitled to be tried if you want to be tried, and that I am here to see that you get your rights."

"No sir, I don't care to be tried," Crawford said. Houston suspected that Crawford had said the things reported by the *Journal and Guide*, but was satisfied that he had recanted thoroughly enough to satisfy Alexander.

"Your honor, may I say here that the motive in having him plead guilty is that he assist in the apprehension of Charlie Johnson, who actually committed the murder," Houston said. "In this article in the newspaper it is stated that he denies having known Charlie Johnson. Your honor, I would like for you to ask him if that fact is true.... There may or may not be a man by the name of Charlie Johnson, but there was another man, and he can identify this man and give any other assistance possible."

"This newspaper quotes you as saying that you do not know any man by the name of Charlie Johnson.... Did you make any such statement?" Alexander asked Crawford.

"No, sir."

"Do you know this man?"

"Yes sir. I know him, or if I saw his picture, I would know him."

"Mr. Galleher, what is the Commonwealth's recommendation?" Alexander asked.

"The recommendation of the Commonwealth is that he be imprisoned for the balance of his natural life, on this indictment, charging him with the murder of Mrs. Mina Buckner," Galleher said.

"Crawford, the court wants it distinctly understood that in accordance to that suggestion it does not think that punishment is adequate in this case," Alexander said. "On the other hand, I am going to adopt that suggestion because of the fact that if you are put to death, Johnson can never be convicted. You understand that, do you?"

"Yes, sir."

"And further, upon the promise that you are willing to assist the commonwealth in every way that you can in the apprehension of this man, Charlie Johnson."

"Yes, sir."

"Have you anything to say before I sentence you?"

"No, sir."

"The judgment of the court on the plea of guilty on the indictment charging you with the murder of Mrs. Mina Buckner, is that you are to be taken from this courtroom to the state penitentiary in Richmond, and there to be confined for the balance of your natural life," Alexander said.

"I wish your honor please would make it clear that it is upon his own responsibility and free will that he has entered this plea of guilty," Houston said.

"I think the record will clearly show all of that, but in order that there will be no misunderstanding, I am asking you now: is this done of your own free will and accord?" Alexander asked Crawford.

"Yes, sir."

That afternoon, Houston sat down to respond to the *Journal and Guide*'s article. By now he had lost patience with his critics. To the *Journal and Guide*, he laid out the details of the case and told them to "keep the facts straight." He had confronted Crawford with their article before entering the courtroom for the Buckner hearing, Houston wrote to the newspaper. "I told him that under the circumstances I would not take the responsibility of pleading him and he must make his own plea." He wrote to White that Boardman needed to "get herself straight." She had bypassed several important facts brought to light at the Leesburg trial, he said.

"Neighborhood gossip is one thing, and the record of the trial itself is another," Houston said.

And Houston had also lost patience with Crawford, who he felt could not be trusted to tell the truth, though he was not ready to completely wash his hands of him. In a letter sent to Crawford at the state penitentiary, Houston enclosed a copy of his letter to the *Journal and Guide* and offered to stay in touch. "When I come to Richmond again I will come in to see you," he told Crawford. He also advised Crawford to be more cautious about jailhouse interviews.

"You are free to talk to anybody you choose now. But if I were in your place I would not talk to anybody except an official of the State of Virginia. Talking to anybody and everybody cannot help you, and may do you a great deal of harm. It is true that your life is safe and that you cannot be put in the electric chair, but things can be made unpleasant for you if you get involved in a lot of lies."

White was convinced that the *Journal and Guide* article was a fabrication and that the ILD had had a hand in it. Statements attributed to Crawford sounded quite similar to ILD doctrine, he thought. He wrote to *Journal and Guide* editor Tom Young, asking who from the newspaper had been in contact with Crawford.

According to Young, the article "was no hoax." The ILD had had no hand in the story, he said. Reporters Josephus Simpson and John D. Bogle had talked with Crawford and written "a good story, and we knew that it would make interesting reading matter ... of course, we rather suspected that Crawford was telling some lies because he told you some and he told his lawyers some, and as for his repudiation of the interview, that is no less astonishing than his repudiation of the confession he made in Boston."[5]

"We are utterly amazed and disgusted at the *Norfolk Journal and Guide*'s story on Crawford," White told Houston. "What could possibly have induced him to make such a statement in the light of the facts? Do you think someone from the ILD has either gotten in to see him or written him?"[6]

But the *Journal and Guide*'s story and displeasure with Houston and White's handling of the Crawford case added to a growing rift within NAACP leadership. Financial problems, strategic and philosophic disagreements, infighting and office politics threatened to splinter the NAACP.

The split had been evident for some time. In October 1933, when the NAACP had reconstituted its board of directors, NAACP co-founder and *Crisis* editor W.E.B. Du Bois had submitted a slate of candidates that included Gruening and other names that seemed designed to pressure White out of power. NAACP president Joel Spingarn turned down Du Bois' proposal to enlarge the board.

"The *Journal and Guide* stirred up the Crawford case but ran against a stone wall," *Crisis* managing editor George Streator wrote to editor-in-chief Du Bois. "Walter White's reaction was characteristic. He wrote the *Journal and Guide* that the whole thing was inspired by the ILD, and that the interview never took place. Needless to say, the maneuver was unsuccessful. He made a fool out of himself with Young, giving us another ally."

The Crisis was crippled by money problems and internal squabbles. Streator fought with printers and paper companies to get each issue bound and distributed; office workers resisted any changes he suggested and he saw Houston, White, Wilkins and Spingarn as enemies conspiring against himself and Du Bois. In the past, White and Du Bois had exchanged charges of wasteful spending.

"This Charley Houston seems to be as crooked as Walter White," Streator told Du Bois. The *Nation* had asked Gruening for a story about the Crawford case, "and they think that it is a clear sell-out," he said.[7]

"Theater Guild is producing a Scottsboro play which I am going to see Tuesday night. It pans the 'NAACP' and Walter. It is rated good. Damned good if it pans Walter," Streator told Du Bois.[8]

Streator continued his behind-the-scenes sniping at White in a February 28 letter to Du Bois. "Martha Gruening called to say that interesting developments in [the] Crawford case will make it hot for Walter to explain. It seems that they are quiet now, and mad as hell. Walter brushed by yesterday without speaking, and Walter's boy Roy has not been over this week. Oh well."

But Streator pulled up short of exposing *The Crisis* to the full glare of the lingering Crawford controversy. "Am withdrawing Crawford editorial on advice of [Howard professor Abe] Harris," he said in a telegram to Du Bois on April 9.

Harris had warned that the editorial "would make an enemy of [fellow Howard professor] Sterling Brown, who admires Houston," Streator explained in a letter two days later.

But the May issue of *The Crisis* did include an opinion piece by Boston lawyer Richard Hale, who said, among other things, that Crawford's extradition differed from Fugitive Slave Law cases only in that it was "lily-white" grand juries that now certified returning African Americans to southern states. And in the same issue, Du Bois fired his own volley, declaring that *The Crisis* had asked Houston to write a statement for the magazine about the trial, "but he was too busy." Du Bois feigned ignorance of the details of the case and ask that Houston "or somebody else" make a public explanation of the NAACP's handling of the case, "because it seems to us that in so grave a case as this, either we should never have taken the case in the first place, or we should have fought it to the last ditch."

In response, White wrote letters to members of the legal team expressing his "profound personal regrets ... I am filled with chagrin that such an article or expression should appear in *The Crisis.*" The NAACP's administrative committee eventually offered an apology to Crawford's defense attorneys—a decision Boardman, predictably, criticized in the pages of the journal.

"As the *Crisis* is the organ of the Association and not merely of any committee or group of members it is appropriate that any matter of interest to the membership should be discussed in its pages. That the Crawford case is of general interest is evident from the many people who have come to me with questions such as those put in the *Crisis* editorial ... it is interesting to note that the administrative committee feels that questions should be apologized for rather than answered," Boardman wrote.

Freda Kirchwey, editor of *The Nation*, forwarded to Houston the manuscript that Boardman and Gruening had submitted to the magazine.

White may have seen the outcome of the trial as a victory, but "to many persons the case seemed, on the contrary, a smashing defeat," Boardman and Gruening wrote. They continued,

> Crawford had been found guilty and had been sentenced by an all white jury; Judge Lowell had died under the shadow of impeachment proceedings in Congress. His decision had been reversed by the circuit court, and the United States Supreme Court had refused to reconsider it. Where was the victory?
>
> Apart from the Boston confession, unsigned, repudiated by Crawford, and obviously obtained by illegal methods, the State had evidence of nothing more than Crawford's presence in Virginia. It had no eyewitnesses to the crime, none who could place him at the scene of the crime within seven or eight hours of it, no fingerprints to connect him with it, no bloodstained clothing, murderous weapon, or recognizable loot found in his possession. Yet Crawford was convicted, and Walter White hailed the result as a victory. Mr. Houston, though he put the matter less strongly, also said he considered it one. It seemed to him a definite victory that Negro lawyers pleaded for the first time in a Virginia court defending a Negro

charged with murdering a white woman, and he also felt that racial relations in Virginia had been definitely improved as a result of the trial. There is no doubt that a very high and unusual degree of surface courtesy and fair play did prevail at the trial. There was no rough stuff as there was at Scottsboro, no gross appeal to race prejudice, no bickering or bad temper. Counsel on both sides displayed good temper, restraint, and sportsmanship, and Judge McLemore's rulings on all minor points were surprisingly fair. Virginia showed sportsmanship, in other words, as long as it did not interfere with Crawford's conviction. But when Crawford evidenced dislike of being unfairly convicted with all the amenities, when he gave the interview complaining that he had been "framed" and — truthfully or otherwise — reaffirmed his innocence, Virginia promptly ran true to form and he got a second life sentence on a forced plea of guilty....

    We realize that this was a difficult case and that any course Crawford's counsel might take had its dangers, but Mr. Houston's failure to appeal shows that he dared not put Virginia justice to any real test. Even if Crawford was guilty, moreover, the constitutional issue remained. Virginia had not "come into court with clean hands," yet an all-white jury had convicted Crawford. Was this a victory for justice? We do not think so. It is possible that some ground was gained when Negroes pleaded as these did in a Virginia county courthouse; it is also possible that racial relations have improved somewhat in Virginia since the trial, but we feel that for both these gains too high a price was paid.

Houston met with *The Nation*'s editors on three occasions to discuss the article and the case. Boardman and Gruening's accusations were "nasty," he told Kirchwey.

"The whole gist of the manuscript is wrong," Houston said. Alibi witnesses would have been guilty of perjury if they had testified; the Leesburg legal team had not been brought into the case over the heads of the Boston team; and Paul Boeing had nothing to do with the murders, he said. He had been presented with testimony and evidence that proved to him, at least, that Crawford was guilty.

"I have in my possession Crawford's clothing which he abandoned in Washington when he fled after the murder ... however, our hands are somewhat tied. We have information which would be quite illuminating, but we got it under confidential relationship and I will have to get Crawford's permission to release it."[9]

The article was deeply revised and published alongside a response written by Houston and Ransom. In it they explained why they had chosen not to appeal Crawford's conviction for Ilsley's murder:

> In the first place, Crawford did not want to appeal. It was his case and his life. He did not get into the mess in order to raise the constitutional issues; and if he was unwilling to gamble with his life to challenge further the issue of jury discrimination in Virginia, quite frankly that was his business. When the question was asked whether he wanted to take the chance on the outcome of another trial if the first sentence was reversed on appeal, he stated that counsel could use their own judgment so long as he did not have to take a chance on the electric chair. As Crawford's counsel, the authors of this article took their orders from him.

It was counsel's best judgment that on a second trial Crawford would probably get a death sentence.... If Crawford had wished to appeal or if he had received the death sentence, counsel would have appealed and fought the case to the end, because then Crawford would have had everything to gain and nothing to lose, but with a life sentence it was different. Crawford's private, personal interests dictated winding up the case as quickly as possible.

Publication of the Boardman-Gruening article and the Houston-Ransom response to it "will close the discussion," *The Nation* said.

On May 5, Houston addressed dozens of female delegates at the National YWCA Convention in Philadelphia on the issue of race.

"The race problem in the United States is the type of unpleasant problem which we would rather do without, but which refuses to be buried," Houston began.

It has been a visible or invisible factor in almost every important question of domestic policy since the foundation of the government, and may yet be the decisive factor in the success or failure of the New Deal. The dominant interests in the South are determined that there shall not be an industrial emancipation of the Negro....

The Scottsboro Cases, the Angelo Herndon Case in Georgia, the impotence of the States to curb or punish lynching; the attempted murder of two negro lawyers near Henderson, North Carolina, for daring to challenge the exclusion of Negroes from a North Carolina jury, reflect the load carried by the Negro in the courts of justice....

The Negro has made some progress under the New Deal; and at least in the federal government there is an increasing tendency to give him a voice in his own interest and to include his requirements in the national recovery. The Attorney General of Ohio has just overthrown the designation of race and use of photographs in Ohio State Civil Service applications by declaring it an unconstitutional discrimination. The State of Maryland in 1933 made a bold attempt to bring the lynchers of George Armwood to justice. The Commonwealth of Virginia is reforming its jury system. Southern women are moving rapidly to the front in interracial work....

The National Association for the Advancement of Colored People under the courageous and aggressive leadership of its secretary, Walter White, represents the most effective fighting force in the Negro group; but the National Association needs certain reorientation and a measure of reorganization.

Houston also called Communism one of the "most significant events which have affected Negro psychology" since prior to the beginning of World War I:

The contribution of the Communists to the Negro has been to turn the race issue into a class issue. They have been the first, at least in recent times, to have appealed to the masses, as distinguished from the classes. Whereas all prior approaches to the masses had been paternalistic, the Communists came and walked among them, like the disciples of old, and offered them full and complete brotherhood, without respect to race, creed or previous condition of servitude ... the fight which [ILD attorney Samuel] Liebowitz and the Communists have made and are making in the Scottsboro cases has caught the imagination of Negroes as nothing else within a decade. And as one of its repercussions it has forced all the rest of us would-be Negro leaders, or, as the Communists would have it, Negro misleaders, to a firmer stand and bolder action than we probably would have been inclined to take otherwise. The Communists have made it impossible for any aspirant to Negro leadership to advocate less than full economic, political and social equality, and expect to retain the respect and confidence of the group. Some day the Scottsboro cases are to be acknowledged as a milestone in the history of America.[10]

Criticism of the NAACP's handling of the case continued, much if it coming from Boardman. She claimed that White had sent a telegram recalling her from her Middleburg investigation prematurely; White denied it. She claimed Nannie Burroughs, president of the National Training School for Women and Girls at Washington, had been asked to look into Crawford's case, but had not followed up on the investigation. Burroughs denied the allegation.

On May 7, White fired off a letter to Du Bois criticizing he and *The Crisis* for not having looked at the records of the Crawford trial and the NAACP team's pre-trial preparation before publishing Boardman and Gruening's criticisms. News of Streator's backstabbing had made it back to White.

"We have heard rumors that a certain individual has been assiduously making wild statements which have no basis in truth whatever regarding this case," White wrote. "For certain reasons he has been trying desperately to cause some sort of scandal. If I personally can get proof of certain stories which have been attributed to this individual I intend to make an issue of it in the court and let this man prove his misstatements or take the consequences. We have not seen fit to answer the irresponsible statements of this particular individual and I fear that either he or someone of similar mind had led you astray."

Attacks on Houston and the NAACP's handling of the case continued, but there were those who supported the NAACP team as well. "I was much provoked by the vicious and shameless attacks on Dean Houston," Freeman told White. "It is incredible that a man who did such a fine work should be so bitterly assailed."[11]

On June 11, Houston wrote a letter to Alexander explaining the pressure that had been building for the NAACP to appeal the outcome of the Ilsley trial and Loudoun County's all white jury system.

"There has been considerable criticism of our action in the Crawford case in allowing Crawford to plead guilty to the Buckner indictment instead of pressing the constitutional issues to the United States Supreme Court. A lot of pressure has been put on us to return to Loudoun County to raise again the issue of jury discrimination. We have repeatedly taken the position that we wanted to give Loudoun County an opportunity to handle the situation with all pressure removed.

"I am not attempting to influence your final action, but I am keeping these facts before you with the hope that you will bear them in mind when you draw your next grand jury list and when you select your next jury commissioners."

On June 12, Freeman wrote to Kirchwey at Houston's request. "Raising the issue of Negro jury service in the Crawford case did more than anything else that has occurred in my lifetime to put Negroes on the jury panels of Virginia," Freeman said. The Richmond and Suffolk circuits—home to Virginia's largest African American populations—had instructed jury commissioners to include African Americans on jury lists, and African Americans had since been drawn for grand jury and petit jury service. Judge McLemore, in Suffolk, was among those who had pushed the issue. "I think it is only a question of time before the Negroes will be restored to jury service everywhere in Virginia, and I do not believe this could have been done at this time but for the impressions made by Dr. Houston in his argument to quash the indictment against Crawford on these grounds ... the appearance of such a Negro lawyer as Dr. Houston in the courts of Virginia was a revelation to bench and to bar," Freeman said. He had talked off the record with Governor Pollard before the trial; Pollard had undercover men at work in Loudoun who were "very much concerned" about race relations, and Pollard had thought there could be a lynching if there was no conviction, Freeman said.

On Sunday, June 24, 1934, Crawford wrote a letter to White, asking him to send tobacco, a pipe and "a pair of radio ear-phones." He also changed his story about the murders, again.

"Since I have been here in prison, it looks like the whole world has turned their back on me. I have written to different parties but fail to hear anything at all," Crawford said. "Well I thank God some day they will find that I was treated badly for this crime they put on me. I am glad God knows all things and some day it will all leak out that I am innocent of the dirty crimes they put on me."

The turmoil at *The Crisis*, much of it driven by differences on segregation—with Du Bois and Streator on one side of the issue and White and Spingarn on the other—was never-ending. Du Bois and Streator were both threatening to resign. Du Bois had made the same threat more than once in the past year. But on June 26, 1934, he made good on it, submitting his resignation as editor of *The Crisis*. His final departure from the magazine came one day after *The Nation* published more of Boardman and Gruening's criticism of Houston.

Even after Du Bois' resignation, Streator kept a steady stream of paranoid reports about the NAACP and *The Crisis* flowing to him at his office at Atlanta University. White and Ransom had been making inquiries about Streator around the country, and were riding him hard at the magazine, he said.

"I received a lecture on the Crawford case from Walter, and a snobbish piece of tripe from Ransom. I told Arthur [Spingarn] that I considered Walter a fool, and the board a fool (collectively) ... Walter is trying to prove that I have claimed that he and Houston divided a large piece of money in the Crawford case. I am certain that Crawford had no defense!"[12]

Despite *The Nation*'s vow to end the debate, Gruening couldn't resist getting in yet another criticism of the NAACP — and the magazine couldn't resist printing her letter to the editor in its July 18 edition.

> Messrs. Houston and Ransom labor under a misunderstanding about the real basis of our criticism. It was not that counsel left the investigation of the alibi to the last, but that they never made any real investigation — at least not with any thoroughness— and then stated in print that the alibi witnesses had been seen and could not substantiate the stories they had told at the extradition hearing.... Messrs. Ransom and Houston say that Crawford did not want to appeal. On all the evidence I have seen this seems to me doubtful. At least it seems to me doubtful without duress or inducement or some misunderstanding of the consequences.

Ransom told White that he thought Gruening and Boardman were "sore" over the lack of publicity that they received during the Crawford case.[13] Hale told White that his impression of Boardman, based on her article and a personal interview, "is that her excellent virtues do not make her a reliable investigator or a wise critic."[14]

Other lawyers continued to attempt to insinuate themselves into the case. Bernard Ades wrote to Crawford directly, and to Josephus Simpson at the *Journal and Guide,* trying to set up an interview with Crawford. Houston was wary of the maneuver. "If you feel you have been mistreated, you are free to make your statement to anybody you want," he wrote to Crawford. "But I would advise you to have a witness present to hear what you say so that people cannot misrepresent you. You recall that the last time some newspaper men came to see you and wrote you up in the paper, you said they put words in your mouth which you never said."

But Houston did not want to rekindle any public war of words about the Crawford case with the ILD or anyone else. "I am disposed to play the same game they have done in going to the public if I get the goods on them," he told White. "Keep quiet and wait."[15]

A few days later, Houston and M.A. Norrell, editor of the *Richmond Planet,* visited Crawford at the penitentiary. Crawford said that in his June 24 letter to White, he had only meant that he had not killed Ilsley and Buckner himself. He was satisfied with the work of the NAACP legal team, he said. While at the prison, Houston met Superintendent Rice Youel, who told him that the *Norfolk Journal and Guide* had telephoned in an attempt to arrange an interview with Crawford for Ades.

In a September 12 letter to White, Associated Negro press feature editor Percival L. Prattis laid out some reasons for the public criticism of the NAACP legal team. It had been a matter of misguided expectations, and the NAACP was at least partly to blame, Prattis said. "We expected you to prove Crawford innocent. There had been no hint even that that was going to be hard to do ... we, the public, were expecting a smashing offense by the defense counsel at the trial. But something happened. Instead of the offense, there was what seemed to the public either surrender or prudent compliance ... no attempt was made at the time to explain the sudden shift in your course. The public was left to conjecture."

The NAACP finally decided not to publish or push the dispute further. "It might arouse a wrangle that will take out time from more important matters," Wilkins said.[16] White agreed.

White and Houston continued to send Crawford tobacco, magazines, toiletries and small amounts of money, and Crawford continued to send them letters asking for more handouts. In a September 23 letter to White, Crawford asked for books and magazines, and said he had heard from Ades. A few weeks later, Crawford wrote both White and Wilson about Ades. "I don't care to see him at all and further more I haven't any talk for no one. I am trying to forget everything so I have nothing to say." White forwarded a copy of the letter to the *Nation*.

Houston was able to see the bigger picture, though, and knew that Ades' efforts on behalf of clients were helping to bring down the all-white jury system in Maryland. He and Marshall defended Ades before the U.S. District Court for the District of Maryland in 1934, when the ILD lawyer was charged with "professional misconduct, malpractice, fraud, deceit and conduct prejudicial to the administration of justice" for his part in the defense of Euell Lee. Ades had attempted to have Lee's body taken to New York following his execution for a politically motivated, ILD-sponsored public funeral, against Lee's stated wishes, according to the charges. The court declined to disbar Ades, though it found that "his conduct was not merely offensive to every instinct of good taste," according to the decision. "It was to a high degree, reprehensible in that he withheld from Lee the real purpose that he had in mind in obtaining the body."

Other Communists kept up their attacks on the NAACP legal team. Gruening became ever more sharply critical, charging in an article in *The Masses* on January 8, 1935, that a possibly innocent man had been given a life sentence for the sake of the NAACP's belief in improved interracial relations in the South. Gruening again trotted out every complaint Houston's critics had created since the trial began: the only "evidence" against Crawford had been his race, his prison record and the disputed confession, she said; the legal system, the media and Middleburg's elite had railroaded him; Houston had been cowardly, outwitted by the establishment, going so far as to lie about attempts to interview witnesses in Boston during the extradition hearing. She contradicted virtually every assertion made by the NAACP during Crawford's trial.

The article was "a shameless tirade," according to Freeman; Virginia Dabney, agreed that it was "unfair." It was an attempt by the Communists "to distract attention from the horrible moves they have made of the Scottsboro cases by throwing mud at the Crawford case," White told Ransom. "This episode merely strengthens my distrust of the professional white liberals and radicals who, way down in their hearts, are just about as bigoted as Georgia crackers."[17]

Houston felt he had no choice but to retaliate. In February he convinced Crawford to allow the NAACP to release what had until then been confidential information about the case: the clothes he had worn on the night of the murders, which he had abandoned at Lessie Hedgepath's home in Washington. "I obtained the clothes from a house in Washington upon information furnished directly by Crawford," Houston said. "The prosecution did not even know the existence of the clothes — which is an answer to Miss Gruening's charge that the evidence against Crawford was planted."[18]

Houston planned to take a half dozen reporters to the Richmond penitentiary, where Crawford would identify the clothes as his own. Houston would then take the reporters to the boarding house where the clothes had been found. All of this, along with a statement signed by the reporters and whatever articles they might write, would help to discredit Gruening, Boardman and the ILD attacks. "Recrimination will do no good," Houston told Freeman. "What I want to present is objective evidence which cannot be denied."[19]

At 3 p.m. on February 28, Houston and a group of reporters met at the penitentiary. Crawford identified the clothes and told the reporters that his alibi had been a lie and the Boston witnesses would have perjured themselves if they had testified in Leesburg.

"I am satisfied with what Dr. Houston did for me," Crawford told the reporters. "I am satisfied with the trial. I am satisfied with the sentence. I am satisfied to stay here the rest of my life, if they'll just let me alone. I am tired of seeing my name in the papers and I am tired of talking to people about the case. If I am satisfied, I don't see why the devil other people don't let me alone."[20]

Houston assured the reporters that — despite the letter-writing campaign by Boardman and Gruening — the NAACP had, in fact, investigated Crawford's Boston alibi.

"We thoroughly checked the alibi later and found it would not stand up in the face of the state's evidence, and we abandoned it," Houston said.[21]

But Crawford, who could not seem to tell his story the same way twice, told one of the reporters that he had left the clothes at Hedgepath's home when he and DeNeal returned from Boston — before the murders.

Days later, in a letter to Boardman, Crawford changed his story again, saying he had left the clothes in Washington a full year prior to the murders. Hedgepath, however, continued to back Houston's story, telling the *Afro-American* and the *Washington Daily News* that Crawford had left the clothes at her home shortly after the murders.

Boardman and Gruening were aided in their campaign to discredit Houston and the NAACP by Crawford's inability to stick to any story. In meetings and correspondence with NAACP members he sang their praises; in letters to Gruening, Boardman and others he claimed to have been railroaded. If they were sincere in their attacks on the NAACP team, they were among the very few in the country not to have discerned something that Houston had understood since the days just before the Leesburg trial began: Crawford was an habitual liar.

"You are, and have been, much closer to him than I have," Percival Prattis told Houston. "But even from this great distance, I was able to discern long ago that Crawford is a dangerously shifty person, skilled in dissembling ... each letter seems to indicate that he is not playing fair with you."[22]

As late as March 14, 1935, Houston said the facts of the case had been so muddled by Boardman and Gruening that "a member of my own family is not satisfied that there is really a Charlie Johnson." Still, "once the facts are out, they spell themselves," he wrote to Wilkins. The confusion, flamed by Boardman and Gruening, could have been avoided if Wilson had done a better job in Boston, according to Houston.

"If he had not acted the dog in the manger in his insane desire to hog the show, we could have got the facts in VA by April 1933, and known exactly how to play our cards," Houston said.

"As it was, he kept us shooting in the dark. Result we put up a huge ballyhoo about Crawford's innocence, and of course the public can't understand how we took low so quickly and pedaled a case which we had proclaimed to be a second civil rights charter."[23]

In April, *The Crisis* yet again took on the issue, printing "A Statement by the NAACP," which rehashed the story of the murders, the extradition battle and the Leesburg trial, and attempted to further vindicate Houston's tactics and strategy.

"George Crawford, from his cell in the Virginia state penitentiary at Richmond, has given permission to the NAACP to make public events in connection with his arrest, trial and conviction on a charge of murder. The Association makes this statement not with the idea of entering into a controversy, but merely to advise its members and friends of what actually took place...."

And Boardman and Gruening went on to publish *Who Is The NAACP?*, a rambling 32-page missive that once again attacked virtually every decision made by Houston and the NAACP. But the public had finally grown tired of the sideshow being put on by Boardman and Gruening. "First, we didn't like their foreign names, second we doubt their sincerity, and third we believe their entire program of subversive propaganda is communistically inspired," the *Washington Tribune* said.

Within just a few months of Crawford's conviction, the significance of the case and of Houston's efforts were finally and irrevocably overshadowed by the

Scottsboro Boys case, when the U.S. Supreme Court declared the exclusion of African Americans from jury pools unconstitutional.

"We find it impossible to accept such a sweeping characterization of the lack of qualification of Negroes," the Court said in its April 1, 1935 decision in the Scottsboro cases. "For this long-continued, unvarying and wholesale exclusion of Negroes from jury service, we find no justification consistent with the constitutional mandate." The death of the all-white jury system was at hand.

"Negroes will be placed on the jury list for services at the June term of the Loudoun Circuit Court, opening Monday, it was indicated this week," the *Loudoun Times-Mirror* reported June 6, 1935. "Judge J.R.H. Alexander said he had the matter under consideration, adding that it was more than probable that respected colored citizens of the county would be called for jury service. Presence of colored citizens on a jury in Loudoun will mark the first time since Reconstruction days in Virginia that negroes have been recognized for such service in Loudoun.

"The recent dictum of the United States Supreme Court in the celebrated 'Scottsboro Cases' is the beacon light guiding the actions of Judge Alexander and other Virginia judges in calling negroes for jury service. The highest tribunal in the land held that failure of Southern courts to place negroes on juries deprived colored citizens of rights guaranteed them under the Fourteenth Amendment to the Constitution of the United States." But there were some who saw Alexander's decision as little more than a clumsy public relations effort designed to end criticism of Loudoun's all-white jury system without actually changing it in practice: the first African American name entered into the jury pool was Gus Valentine, the husband of Alexander's maid, and Valentine was never seated on a jury.

In 1935 Houston became chief counsel for the NAACP, and drove the organization in its legal battles for quality in education, focusing on a series of cases meant to lead to the overturning of *Plessy v. Ferguson*. Among the cases Houston and his protégés took on was *Murray v. Maryland*, a case that allowed Marshall, who had been denied admission at the all-white University of Maryland Law School, to open the school's doors to African Americans.

Also in 1935, Houston successfully challenged the exclusion of African Americans from juries in *Hollins v. Oklahoma*. In the first Supreme Court victory by an all–African American counsel, the court ruled that systematic exclusions from juries was unconstitutional and overturned the conviction.

Houston returned to Loudoun County in 1940 to assist the County-Wide League (CWL), a group of mostly African American parents, in their fight for better schools for minority students. Since 1884 the only school for African Americans within the county seat had been the Leesburg Training School, a facility with conditions so bad that the state refused to grant accreditation. Houston and the CWL fought to get the county to agree to a new high school for African American students. The CWL raised enough money to buy a few acres for the school and, after Houston persuaded the State Literary Fund to loan the county money for construction costs, the Board of Supervisors acquiesced. The new school was built on a flat patch of land on the town's eastern edge, just across the road from the potter's field cemetery where the indigent and unwanted, including lynching victims Owen Anderson and Charles Craven, had been buried for a century. The Douglass High School opened its doors in 1941. The half-acre cemetery was paved over in 1983. More than 400 graves—some of them already lost beneath the now-paved Market Street — were probably all that remained of the neglected cemetery, according to an archeological team that investigated the site. The few remains that could be found were retrieved by a bulldozer, dumped into a communal vault and reinterred in a small plot in a corner of Leesburg's Union Cemetery.

Houston's marathon working hours eventually exhausted him. Even as he had led Crawford's defense, he had continued to meet all of his responsibilities as dean and professor at Howard. It was the kind of work schedule that some said would bring him to an early grave. Failing health forced him to step down as NAACP chief counsel in 1938; he left the NAACP in 1940, eventually moving on to a position with the Fair Employment Practices Committee. He suffered a serious heart attack in 1948 and died of heart failure in Bethesda, Maryland, April 22, 1950. In 1958 Howard University renamed its main law school building in his honor. The NAACP posthumously awarded him its Spingarn Medal.

Thurgood Marshall, the promising law student who assisted Houston during the Crawford trial, went on to serve as chief counsel for the NAACP Legal Defense and Education Fund. In 1954 he successfully argued against school segregation in *Brown v. Board of Education*. He became a judge on the United States Second Circuit Court of Appeals in 1961, the first African American solicitor general of the United States in 1965, and the first African American justice on the U.S. Supreme Court in 1967.

Changes in race relations came slowly in Loudoun County. Blacks continued to be denied entrance to Middleburg restaurants until 1961, when Ernest deBordenave, rector of Emmanuel Episcopal Church, integrated the Red Fox Inn by sitting down to lunch with a group of parishioners and Maurice Brittian King Edmead, a doctor who had opened an office in town in 1933 but had never been allowed to practice at Loudoun Hospital. Despite Marshall's victory in *Brown v. Board of Education*, Loudoun schools remained segregated for years. In 1962, black students who had been denied entrance to the county's two white high schools sued in U.S. District Court. Loudoun ignored a resulting court order to implement a "Freedom of Choice" plan. The U.S. Justice Department sued Loudoun in 1965, and the county school system was ordered to desegregate. When classes began in September 1968, Loudoun County schools were finally integrated, with black teachers on the payroll and black students in the classrooms.

Out in Purcellville, the annual Emancipation Day meetings continued to draw large crowds during the Civil Rights battles of the 1960s. Mahalia Jackson sang at one Emancipation Day ceremony. But the aging tabernacle, built in 1914, was falling apart. The last Emancipation Day ceremony was held in 1967. The tabernacle collapsed a few years later, it's remains eventually sold for scrap.

The Tally Ho movie theater in Leesburg remained segregated, forcing its African American patrons to buy their tickets at a separate window and sit only in the balcony until 1965. Integration came to the theater when a group of African Americans challenged the seating policy by sitting in the whites-only downstairs gallery. They were not challenged.

The search for Charley Johnson turned up few leads. On April 19, 1935, Galleher traveled to Fredericksburg, Virginia, to talk to a police officer who said he might have information about the man who Crawford had claimed was the actual killer of Agnes Boeing Ilsley and Mina Buckner. Nothing came of it. Despite all of the details Crawford had provided in his confession — the photographs that he said had been taken at the shelter for vagrants in Pittsburgh in the days after the murders, the address of Johnson's relatives in Washington, the time he said Johnson had spent in jails in Baltimore and Raleigh — Johnson was never found.

Crawford died in the Virginia Penitentiary of a cerebral hemorrhage on August 15, 1955. Over the years he had continued to write letters to NAACP lawyers, asking them to send him money, cigarettes and other items. And, despite the wrenches he had repeatedly thrown into their efforts, Houston and White usually sent him everything that he asked for.

"We have a letter in the mail this morning from your mutual friend, George Crawford, now confined in the Richmond, Virginia Penitentiary," Marshall told Houston and White in 1937. "Crawford states, 'I am asking if you would please send me some cigarettes to smoke and some Colgate's tooth paste and some Gillette razor blades ... please don't turn me down.'"[24]

A few hundred folks brave the cold each January to march in the Martin Luther King, Jr., Day Parade in Leesburg. An informal event, the parade begins on the courthouse lawn, literally in the shadow of the "silent sentinel" Confederate Soldier's memorial statue, and ends at Douglass High School, which is now a community center.

In 2008, with the 100th anniversary of the statue approaching, the Lee Chapter of the United Daughters of the Confederacy asked the Loudoun County Board of Supervisors for $6,300 for a "celebration event." When some Supervisors criticized the request and the statue, the UDC withdrew the funding request, saying it had been able to raise the money for the event by itself.

Bagpipes played on the west lawn of the courthouse as the names of Loudoun's Confederate dead were read aloud on May 28, 2008. "Today I rejoice, because this celebration is not about hate or racism or to resurrect a debate about a war fought nearly 150 years ago," Becky Fleming, president of the chapter, said during the ceremony. "It's simply a chance to be a part of our great county's history."[25]

Chapter Notes

Much of the story was built using documents found in *Papers of the NAACP*, Part I, Boxes D51, D52, D53 and D54 at the Library of Congress. Extensive quotes in chapters ten and eleven are verbatim from the transcript of the Leesburg trial.

Chapter Two

1. Bank of Montreal acquired Marshall & Ilsley Corp. for $4.1 billion in 2010 ("Bank Bid Sparks Talk of Who's Next," *Wall Street Journal*, Dec. 18, 2010).

Chapter Three

1. "A Colored Mass Meeting," *The Mirror*, May 17, 1883, 1.
2. "Lynching in Leesburg," *The Mirror*, Nov. 14, 1889, 3.
3. Ibid.
4. Ibid.
5. "November Court," *The Mirror*, Nov. 14, 1889, 2.
6. "Mob Hangs Craven," *Washington Post*, Aug. 1, 1902, 1.
7. Diary of Ida Lee Rust, Rust Papers, Thomas Balch Library, Leesburg, VA.
8. "Mob May Attack Jail," *Washington Post*, Aug. 5, 1902, 4.
9. There were reportedly other, undocumented lynchings in Loudoun County. In 1917 a young African American man was reported to have pled for his life as a crowd carried him past his family home on King Street and on to the grounds of the whites-only Leesburg High School, where he was hung. And there are members of families who have lived in the county for generations who say they have seen photographs of four white men standing proudly next to the body of an African American man dangling at the end of a rope on the front porch of a pool hall that stood near the Ashburn railroad stop, a few miles east of Leesburg.
10. Hugh Lee Powell, "Unveiling of Monument at Leesburg, VA," *Confederate Veteran*, October, 1908.
11. "Band Minstrel Shows Very Highly Enjoyed," *Loudoun Times*, April 12, 1923, 1.

Chapter Four

1. Douglas Waller, *A Question of Loyalty* (New York: Harper Collins, 2004), 20.
2. Ibid., 337.
3. Ibid., 57.
4. "Mrs. Spencer Isley and Companion Slain by Midnight Intruder in Middleburg Home," *Loudoun Times-Mirror*, Jan. 14, 1932, 1.
5. Helen Boardman deposition, Feb. 1, 1933, Papers of the NAACP.
6. Notes taken by Walter White during the Leesburg trial, Dec. 12, 1933, Papers of the NAACP.
7. Helen Boardman, "The South Goes Legal," *The Nation*, March 8, 1933, 258.
8. Katrina McCormick, telephone interview by the author, Dec. 9, 2004.

Chapter Five

1. Boardman, 258.
2. Walter White, *A Man Called White* (Athens: University of Georgia Press, 1948), 152.
3. Boardman deposition.

Chapter Six

1. "$3,025 is Offered as Reward for Double Slayer," *Loudoun Times-Mirror*, Jan. 28, 1932, 1.
2. Ibid.
3. "Tips Prove Futile in Double Murder," *Washington Post*, Jan. 17, 1932, 2.
4. "Murderer Eludes Police; Larger Reward is Sought," *Loudoun Times-Mirror*, Jan. 21, 1932, 1.
5. "Policeman Slugs Photographer at Funeral of Slain Woman," *Evening Star*, Jan. 15, 1932, 1.

Chapter Seven

1. "Ilsley Janitor at Liberty After Long Questioning," *Loudoun Times-Mirror*, Feb. 4, 1932, 1.
2. The conversation between Galleher and Crawford is from a transcript of the unsigned confession, transcribed at the Suffolk County jail on Jan. 19, 1933.
3. "Crawford Return Fought in Boston," *Loudoun Times-Mirror*, Jan. 25, 1933, 1.
4. Ibid.
5. Ibid.
6. Ibid.
7. J. Douglas Smith, *Managing White Supremacy* (Chapel Hill: University of North Carolina Press, 2002), 184.
8. White, 13.
9. Mark V. Tushnet, ed., Thurgood Marshall: His Speeches, Writings, Arguments, Opinions and Reminiscences (Chicago: Lawrence Hill Books, 2001), 415.
10. Carl Rowan, Dream Makers, Dream Breakers: The World of Justice Thurgood Marshall (Boston: Little, Brown, 1993), 68.
11. Geraldine Segal, *In Any Flight Some Fall* (Rockville, MD: Mercury Press, 1975), 34.
12. Michael D. Davis and Hunter R. Clark, *Thurgood Marshall: Warrior at the Bar, Rebel on the Bench* (New York: Carol Communications, 1992), 45
13. Mark Tushnet, "The Politics of Equality in Constitutional Law: The Equal Protection Clause, Dr. Du Bois and Charles Hamilton Houston," *Journal of American History* 74, December 1987: 901.
14. Wilbur Hall letter to William Mitchell, Jan. 27, 1933, Papers of Gen. William Mitchell, Library of Congress.
15. All of Boardman's recollections of conversations she had in Loudoun County in this section are taken from her Feb. 1, 1933 deposition.
16. Boardman, *The Nation*, 258.
17. Charles Tittmann, "The Crawford Case," *The Nation*, April 5, 1933, 375.
18. "Negro Group Goes Into Court to Keep Crawford in Mass," *Loudoun Times-Mirror*, Feb. 23, 1933, 1.
19. Alfred E. Cohen letter to Butler Wilson, Feb. 16, 1933, Papers of the NAACP.
20. Walter White letter to James Dillard, Feb. 20, 1933, Papers of the NAACP.
21. Petition for Writ of Habeas Corpus filed in Boston February 1933, Papers of the NAACP
22. Walter White letter to Charles Houston, April 29, 1933, Papers of the NAACP.
23. A. Harry Moore letter to Charles Houston, March 1, 1933, Papers of the NAACP.
24. Walter White letter to Charles Houston, March 6, 1933, Papers of the NAACP.
25. Charles Houston letter to Walter White, March 8, 1933, Papers of the NAACP.
26. Walter White letter to Butler Wilson and J. Weston Allen, March 7, 1933, Papers of the NAACP.
27. Charles Houston/Edward Lovett affidavit, March 10, 1933, Papers of the NAACP.
28. Ibid.
29. Ibid.
30. Charles Houston/Edward Lovett memorandum, March 10, 1933, Papers of the NAACP.
31. Ibid.
32. Houston/Lovett affidavit.
33. Walter White letter to Butler Wilson, March 20, 1933, Papers of the NAACP.
34. Butler Wilson letter to Walter White, March 21, 1933, Papers of the NAACP.
35. Walter White letter to Butler Wilson, March 22, 1933, Papers of the NAACP.

36. Unsigned memorandum, March 28, 1933, Papers of the NAACP.
37. Ibid.
38. Charles Houston letter to J. Weston Allen and Butler Wilson, April 2, 1933, Papers of the NAACP.
39. Walter White letter to Butler Wilson, March 29, 1933, Papers of the NAACP.
40. Houston to Allen and Wilson.
41. Walter White letter to Charles Houston, April 17, 1933, Papers of the NAACP.
42. Charles Houston letter to Walter White, April 21, 1933, Papers of the NAACP.
43. Ibid.
44. Ibid.
45. Walter White letter to Helen Boardman, March 2, 1933, Papers of the NAACP.
46. Elaine E. Thompson address, "Charles Hamilton Houston and Loudoun County," Eastern Loudoun Regional Library, Feb. 2004.
47. "Bars Extraditing Negro to Virginia," New York Times, April 25, 1933, 1.
48. "New Fugitive Slave Law Seen," New York Times, April 26, 1933, 1.
49. Butler Wilson letter to Walter White, April 24, 1933, Papers of the NAACP.
50. J. Weston Allen letter to Walter White, April 25, 1933, Papers of the NAACP.
51. Walter White letter to Charles Houston, April 25, 1933, Papers of the NAACP.

Chapter Eight

1. Allen to White, April 25, 1933.
2. "Ruling Releasing Crawford Arouses Storm of Protest," Loudoun Times-Mirror, April 27, 1933, 1.
3. "Smith and Dies Move to Punish Judge Lowell," Washington Post, April 26, 1933, 1.
4. "Inquiry on Lowell for Freeing Negro is Voted by House," New York Times, April 27, 1933, 1.
5. "House Plans Probing of Ilsley Case Ruling," Washington Post, April 27, 1933, 1.
6. "Boston Bar Council Upholds Judge Lowell; Says He Acted Impartially in Negro's Case," New York Times, April 30, 1933, 3.
7. "Judge Ignores Moves," New York Times, April 26, 1933, 1.
8. Butler Wilson letter to Charles Houston, May 4, 1933, Papers of the NAACP.
9. Waller, 343.
10. "Influence of Reds Charged in Ruling

Freeing Crawford," Loudoun Times-Mirror, April 27, 1933, 4.
11. William Mitchell letter to John Garland Pollard, April 25, 1933, Papers of Gen. William Mitchell, Library of Congress.
12. William Mitchell letter to Fitzhugh Lee, April 29, 1933, Papers of Gen. William Mitchell, Library of Congress.
13. William Mitchell letter to John Cudahy, May 12, 1933, Papers of Gen. William Mitchell, Library of Congress.
14. Waller, 343.
15. Walter White letter to Roy Wilkins, April 26, 1933, Papers of the NAACP.
16. Walter White letter to Arthur Spingarn, May 1, 1933, Papers of the NAACP.
17. Charles Houston letter to Walter White, May 9, 1933, Papers of the NAACP.
18. Walter White letters to Mack Taylor, John Moten and William Hall, June 21, 1932, Papers of the NAACP.
19. Ibid.
20. Felix Frankfurter letter to Walter White, June 23, 1933, Papers of the NAACP.
21. June Guild letter to Roger Baldwin, undated, Papers of the NAACP.
22. "Crawford Case Now Before the Supreme Court," The Afro-American, Sept. 9, 1933, 3.
23. "Judge Charges Subject," Washington Post, Oct. 17, 1933.
24. NAACP press release, Oct. 16, 1933, Papers of the NAACP.

Chapter Nine

1. "Maryland Witnesses Wildest Lynching Orgy in History," New York Times, Oct. 19, 1933, 1.
2. Charles Houston/Leon Ransom letters to American Legion Posts, Oct. 23, 1933, Papers of the NAACP.
3. "At Princess Anne," Time, Oct. 39, 1933, 14.
4. White, 152.
5. Douglas Freeman letter to Walter White, Nov. 2, 1933, Papers of the NAACP.
6. Charles Houston, affidavit in support of Motion to Quash, Oct. 26, 1933, Com. v George Crawford.
7. "Fear of Mob Bars Lynching Arrests," New York Times, Nov. 18, 1933, 1.
8. Ibid.
9. Charles Houston letter to Richmond

Times-Leader, Nov. 9, 1933, Papers of the NAACP.

10. "Caste System Excludes Negroes from Juries Here, Says Houston," *Loudoun Times-Mirror*, Nov. 9, 1933, 2.

11. Charles Houston letter to Butler Wilson and J. Weston Allen, Nov. 11, 1933, Papers of the NAACP.

12. "Make Appeals for Crawford," *New York Amsterdam News*, Nov. 22, 1933, 1.

13. Walter White letter to Charles Houston, Nov. 13, 1933, Papers of the NAACP.

14. Ibid.

15. Roy Wilkins letter to Charles Houston, Nov. 18, 1933, Papers of the NAACP.

16. Unsigned note, Papers of the NAACP.

17. William Mitchell letter to S. Gardner Wallace, Nov. 24, 1933, Papers of Gen. William Mitchell, Library of Congress.

18. James McLemore letter to E.O. Russell, Nov. 18, 1933, *Com. v George Crawford*.

19. Walter White letter to Charles Houston, Nov. 24, 1933, Papers of the NAACP.

20. "Crawford Defense to Demand Negroes on Death Trial Jury," *Washington Post*, Nov. 19, 1933, 12.

21. White, 153.

22. White 154.

23. Charles Houston letter to Walter White, Nov. 10, 1933, Papers of the NAACP.

24. Charles Houston memorandum, Nov. 6, 1933, Papers of the NAACP.

Chapter Eleven

1. Juan Williams, "Marshall's Law," *Washington Post Magazine*, Jan. 7, 1990, 12.

2. Walter White letter to Douglas Freeman, Dec. 18, 1933, Papers of the NAACP.

3. Walter White letter to A.E.O. Munsell, Dec. 18, 1933, Papers of the NAACP.

4. Walter White letter to Helen Boardman, Jan. 18, 1934, Papers of the NAACP.

5. Tom Young letter to Walter White, Feb. 15, 1934, Papers of the NAACP.

6. Walter White letter to Charles Houston, Feb. 13, 1934, Papers of the NAACP.

7. George Streator letter to W.E.B. Du Bois, Feb. 23, 1934, W.E.B. Du Bois Library, University of Massachusetts Amherst.

8. Ibid.

9. Charles Houston letter to Fred Kirchway, May 1, 1934, Papers of the NAACP.

10. Charles Houston, "An Approach to Better Race Relations," Address to National YMCA Convention, Philadelphia, May 5, 1934.

11. Douglas Freeman letter to Walter White, May 17, 1934, Papers of the NAACP.

12. George Streator letter to W.E.B. Du Bois, June 28, 1934, Papers of the NAACP.

13. Leon Ransom letter to Walter White, July 13, 1934, Papers of the NAACP.

14. Richard Hale letter to Walter White, July 20, 1934, Papers of the NAACP.

15. Charles Houston letter to Walter White, July 31, 1934, Papers of the NAACP.

16. Roy Wilkins letter to Walter White, Oct. 7, 1934, Papers of the NAACP.

17. Walter White letter to Leon Ransom, Jan. 24, 1935, Papers of the NAACP.

18. Charles Houston letter to Douglas Freeman, Feb. 17, 1935, Papers of the NAACP.

19. Ibid.

20 "'Lifer' Defends His Attorney From Criticism," *Washington Post*, March 1, 1935, 5.

21. Ibid.

22. Percival Prattis letter to Charles Houston, March 8, 1935, Papers of the NAACP.

23. Charles Houston letter to Roy Wilkins, March 14, 1935, Papers of the NAACP.

24. Thurgood Marshall memorandum to Charles Houston and Walter White, Aug. 10, 1937, Papers of the NAACP.

25. Kara Clark, "Confederate Statue Rededication Celebrated," *Leesburg Today*, June 2, 2008, 5.

Bibliography

Books

Appiah, Kwame Anthony, and Henry Louis Gates, Jr. *Africana: The Encyclopedia of the African and African American Experience.* New York: Basic Civitas Books, 1999.

Ayers, Edward L., and Anne S Rubin. *The Valley of the Shadow: Two Communities in the American Civil War.* New York: W.W. Norton & Company, 2000.

Bearss, Sara B., senior editor. *Dictionary of Virginia Biography.* Vol. 3. Richmond: The Library of Virginia, 2006.

Birch, Frank V., ed. *The Badger.* Vol. 32 (1918). Madison: University of Wisconsin Press, 1917.

Black History Committee of The Friends of the Thomas Balch Library. *The Essence of a People: Portraits of African Americans Who Made a Difference in Loudoun County, Virginia.* Leesburg, VA: The Friends of the Thomas Balch Library, 2001.

_____. *The Essence of a People II: African Americans Who Made Their World Anew in Loudoun County, Virginia, and Beyond.* Leesburg, VA: The Friends of the Thomas Balch Library, 2002.

Broadfoot, Grover L., ed. *The Badger.* Volume 30 (1916). Madison: University of Wisconsin Press, 1915.

Brundage, W. Fitzhugh. *Lynching in the New South: Georgia and Virginia, 1880–1930.* Chicago: University of Illinois Press, 1993.

Cemetery Committee of Thomas Balch Library. *Middleburg Cemeteries, Loudoun County Virginia.* Westminster, MD: Willow Bend Books, 2000.

Civics Club (compiled). *Brodhead's Tribute to Her Men of the Service, 1914–1918.* Madison, WI: Cantwell Printing Co., 1921.

Crawford, J. Marshall. *Mosby and His Men: A Record of the Adventures of That Renowned Partisan Ranger, John S. Mosby.* New York: G.W. Carleton & Co., 1867.

Divine, John, Wilbur C. Hall, Marshall Andrews, and Penelope M. Osburn. *Loudoun County and the Civil War.* Leesburg, VA: Willow Bend Books, 1998.

Dray, Philip. *At the Hands of Persons Unknown: The Lynching of Black America.* New York: The Modern Library, 2002.

Ellis, Catherine, and Stephen Drury Smith, eds. *Say It Plain: A Century of Great African American Speeches.* New York: The New Press, 2005.

Frain, Elizabeth R. *Union Cemetery, Leesburg, Loudoun County, Virginia.* Westminster, MD: Heritage Books, Inc., 1995.

Ginzburg, Ralph. *100 Years of Lynchings.* Baltimore: Black Classic Press, 1962.

Hallam, Arthur, ed. *The Badger*. Vol. 28 (1914). Madison: University of Wisconsin Press, 1913.

Hurley, Alfred F. *Billy Mitchell, Crusader for Air Power*. Norwalk, CT: The Easton Press, 1964.

Janken, Kenneth Robert. *White: The Biography of Walter White, Mr. NAACP*. New York: The New Press, 2001.

Jones, George O., Norman S. McVean, et al., comp. *History of Lincoln, Oneida, and Vilas Counties Wisconsin*. Minneapolis-Winona, MN: H.C. Cooper, Jr., 1924.

Lewis, David Levering. *W.E.B. Du Bois: The Fight for Equality and the American Century, 1919–1963*. New York: Henry Holt, 2000.

Low, Chet. *One Hundred Fiftieth Anniversary of the Consecration of Emmanuel Episcopal Church*. Middleburg, VA: Emmanuel Episcopal Church, 1993.

Mack, Kenneth W. *Representing the Race: The Creation of the Civil Rights Lawyer*. Cambridge, MA: Harvard University Press, 2012.

MacLean, Nancy. *Behind the Mask of Chivalry: The Making of the Second Ku Klux Klan*. New York: Oxford University Press, 1994.

Margulies, Phillip, ed. *The Roaring Twenties*. San Diego: Greenhaven Press, 2004.

McNeil, Genna Rae. *Groundwork: Charles Houston and the Struggle for Civil Rights*. Philadelphia: University of Pennsylvania Press, 1983.

Melville, Herman. *Battle-Pieces and Aspects of the War*. New York: Harper & Brothers, 1866.

Miller, Kristie. *Ruth Hanna McCormick: A Life in Politics, 1880–1944*. Albuquerque: University of New Mexico Press, 1992.

Phillips, John T. II, ed. *The Bulletin of the Historical Society of Loudoun County, Virginia, 1957–1976*. Leesburg, VA: Goose Creek Productions, 1997.

Saffer, Wynne C. *Loudoun Votes 1867–1966: A Civil War Legacy*. Westminster, MD: Willow Bend Books, 2002.

Scheel, Eugene M. *The History of Middleburg and Vicinity*. Warrenton, VA: The Piedmont Press, 1987.

_____. *Loudoun Discovered: Communities, Corners & Crossroads*. Leesburg, VA: The Friends of Thomas Balch Library, Inc., 2002.

Smith, Kathryn Gettings, Evelyn D. Causey and Edna Johnston. *Exploring Leesburg: Guide to History and Architecture*. Leesburg, VA: Town of Leesburg, 2003.

Swoboda, Marian J., and Audrey J. Roberts. *Wisconsin Women, Graduate School and the Professions*. Madison: Board of Regents of the University of Wisconsin, 1980.

Thompson, Elaine E. *In the Watchfires: The Loudoun County Emancipation Association, 1890–1971*. Leesburg, VA: The Thomas Balch Library, Inc., 2005.

Tolnay, Steward E., and E.M. Beck. *A Festival of Violence: An Analysis of Southern Lynchings, 1882–1930*. Chicago: University of Illinois Press, 1995.

Turner, Fitzhugh. *Loudoun County and the Civil War: A History and Guide*. Virginia Civil War Centennial Commission, 1965.

Wade, Wyn Craig. *The Fiery Cross: The Ku Klux Klan in America*. New York: Oxford University Press, 1987.

Waller, Douglas. *A Question of Loyalty: Gen. Billy Mitchell and the Court-Martial That Gripped the Nation*. New York: HarperCollins, 2004.

Wells, Chester Caesar, ed. *Ye Badger*. Vol. 27 (1913). Madison: University of Wisconsin Press, 1912.

White, Walter. *A Man Called White*. Athens: University of Georgia Press, 1995.

Williams, Juan. *Thurgood Marshall, American Revolutionary*. New York: Times Books, 1998.

Williamson, James J. *Mosby's Rangers*. New York: The Polhemus Press, 1895.

Younger, Edward, and James Tice Moore, eds. *The Governors of Virginia, 1860–1978.* Charlottesville: University of Virginia Press, 1982.

Other Documents

Annual Report on State Banks, Mutual Savings Banks and Trust Companies of Wisconsin. Madison, WI: Democrat Printing Company, State Printer, 1908.

Commonwealth of Virginia v George Crawford. Loudoun County Circuit Court, Leesburg, VA.

Fifth Annual Report of the Bank Examiner of the State and Private Banks of Wisconsin, Submitted to the Governor December 12, 1899. Madison, WI: Democrat Printing Company, State Printer, 1900.

Moody's Manuel of Railroads and Corporation Securities, Issue of 1917, Vol. 18, Part 1. New York: Moody's Manual Company, 1917.

Papers of the NAACP. Part I, Boxes D51, D52, D53, D54. Library of Congress.

Public Documents of the State of Wisconsin, Being the Reports of the Various State Officers, Departments and Institutions for the Fiscal Term Ending June 30, 1902. Madison, WI: Democrat Printing Company, State Printer, 1903.

Seventh Annual Report of the Bank Examiner of the State and Private Banks of Wisconsin, Submitted to the Governor January 23, 1902. Madison, WI: Democrat Printing Company, State Printer, 1902.

Transcripts of the United States Congress: Authorizing the President to Issue Posthumously to the Late William "Billy" Mitchell a Commission as Major General, United States Army (House of Representatives—October 8, 2003).

U.S. Department of Commerce, Bureau of the Census, Manuscript Federal Census, Loudoun County, Virginia, 1830.

U.S. Department of Commerce, Bureau of the Census, Manuscript Federal Census, Loudoun County, Virginia, 1930.

U.S. Department of Commerce, Bureau of the Census, Manuscript Federal Census, Milwaukee, 1880.

W.E.B. DuBois Papers, 1803–1979 (MS 312). Special Collections & University Archives, W.E.B. DuBois Library, University of Massachusetts–Amherst.

Index

193